COME DUNGEONS DARK

John Taylor Caldwell

COME DUNGEONS DARK

By

John Taylor Caldwell

Luath Press Ltd.,
Barr, Ayrshire. KA26 9TN.

First Edition 1988

The Publisher acknowledges subsidy from the Scottish Arts Council towards publication of this volume.

Cover Design & Chapter End-Pieces by John Mower

CONTENTS

Guy Alfred Aldred

MEDITATION

(Written by Guy Aldred on the eve of his first Court Martial at Fovant Military Detention Barracks, May 16, 1916.)

To the destiny of man,
to the instinct of my own nature,
to the martyred spirit of all dead pioneers,
let me pray.

Let me commune for health and strength and endurance in captivity.
Let me pray for zeal of spirit and power of faith.
Let me pray for intellectual vision and fervour of passion.
Let all vulgarity slip from me, and the word, the spirit of truth, become
incarnate in me.

Let me never deny the truth either in word or spirit.
Let me work for the overthrow of scoffers in high places,
for the destruction of the scoffing.
Let me become a prophet against the scepticism of worldly piety and
social unbelief.

Let me become a son of man,
the enemy of God,
the foe of kings,
the destroyer of ritual, ceremony, and all useless form.

Let truth, and truth alone, be my mistress,
and that I bring witness to her integrity
for all lands and climes.   May no worldly ambition,
no temptation in this wilderness of understanding,
lead me to serve the enemy of man,
the principle of power and domination.

(From Voices of Dissent, introduced by Farquhar McLay, Clydeside Press, 1986)

THE RED FLAG
(Air: *Maryland)*

The peoples' flag is deepest red:
It shrouded oft our martyred dead,
And ere their limbs grew stiff and cold,
Their heart's blood dyed its every fold.

Chorus
Then raise the scarlet standard high!
Within its shade we'll live and die!
Tho' cowards flinch and traitors sneer
We'll keep the Red Flag flying here.

Look round: the Frenchman loves its blaze,
The sturdy Russian chants its praise,
In German vaults its hymns are sung,
Chicago swells the surging throng.

It waved above our infant might,
When all ahead seemed dark as night:
It witnessed many a deed and vow:
We must not change its colour now.

It well recalls the triumphs past;
It gives the hope of peace at last:
The banner bright, the symbol plain
Of human rights and human gain.

It suits today the weak and base,
Whose minds are fixed on pelf and place,
To cringe before the rich man's frown,
And haul the sacred emblem down.

With heads uncovered swear we all
to bear it onward till we fall.
Come dungeons dark or gallows grim
This song shall be our parting hymn.

FOREWORD

My qualifications for writing a biography of Guy Alfred Aldred are that I worked with him, and was part of his household for twenty-seven years. I was his election agent on four of the seven occasions on which he stood as a parliamentary candidate; I was secretary of his group — The United Socialist Movement — for a number of years, and I frequently took the chair at his public meetings. I was one of the staff who opened The Strickland Press in 1939, and carried it on for five years after Aldred's death in 1963, turning the key in the lock for the last time in May, 1968. Thus, I was intimate with Guy Aldred longer than anyone now alive, and I think I understood him better than most of his colleagues — or opponents.

There are several reasons why a life of Guy Aldred should be written. He was an outstanding man, and there are too few of such for us to allow them to be forgotten lightly. He persistently represented an aspect of left-wing thought which had been — and still is — crushed off stage by the parliamentary socialism of the Labour Party and the Independent Labour Party, and by the dictatorial centralism of the Communist Party. He was an anti-parliamentarian socialist who believed in Communes rather than Parties, and put forward his own scheme for the non-violent establishment of those Communes. He did not consider his ideas as deviations from socialist thought, but condemned as aberrations both reformist parliamentarianism and conspiratorial communism. The ideas he stood for are still around, though not connected with his name, and somewhat affected by recent history and modern attitudes. A reason for writing the 'life' of Guy Aldred is that it articulates ideas that have become incoherent and corrupted; ideas which will surely loom larger in importance in the years ahead.

Another reason why Guy Aldred should be known, especially by Glaswegians, is that he was part of the history of that city. He was a well-known figure in the streets of Glasgow, and in the public life of the city from 1920 till his death in 1963. He had first come from London to speak in the Pavilion Theatre, Glasgow, in 1911, when he was twenty-five years of age. He liked the city, and the people he

1

met there, so he returned often, and eventually made Glasgow his home and headquarters. It was not a peaceful haven, for he fought many battles on the city's historic Green, and at its street corners; wordy battles on the right to speak freely, and sometimes bloody battles, and often legal battles.

A difficulty in portraying the character and personality of Guy Aldred is that he cannot be categorised. Intellectually, he was a unique amalgam of Marx, Proudhon, Bakunin and Jesus, all processed and refined by the originality of Guy Aldred. As a Boy Preacher he was a puzzle and an embarrassment to his elders. All they wanted to do as non-conformist evangelists was to proclaim their own personal salvation and to save other souls from the wrath to come. Young Aldred was more concerned with service than salvation. He spoke with particular fascination on the mystic concept of *The Word*. When he became an atheist he transformed, but did not relinquish this idea.

This atheistic mysticism, shared by his predecessors Godwin and Proudhon, often disconcerted his supporters and gave a point for derision among his opponents. He was not perturbed by either reaction, though he would rather have been understood than misrepresented. He had studied Hellenic philosophy privately under a very learned clergyman, and the concept of the *Logos* which had fascinated him in his Boy Preacher days remained with him during his atheist years. But the *Word* was transformed from a godly emanation from transcendental realms to an inexplicable element in human experience. It was the factor in human evolution which was not explained by biological development alone; nor did the dialectics of materialism explain it.

The improvement of the species did not come from the blind clash of material forces. There was something else, not supernatural, but germinating in experience, which was overlooked by the exponents of the dialectic. It was not just the *Will to Live,* nor the *Will to Power,* in prevailing forms. It was the *urge to surpass*; not to promote life's quantity, but to enrich its quality. Not to *improve* life by existing values, but to create new values. The aspirations which affect some persons, particularly when young, driving them towards goals neither worldy nor spiritual in any usual sense — these Aldred called *Vision*. He said in what was almost his last public speech:

> 'All the realities around us, all the differences in our lives from that of our forefathers, the development of man from the brute animal, is due to the faculty of *Vision* — as opposed to the mere observation of Reality......It means that the animal has

developed a new understanding and has therefore changed into a new being......'

And the *Word* was the articulation of that *Vision*.

A critic of this manuscript commented that Guy Aldred was 'someone whose career was, by conventional standards, a total failure.' This indicates an absurd reversal of Aldred's ideas. He was not quite seventeen when he stated publicly what he thought of conventional success. 'The purpose of life is not success, but service.' Aldred spent his life denouncing success, for such denunciation was implicit in all his attacks on careerists. He wrote an essay on the subject of failure which argued that the heritage of the common people runs in a line through history's conventional failures, when they showed themselves as rebels against conventional success, opposed to the Establishment. Only as long as they are failures do they have any communion with the people. When Socrates is promoted from the prison cell to the Academy, or Jesus taken from the Cross and made a fetish at the Altar, their appeal to the common people is over. They become the study of aspiring pundits and priests.

Aldred believed that a change of mood and direction came over the socialist movement after the Paris Commune. Following that holocaust of martyrs, the ideal of international socialism died, and with it the First International. It was replaced by the Second International, the promotion of socialism with State boundaries, and hence State socialism, parliamentarianism and war patriotism. The ideal of *sacrifice* gave way to the aspiration of *success*, to the proliferation of important little people with 'thimble-rattling souls' who busied themselves becoming socialist Town Councillors or socialist Members of Parliament, to the delight of their friends and the jubilation of their families. 'Socialism' meant advancing from back streets to suburbia, from back bench to Treasury Bench, from work bench to the House of Lords. And the workers remained where they were. Aldred was a youth of twenty when Social Democracy began to take shape in Britain, and he saw in it the debasement of the socialist idea; he saw it produce the pantomime of MacDonald, first 'socialist' Prime Minister, arrayed in knee breeches and cocked hat parading the failure of his success; and J.H. Thomas, of contemptible memory, tripping over his ceremonial sword in embarrassment when His Majesty actually spoke to him. Aldred, who grew to manhood when careerism was a developing trend, had the opportunities for political advancement, but he stood against the tide. He denounced the careerists, and was in turn denounced by them. He believed it better that his name be not mentioned in the biographies of success, and hence he is not widely known to a later generation.

Guy Aldred was well-known, especially in Glasgow, for his political activities, but also for his great debates as a militant atheist. He was a Boy Preacher (though an unorthodox one) at sixteen, an agnostic at seventeen, and an atheist at eighteen. By that time he had founded the The Clerkenwell Free-thought Mission, and for two years conducted meetings under its auspices. It was still in operation when he joined the Social Democratic Federation — and incurred the displeasure of Hyndman by combining freethought with his socialism.

During the long years of his propaganda activity, Aldred, on occasion, gave himself a descriptive appellation. This is not surprising when we remember that his father was an aspiring dramatist, and Guy an ardent evangelist. So the dramatic and the ecclesiastical combined. In 1910, an uneasy year when the clouds of war began to gather, and the Labour Party began to take on a definitely orthodox political character, Aldred started his first monthly journal with the title *The Herald Of Revolt*. When the Russian revolution raised socialist hopes, he set out on a nation-wide speaking tour as *'The Red Evangel'*. When these hopes were dashed by the new Communist Party's support of parliamentarianism, he attacked the place-seeking town councillors and aspiring parliamentarians above the signature of 'The Red Scourge' — the reference being to the scourge of forty cords which whipped the money-changers out of the Temple. Although his optimism usually defied the logic of events, towards the end of his life it wavered a little when the political struggle had run into the quick-sands of Welfarism, the industrial battle had built the Unions into an edifice of the Establishment, and militarism had blown itself into the size of a mighty Atom, immobilised only because it was afraid to move. Then, just a touch of weariness in his pen, he wrote: 'I am a rejected corner-stone.....I have been rejected all the days of my life.....I think that I am right to say that I am the stone that the builders refuse, and that I am the headstone of the corner. Egotism? Maybe. Truth? Yes; and I dare assert, truth without question.'

Almost his last public utterance was: 'Of course I am bitter. I am bitter at the lack of support. I am bitter because I am growing old, and because the voice I have used so long has not had the effect it should have had. In this I am wrong. There should be no bitterness, for I know that finally the Cause shall triumph.'

To be brought back into a frame of mind where there is a cause is a refreshing experience for the elderly, and should be rich in exciting prospects for the young. Guy Aldred has been dead for twenty-five years, but if we accept his definition of socialism (It is the next step in evolution....It is the next station to Capitalism in man's forward march....It embodies all religion, and includes all ethics.....) then we cannot long be pessimistic. As far back as 1916, Guy Aldred wrote: '*The Word* must be whispered in the shadows before it is proclaimed from the housetops.' He thought it had been whispered in the shadows long enough.

John Taylor Caldwell.

Book One:

THE HERALD OF
REVOLT

Dare to be a Daniel,
Dare to stand alone.
Dare to have a purpose firm.
Dare to make it known.

BOOK ONE
THE HERALD OF REVOLT

CONTENTS

The Iron Infants' School, Farringdon Road, London. The teacher seems to be holding Guy Aldred down!

1:   The Dreaming Boy.

Guy Alfred Aldred was born in Clerkenwell, London, on November Fifth, 1886.   His father was a 22-year-old Naval lieutenant who had resigned his commission to become a dramatist.   His ambition, never realised, was still green in the early days of 1886 when he met a nineteen-year-old parasol maker named Ada Caroline Holdsworth. She was, of course, socially unacceptable, and nothing would have been known of the meeting if the evidence had not grown big with the advancing year.   Like an officer and a gentleman, the budding dramatist who never flowered married the girl on September 13th, 1886, and, saying goodbye on the church steps, went home with his widowed mother.   Seven weeks later a baby boy was born.   Because it was November the Fifth — Guy Fawkes Day — they called him Guy, with Alfred as a middle name to show that he had a father who was called Alfred.

Guy was reared in the house of his maternal grandfather, Charles Holdsworth, at 24 Corporation Buildings, Farringdon Road, Clerkenwell.   Charles was a bookbinder, and a Victorian radical.   He did not belong to any group, but took an interest in social matters.   He championed the rights of Italian immigrants in Clerkenwell.   He was a nominator of Dabhabai Baorji, the M.P. for Central Finchley in 1892, the first Indian to be elected to the House of Commons.   Grandfather's political hero was Gladstone, whose portrait dominated one wall of the sitting-room.   Charles was a supporter of Charles Bradlaugh, and an atheist; but grandmother Emma was very orthodox, and for her sake Charles went to Church on Sunday, dressed in frock coat and tall hat.

It puzzled little Guy, who didn't know that his beloved grandfather was an infidel, when the old man, on coming home, undid and discarded all his respectable trappings, and exclaimed: 'Thank God that's over.'

After dinner he read to the family, which consisted of Em, who kept dozing off and waking up and exclaiming 'Yes, Charles dear', to show that she had heard every word, a married daughter and her husband Sunday visiting, Guys' mother Ada, and a younger sister — and Guy.   The reading choice was usually Thackeray or Dickens, because these were the old man's favourite authors.   Guy sat on the floor making model theatres from cut-outs which could be bought at the newsagents, penny plain and twopence coloured. At the age of five he was sent to the Iron Infants' School in Farringdon road, and two years later was transferred to the Hugh Myddleton School.

Guy was a solitary, dreamy boy. He took long walks round Clerkenwell, filling the streets with figures, buildings and events of the past. The impermanence of people and things fascinated and frightened him, and thoughts on the why and wherefore of existence occupied his mind at an early age. Grandfather was too much mindful of Em, or too afraid of hurting her, to be their grandson's heretical mentor. But he kept abreast of the boy, or just a little ahead of him, as he found his own way through paths which might lead to enlightenment. Guy started with Holy Writ, for therein lay the revelation of Truth. His questioning nature soon caused him to leave aside the accepted, pending further investigation, and his main reading became works of non-conformists. On his book shelves nearly seventy years later he still had some of the volumes he studied so avidly under the fan-like gas jet in his cold bedroom all those years ago, before the old Queen died, or the new century was born. To modern youngsters, some of these books would be, not just dry and difficult, but pointless. They were the works of Theodore Parker, of Joseph Parker, of Ellery Channing, Moncur Conway, and three volumes of Mosheim's *Ecclesiastical History,* and, equally well thumbed through the long solitary hours, Eusebius' *History (324 A.D.).* Of secular works, the *Essays* of Emerson still survived the assaults of penury upon his depleted bookshelf. Guy attended the Hugh Myddleton school till he was fifteen.

Between the ages of thirteen and sixteen Guy struggled from Anglican High Church conformity to the near-blasphemy of non-conformity. It gave him much soul-searching. When he was confirmed in St. Paul's Cathedral he was an unhappy boy with a troubled conscience. He did not believe in 'kneeling before my God on cushions of red silk.' He thought it would not be so bad if he only pretended to kneel on one knee.

It was not in his nature to be at odds with himself. The time had to come when he refused to go to church. His mother had ceased attending church since she had formed a bigamous union with a young man who was lax in religious concerns, and his grandmother had the dinner to prepare, but they both berated Guy. His grandmother foresaw a life of crime and a bad end, followed by a worse eternity. His mother said the cross of Christ was slipping from Guy's hands. They appealed to grandfather. Grandfather, all dressed up in silk hat, dickie and cuffs, awaiting the pleasure of his little grandson's company, delivered his judgement. 'Leave the boy alone. God is not praised by an unwilling worshipper.' Then he went his lonely way, to kneel on the plush cushion, not to praise God, but to please Em.

Guy was born with a crusading zeal. When he was ten he formed an Anti-Nicotine League among his class-mates, and later had them sign a Pledge not to indulge in Strong Drink. Despite this, and his refusal to put up his fists in a fair fight, he was reasonably popular. This popularity was enhanced enormously when he threw an inkwell at Mr. Hodges. Mr. Hodges was the singing teacher, and he was a back-thumper. He thumped the backs of boys who did not sing, which may have had some justification, but he also thumped the backs of boys whose voice was made to out-shout hecklers in Hyde Park, and for this there was no excuse. One day Mr. Hodge thumped Guy's back. Guy's instinct for fair play made him wait till Mr. Hodges had made his back-thumping way to the front of the class and had turned to face his captives. Then young Aldred took aim. The heavy glass bottle whizzed past the teacher's ear and splattered on the blackboard, a near miss. When the shaken Mr. Hodges had regained control of himself, he sent Guy to the headmaster.

There was quite a row about the incident. The headmaster convened a Court comprising himself, two school governors, and Mr. Hodges. The culprit's parents were notified to attend. If the headmaster had expected an apologetic father or a timid mother, he had a surprise in store. Grandfather Holdsworth was an elderly greybearded Victorian who carried himself with that dignity and presence which was not uncommon among elderly Victorians, but which was always impressive. Mr. Hodges found himself apologising for assaulting a pupil who could not do the impossible. Nothing happened to Guy. The boys never mentioned the fact that he had missed.

2: THE DARING DANIEL

His mother's 'marriage' put Guy under the strain of divided loyalty. Should he stay with her and his step-father, or should he remain with his grandparents? He settled the question by staying with his mother at weekends. Guy and his grandfather were great friends still, as they had been when Guy was little. When he was old, Guy still spoke of his grandfather with a fresh intensity of affection.

Every morning at six o'clock Guy rose and spent two hours in concentrated study before going to school. The subjects were of his own choosing: theology and church history. Deep in his books he was lost to the world, and was not easily brought back to the reality of his position as junior member of the household. He had certain tasks to perform as his contribution to the efficient running of the house. He had all the shoes to clean, and he had to go for the 'messages'. Grandma insisted.

Grandpa intervened. 'Let the boy study. I will clean the shoes, and I will go for the messages.' And he did, every morning for several years. He got out of his bed an hour before his time, and on his knees before a heap of family footwear, he performed Guy's task. Then, with the message basket on his arm, the money and list in hand, he joined the gatherings of sleepy-eyed children in the neighbourhood shops. An observant friend of Guy Aldred in later life may have noticed that he spent some time every morning, whatever the pressures of the world, in polishing his shoes. Shining shoes were as much part of his dress as the knickerbockers and long woollen stockings by which the newspapers often characterised him.

This outfit had a similar explanation. In October 1900, Guy's grandmother, the beloved Emma, died. This was the young boy's first bereavement. His sorrow was intense. During the last year of her life, Grandma and Guy had become special friends, and he was forgiven for not going to church. A few days before the onset of her final illness, grandma had taken him to a Boys' Outfitter, and had fitted him out in a Norfolk jacket, woollen stockings and boots. Then, looking at the result admiringly, she had exclaimed that he was a 'Little Toff'. Guy, never, during the sixty-five years of life that followed, dressed in any other style; and he never explained why.

As Guy's reputation as a theological scholar spread among his relatives, several persons with ecclesiastical connections emerged from the family background. One of these was the Reverend Hart, later vicar of Stepney. He drew from other interested parties an undertaking to bear a share of the cost of seeing Guy through college and university till he was eligible for ordination in the Church of England at the age of twenty-three. Guy turned down the offer disdainfully. 'Did Jesus go to university?' It was his first challenge to careerism. But he joined the *Lamb and Flag Mission* to which this relative belonged, and under its auspices visited back street hovels and doorways where outcast wretches lived and lurked, dispensing to them bread, soup and blankets.

With the death of Emma, Grandfather and Guy continued living in the old family house for some months, then Charles closed the house, and he and Guy went to live with Ada, Guy's mother. She had need of help. Her husband by bigamous contract could not, or would not, find work. Yet he was seldom sober. And Ada was pregnant, and had to give up the job that had kept them both. So grandfather joined the house with the status of lodger, although he was really the breadwinner. Guy, of course, accompanied him.

These events, marriage, death and birth, put the brilliant young Guy into the background. Nobody was interested in his future, and nobody objected when he left school before he was fifteen. He felt that he must find work. He objected to the strain being placed on his elderly grandfather. There was a notion in his young head that he might launch himself upon the world as a great non-conformist preacher. There were also the first signs of an emerging political consciousness. Now that Em could no longer berate him, the gentle Charles was free to assert his convictions. He was opposed to war, and, as the Boer war was on, he was opposed to that. He took Guy to anti-war meetings, and the pair of them paraded with placards — which perhaps, by their inscriptions, might have been considered more pro-Boer than anti-war.

The Boer war ended, but there were already distant rumblings of what was to come. Guy resolved to conduct a one-boy campaign against war. He would, of course, do so from, the standpoint of his religious convictions. Aldred later wrote of this time: 'I was beginning to feel the urge to preach. The story of the boy Jesus in the Temple fired my imagination.'

The year was 1902, Coronation year. London was full of dignitaries from all parts of the Empire. Many of them were heathens. There was a public wonder at the wealth and splendour and the civilised behaviour of these people. It seemed a violation of nature that unbelievers should be dressed beyond loin-cloths, and should worship strange gods with dignity.

Guy was fascinated. He had not given much thought to the possibility that there was a world outside London, or that people really did have other gods than the Biblical one.

The Rev. Septimus Buss, ancient rector of St. Anne's and Saint Agnes', the church Guy and his grandfather had attended till Emma died, decided that it would be a change from intoning to dust motes and cobwebs and a congregation as old as himself, if he were to take advantage of this public interest and deliver a series of lectures on 'Religions of the World'. Guy read the advertisement, and bought a special notebook.

He attended every one of the lectures, which were delivered between 9th April and 25th July, 1902, making notes and afterwards writing an essay on each subject for criticism by Mr. Buss. In his biography, Aldred wrote: 'My notes reveal the narrowness and bigotry of my mind, but they promise a broadening of vision. Here and there were flashes of heresy.'

The old clergyman cannot have been pleased with some of the young man's remarks, but nevertheless, when the lectures were over, he kept up a correspondence with the boy, urging him to return to the Anglican Church. This Guy could not do, because, apart from his objection to the ritual, the Church did not approve of boy preachers. One had to be twenty-three before one spoke for the Lord. Guy could not wait that long. The fate of Christendom demanded that he speak now. So in June 1902 he set out to save the Christians from their own folly. First he surveyed the large empty basement which was part of his mother's house. A splendid headquarters. Here he wrote his first public utterance, and duplicated it by the time-honoured gelatine process. The leaflet read:

THE LAST DAYS: War or Peace? Throughout this great Christian land — nay, throughout all the lands where white men rule, and over which the 'Christian Flag' flies — there are to be found goodly men who cannot understand why men allow themselves to be dragged down the 'road to ruin' without making an effort to save themselves.

It went on to explain that the 'road to ruin' is the road to war, and it was against the folly of embarking on this road that Master Aldred warned his fellow-Londoners. Having written the Word, he now had to proclaim it. Time was pressing. Instinctively he knew that

14

which Jesus had had to learn from experience: a prophet is without honour in his own village. So he set out for 'various parts of Holloway', which were sufficiently far from Clerkenwell, 'to overcome this shyness, and yet not be too far away to have easy access to my home.' Thus he 'drifted into real and serious contact with the world'. In fact, he did not drift; he marched. With his precious leaflets in his hand, a bible in his pocket and a box-platform under his arm, he went forth with faith, hope and courage (and youthful innocence) to save mankind from the fate awaiting it, the fate hammered out on neccessity's anvil for over a thousand years. Surely his young heart was pounding at the enormity of the task, and his mind aflame with the sublime purpose of it. He walked — he strode — with a peculiarity of gait which gave him a springing motion as his right foot on contact with the ground raised him a little higher than did the contact of his left. He bounced along. His vocal cords had no music, but an anthem was ringing in his soul:

Dare to be a Daniel,
Dare to stand alone.
Dare to have a purpose firm.
Dare to make it known!

He *had* a purpose firm, and he *would* make it known. He strode into the concrete jungle, where the miasma of indifference and the jackass laughter of ridicule awaited him. Who cared if the storm-clouds were gathering and a youthful Daniel warned them of impending disaster? His voice blew back in his face and was as unheeded as the traffic din around him. Passers-by passed on, crushing his leaflet unread in their hands, stuffing it into their pockets, casting it on the pavement. A gang of rough boys jeered and made his jaunty gait the occasion of their derision. 'Jumping Jimmy Jesus!' they cried, 'Jumping Jimmy Jesus!'

Guy was not mocked. Neither was he provoked, though he was persecuted and reviled. So it was with the prophets which went before him. Did not ill-mannered little urchins shout 'Baldy Head! Baldy Head!' after Elijah? And did not the good God send two she-wolves forth from the thicket to tear forty-two of the little monsters apart for their impertinence? God has a brisk way with children. He drowned them in the Flood, plagued them in Egypt, burned them in Sodom, massacred them in Judea, and crucified his own son, who loved little children. Perhaps in never having been a child himself lies some (Freudian?) explanation.

However, Guy continued his meetings through the summer months, and one leaflet fell, as it were, on good soil. It was cherished, and passed from hand to hand till it reached the horny hand of a labourer in the Borough market, and he pressed it into the gentle hand of the Rev. George Martin. It took six months to return to Guy again, in hundred-fold blessing.

3: THE HERETICAL BOY PREACHER

Guy eventuallly found a job — as an insurance doctor's reception-ist. It was an easy job; the doctor was not kept busy, so neither was Guy. He resolved his indecision as to whether to spend his spare time in serious study or relaxation by going to work with a Bible in one pocket and a second-hand Nick Carter in the other.

Nick Carter was the Sherlock Holmes of juveniles, a fore-runner of Sexton Blake. He did not solve crime by tiresome deduction, but by direct action. At that particular time, Nick was dealing with a band of international anarchists in a continuing battle of cunning, daring and mayhem. The anarchists were led by the beautiful, seductive, but suitably sexless Emma Silverman. This was a slanderous fictional representation of the American anarchist Emma Goldman, whom Guy met a few years later – and found not so beautiful, not particularly seductive and certainly not sexless.

After a few months in this splendid job Guy was paid off. The doctor went away to darkest Africa where he felt he was more needed. He gave Guy a month's wages in lieu of notice.

Guy records that his mother was 'affectionate, and not in the least mercenary', but 'she made demands on me which in justice, she had no right to make.' Her false marriage declaration robbed him of legal existence, yet she made him feel that he had a duty to contribute to her support and the support of her new family. As one day of idleness followed another, the atmosphere of disapprobation thick-ened. Resentment, guilt and disappointment burned within him. Finally he resolved after yet another day of fruitless job-seeking not to go home till he had found work. So in the evening, empty of pocket and in stomach, he made his way to the Thames embankment to spend the night with other rejects and social misfits. He was not on unfamiliar ground. He had often been there with other members of the *Lamb and Flag Mission*, distributing cocoa and bread to the hungry outcasts. Now he was one of them. Of course, neither his mother nor his grandfather approved of this foolishness. This was an adolescent indulgence in self-punishment. Fortunately, after a few nights of hunger and cold he found a job.

17

It was not much of a job — office boy with the National Press Agency in Whitefriars House. But he did not remain an office boy for long. In the outer office of the Agency there was a letter-box slot which led into the inner office. It was not for use by postmen, but by an assortment of individuals in varying degrees of decreptitude or affluence who came into the office at intervals and dropped an envelope therein. At the end of the week those same individuals called at the cashier's window and received money. Guy soon discovered that these were free-lance journalists who earned a few shillings by selling items to the Agency, anything from household hints and gossip paragraphs to feature articles. These were syndicated to provincial newspapers. The authors were paid for such material as the Agency considered usable. It was not long before Guy was neglecting the ink-wells and postage stamps to write paragraphs for this wondrous letter-box. He wrote of everything from *Quaint Heathen Customs* to *Gems From English Literature*. In a matter of weeks he was promoted to a sub-editor's job, going through the piles of newspapers and magazines, finding and writing up material for syndication. It was interesting. He liked it. But he did wish he could be a non-conformist preacher.

The opportunity came (more correctly, he *made* it) a week or so before his sixteenth birthday. He was going through a newspaper looking for snippets for the Agency when he noticed an advertisement inserted by a Mr. Willoughby Masters. Mr. Masters was looking for a hall in which to hold evangelical meetings. Guy knew of such a hall. He suggested an alliance with Mr. Masters. The idea was not too absurd. There were several Boy Preachers around, mostly Welsh, the result of one of the several evangelical missions which swept Wales in the last century. They all drew in the customers. Mr. Masters probably considered himself lucky to have found one. He billed his Boy Preacher as the *Holloway Boy Preacher*, most likely to put the best face on his being a cockney, and not Welsh. But this Boy Preacher was different. He could write as well as speak and he had a penchant for drawing up sets of principles.

The name would be *The Christian Social Mission*. The 'social' indicated a subtle secularism which was invading Guy's subconscious. Mr. Masters wanted to call it the *Lyric Gospel Mission*, because he had a beautiful singing voice, and thought that everybody should sing their joy at being saved. Young Guy pressed on regardless: 'The object of the mission will be to walk out of the old rut; to be in sympathy with the best in every sect, and in no sect; to draw together companionable souls by the common bonds of spiritual brotherhood and mutual consideration.'

Mr. Masters was in his fifties and not a bit anxious to walk out of common ruts. He had been in one comfortably for a long time, but he had to humour the boy. Guy humoured Mr. Masters a little in return. The old man knew a number of non-conformist ministers and to Guy these were rebel souls: he was anxious to meet them. Besides, Mr. Willoughby Masters had in his group a young lady who played the harmonium, and who had little to say, but who looked at the vigorous, self-assured boy 'with coy glances.' Guy remembered her all his life.

The Christian Social Mission established its headquarters at the Assembly Rooms, 5, Russell Road, Holloway. In the advertisements Mr. Masters described himself as 'The Lyric Gospel Herald', and conceded that he was assisted by Master Guy Aldred, the Holloway Boy Preacher. The first meeting was held on 10th November, 1902, five days after Guy's sixteenth birthday.

After a hymn and a prayer, Mr. Willoughby Masters spoke. His beautiful voice gave pleasure, and he said nothing to disturb the mind. When he sat down, the pious people in the audience settled themselves to hear the next turn on the bill. The most attractive feature of Boy Preachers was the gusto with which they proclaimed themselves wicked sinners, saved by the Blood of Christ. Guy was diffferent. They watched him rise and take his place at the improvised pulpit. He was pale complexioned, one-eighth Jewish, large-eyed, generous-lipped, holding in leash a merry smile, like that of his grandfather incarnate. He wore a Norfolk jacket, pleated and high-lapelled. He had a starched Eton collar and a starched shirt front. The ends of his black bow tie were tucked under his wide collar. He wore knickerbockers, thick grey stockings and heavy, highly polished black boots.

For perhaps the only time in his life, he carefully wrote out his text, and, perhaps sentimentally, and certainly uncharacteristically, he carefully preserved it as a record of his first public address.

He began quietly, rather limply. He said his text would be found in Apostle Pauls's Epistle to the Galatians, Chapter Six, Second Verse: *'Bear ye one another's burdens, and so fulfill the law of Christ.'* Then he went on to say:

'Paul is not the best interpreter of Jesus, and some of the earliest Christians regard him as an apostate rather then an apostle. He was the founder of Christian dogma, and not the teacher of Christian thought. He breathes submission to authority, whereas Jesus brought liberty, and challenged authority. But he experienced rare intervals of grace, and enjoyed

19

glimpses of truth. His picture of charity is epic literature, and is assured of immortal rank in the thought of the world. It is as useful to remember as it is beautiful to conceive. To the same high order of understanding belongs Paul's definition of the Law of Christ. Paul may have defended and urged servititude. If he did so, let his teaching be rejected and condemned. But he defined the message of Jesus as Service....

'....Christianity has been preached as the Gospel of Success, whereas Jesus made the Word Incarnate identical with failure, was himself a failure without qualification, and taught that the purpose of life was not success, but service....

'....Not grandeur, but grandness....not power, but power to serve. Jesus filled the world with *compassion*, the Christian ages have filled it with *passion. Creed and Greed*, where Jesus taught and exuded Love.....

'Down the ages men have persecuted genius and not known what they did....To be a Son of Glory, to have genius and to be truly great one must *serve*, and not seek to *rule* the people.

'This teaching of service destroys the Christian Church, but it *founds* Christian Society. It undermines throne and altar, but honours struggle....Churches may totter, kingdoms fall, social systems change but all down the ages — until at last Man shall know and live the Truth — will thunder the message: *Bear ye one another's burdens, and so fulfill the Law of Christ.*

'Service is not just the *message of Jesus*, it is the *Law of Christ.* And who, or what, is Christ? Jesus is the man, the messenger, the bearer of the Word, the torch-carrier, but not the torch, the in-dwelling urge, the inmost *must*, the concentrated enlightenment. Jesus was possessed with Christ-spirit, and is called the Christ....Jesus died, but the Christ-spirit survived his betrayal and execution....

'....The Law of Christ is the law of human well-being. Until and unless we do bear each others' burdens society will continue in crime, folly and disease. War, prisons, poverty and hypocrisy must flourish....The devil will rule where God should influence.... The day we bear each others' burdens the Devil will disappear from society. The New Dispensation will dawn, and we will enter into the inheritance of the Kingdom — a new Heaven, and a new Earth.'

Such, in brief, was Master Guy A. Aldred's first sermon. The audience was baffled and uneasy. With a hymn and a prayer the service ended, and Guy was left to face his fellow evangelists. No congratulations, but just embarrassed silence. The harmonium girl, of whom Guy seems to have been uneasily aware 'looked askance, but said nothing.' When criticism took courage and tongues were loosened, Mr. Willoughby Masters and his colleagues accused the Boy Preacher of blasphemy, almost of heresy. Guy had not spoken to please. The Christ-spirit had moved him as he spoke. The *inward must* was imperious in its demands. This concept probably came from his New England reading and is expressed in one of his favourite poems, by James Russell Lowell, on William Lloyd Garrison:

Who is it will not dare himself to trust?
Who is it that has not strength to stand alone?
Who is it thwarts and bilks the *inward must?*
He, and his works, like sand from earth are blown.

Lowell, Emerson, Channing and Parker were his companions, the fellows of his mind. Mr. Masters· and his colleagues spoke a different language. Then Guy found someone who *did* speak his language; and they disagreed.

4: THE PRIEST WITHOUT A PARISH

One day in January 1903 there came to the door of 133 Goswell Road a character so strange in appearance that Guy's stepfather, who opened it, promptly shut it again. He was not an ill-natured man, but he lacked imagination. 'There's a man to see Guy,' he said in bewildered alarm. 'He looks a damned queer character to me.'

Guy went to the door and opened it. The queer character was used to doors being shut in his face, so he was still there. He knew slammed doors usually opened again. He was about forty, dressed in clerical hat, clerical coat, waistcoat and collar. Which was quite proper, for he was an ordained priest of the Anglican Church. Below the waistline he wore heavy porter's corduroy trousers, strapped in below the knee, and heavy, worn, dirty boots. Which was also quite proper, because he was a porter in the Borough Market. It was the combination which had confused Guy's stepfather. But the Reverend George Martin was not dismayed. He knew and understood people, their reactions and their antics. He said not a word till Guy had noticed the handbill he held in front of him, like a miniature placard. It was familiar. Guy had almost forgotten it. *THE LAST DAYS. War or Peace, by Guy A. Aldred..* The seed on good soil had taken root.

The strange-looking character introduced himself as the Reverend George Martin, ordained Anglican minister, and on these credentials Guy's mother invited him in. He said the leaflet had been given to him in the Borough Market, and he had seen the advertisement of the Christian Social Mission. He wanted to meet the Holloway Boy Preacher. So a friendship began which greatly advanced young Aldred's education in theology and philosophy and lasted till he went to jail six years later.

George Martin had been a Minister in Cornwall, but had persuaded himself that a Christian minister must live the life of the people, and if there are social depths, he must sink to them with the people. He moved to that very tough district of London, and moved about it fearlessly. He was very gentle to all who erred and all who suffered. Every day he worked in the Borough Market as a porter, and each evening when he left the market he would take a troop of eighteen derelict men to a tea-room for cocoa, bread and butter. He gave away all that he earned, and much of his allowance from home.

'He loved scholarship,' Guy Aldred wrote, 'and his society was a joy for its quaintness, his classical digressions, and his broad human understanding. His studies had little effect on his superstitions. His love of Greek, and his interest in it amazed me — for I was his victim....He was a most lovable and sincere individual. His attitude towards life influenced me greatly and explains much of my later propaganda reaction. He taught me, by example, to be unafraid of consequences; and to serve the poor.' (*No Traitor's Gait. Autobiography of Guy Alfred Aldred.* Strickland Press, Glasgow, 1955. p. 66)

During their friendship, George Martin had to go to prison. He refused to give evidence against a man who had stolen some trifle, and had confided in Martin as his priest. Martin considered the confidence as sacred as a confession. The court did not agree, and sentenced him to six months imprisonment for contempt of Court.

The slumland of south London was dear to the heart of George Martin. He loved every worn grey stone, and he exuded understanding and compassion for all he met. He and Guy walked together in pleasurable companionship. George was a scholar, but he was no heavy pedant. He carried his classical learning lightly, and revealed it easily, naturally, in conversations which were delightful and fascinating. George Martin loved children. He told Guy: 'Whenever I can, I gather them together, about a dozen or so. Then I look at their hands. If they are dirty, I send them home to wash. And when all have clean hands I give them a cake each, and offer up a little prayer.'

Perhaps he had forgotten that Jesus, who also loved little children, was less particular about washed hands; he had said something to hand-washing Pharisees about whited sepulchers. He would have fed the hungry children first. Young Aldred had discussions with Martin on that very point.

So, in the attic where George Martin lived, amid the damp roofs and smoking chimney pots of a London winter, the adolescent Guy's mind took flight to realms of wider scenes and purer air, to ancient Greece, where men spoke like gods and gods acted like men, and from a maze of imagery came substantial ideas. From the evanescent came the rational, from mystery came understanding, from the speculative came the dogmatic, and from the shadows came reality. The boy's

23

guide was not a silk-robed magi, nor a subtle philosopher in chiton, but a simple, heavy-footed, hobnailed priest who, for all his learning, accepted in faith the belief that a good God had made Plato to prepare the world for Christianity and the miracle of the eucharist.

In his *Historical and Traditional Christianity*, written when he was twenty, Guy Aldred revealed the results of his studies at that time. He also wrote an autobiographical sketch (at that age it could hardly be anything more than a sketch!) called *From Anglican Boy Preacher to Socialist Impossibilist*. This shows that he had departed from the dogmas of his reverend mentor. So we must follow him. But there were other important ecclesiastical episodes still to relate.

5: The Gospel of Hellfire.

At the time Guy wrote to Mr. Willoughby Masters offering his help in forming a Christian Social Mission, he also wrote to the Reverend Charles Voysey, B.A. Charles Voysey was well-known as the former Vicar of Healaugh, whose indictment before the Privy Council on the charge of heresy in 1871 had badly shaken the Anglican Church. He was not burned at the stake, not because there was any shortage of those with ready matchboxes, but simply because the practice had gone out of fashion. He was ordered to pay costs and deprived of his living. He then became the founder of the Theistic Church in Swallow Street, Piccadilly. This Church advertised regularly in *The Times* offering a free batch of literature to truthseekers. There was no more ardent young truth-seeker than Guy Alfred Aldred, who eagerly availed himself of this opportunity. In due course he received a number of printed sermons and a pamphlet entitled *A Lecture on the Theistic Church: Its Foundation and the Bible*. The author invited criticism.

Guy Aldred obliged in a forty-eight page letter, closely written on foolscap. He ended by asking for an interview. Mr Voysey replied promptly. He feared there would be little use in meeting one who saw no contradictions in the narratives of the life of Jesus. Guy wrote back, and again pressed for an interview, giving no indication that he was but a teenage boy. Mr. Voysey relented and on Saturday 20th December 1902 the Holloway Boy Preacher set out to meet the respectable defrocked Anglican.

When Mr. Guy Alfred Aldred apppeared on the doorstep of the upper-class residence of the Reverend Charles Voysey, Annesley Lodge, Platt's Lane, Hampstead, the housemaid was visibly taken aback, and we may surmise a smirk on her face when she opened the drawing-room door and announced him to her master. Then it was the Reverend Charles who was taken aback.

His impulse was to send the boy packing immediately. It was an absurd and humiliating position. He was seventy-four years of age, and a gentleman — he was very conscious of one's position in society — the author of sermons with a circulation of two millions, the writer of several books, one of which had sent ecclesiastical blood pressures soaring; and here he was, confronted by a sixteen-year-old boy, obviously of the working class, dressed in bargain-store Norfolk jacket, knickerbockers, coarse wooollen stockings, and heavy boots with the pull-on tabs sticking out at the back. He suspected some evil intention.

Guy was too innocent to realise that there *could* be any suspicion. The old man questioned him closely; his school, his family, his place of work, his associates, the contents and meaning of the letters he had allegedly written, his purpose in pressing for an interview. Guy's mention of George Martin was greatly in his favour, for George was a character above reproach. So finally Charles motioned Guy to a chair on the opposite side of the fire and the first of many mutually enjoyable talks began. It lasted for three hours, during which time two tray-loads of tea and cakes were devoured, and Charles stopped asking Guy if he was sure his mother knew where he was.

The friendship lasted till the old man's death in 1912, and survived Guy's progress through Theism to atheism and to anarchism. When Guy was gaoled in 1909 for seditious libel, Voysey, nearly eighty years of age, made the journey across London, in his horse-carriage, to visit him in Brixton, having the Home Office over-rule the Governor's objection that Aldred, as an atheist, could not have a 'Spiritual Adviser' with special visiting privileges. When Guy's son was born in 1909, he was called Annesley — one of Voysey's family names — as a mark of friendship. When Guy's grand-daughter was born many years later, she was also called Annesley. So the warmth generated by that meeting between the shy boy and the learned old man in December 1902 was kept alive for half a century.

Voysey did not have a high opinion of the Christian god. He contended that the Gospel which it preached to the heathen and in the majority of churches in the very heart of civilisation (he meant London) is a gospel of Fear, and not a gospel of Love; a gospel, not of Hope, but of Despair; not of Salvation, but of Damnation. Behind the Cross of Calvary, out of the thick darkness there looms the dread image of One who is man's natural foe; whom no-one dare approach in his naked weakness with unshielded breast. The Great Supreme, in bitter irony callled the Father of Jesus and of man, is drawn in outlines so ghastly and painted in colours so lurid that the soul cannot look on that face and live.

For it is cardinal doctrine — the one on which the whole Christian scheme of salvation stands, and without which it falls to the ground — that Almighty God is cruel beyond all human language and thought; and that no human heart in its bitterest paroxysms of revenge ever invented, no savage skill ever put into practice, one millionth part of that cruelty which they say is part of God's honour and glory.

'If all the cruel acts of violence and slow torture inflicted on men by each other were gathered together in one gigantic act of sorrow and then multiplied a thousand times, it could be but a drop in the ocean of cruelty and injustice ascribed by the Christians to their Supreme God. Baal or Moloch? Human sacrifices might load their altars, the flesh of young men and of maidens might writhe in the withering, piercing flame, to gloat their nostrils with the noisome incense. Those ancient gods were loving, compassionate and tender by the side of Him from whose eternal wrath and burning fiery vengeance we are bidden to flee to the Cross of Christ....The Christian God is evil; he loves to be feared, and to be praised for the little mercy that shines dimly through his cruelty. He can be approached only through His Son, whom he humiliated and tortured in a scheme of salvation which is neither wise nor magnanimous. The Theist God is good. He is not good because he can do no other. There is no virtue in that. Goodness is a matter of choice, and implies free-will. God chooses to be good. He has created us and has given us a similar choice....'

Voysey insisted that Christianity was organised atheism, for one could not believe in such an incredible god. Aldred did not entirely agree. He spent a year in study and in debate with Voysey before he was able to write: 'I think that fundamentally the Christian Church is an atheist institution. Jesus as the son of man is a glorious protest against God the upholder of Crown and State and Church, the advocate of war. I begin to realise that Christianity should not be an attempt to *explain* the creation of the world, but a living atttempt to *recreate* human society. If God is Being in the Abstract, Jesus is Becoming in the Concrete.'

Guy put a question to Voysey: 'If Theism is founded on Reason, why does it differ from Deism, the belief of Thomas Paine, and in fact the belief that was the outcome of the Age of Reason?' The difference between the Deist and the Theist, as Aldred understood the terms, is that the Deist believes that God, acting as First Cause, set the Universe in motion, and then withdrew from it, leaving it to unwind itself in a chain of Cause and Effect. He is like a watchmaker who has made a fine instrument, and who, if he so wills, may smash it to bits, but who, having wound it up, may not alter the principles of spring tension and ratchet ratio on which it operates. It was a popular belief among the thinkers who prepared the way for the French Revolution, though Deists were sometimes accused of being timid atheists. The Theist believes that the God who created the world is also concerned with its operation. He is like the Deist's watchmaker, except that he is not content with the working harmony of his instrument's parts, and is anxious about its time-keeping (moral perfection), and is not averse to the adjustment of a screw, either by his own hand in direct intervention, or by that of any agent — priest, prophet, saint, sage or martyr.

The question was not as innocent as it may have seemed. It was the spear-head thrust of a two-pronged attack. If Voysey's theology was based on Reason, as he claimed, were not the prayers which were part of its ritual therefore pointless? And was it not opposed to reason (or Reason) to believe that the watch kept better time than ever when its spring had broken — that is, that human beings lived on after death? Voysey was not trapped by the young man's question. He pointed out that Theism was based not on Reason alone, but also on Conscience and Love. This was the triune of his monotheistic religion. Reason only made clear to our understanding that which was apprehended by Conscience and Love. This begged so many questions, and demanded so much definition, that it is little wonder that the interview continued for three hours.

In that discussion, as in all subsequent discussions, Charles Voysey stressed one point particularly: Religion is Virtue. Not necessarily the *good* of prevailing social morality, but the *passion for good* however that *good* may be interpreted. It is a passion which generates in the mind of man and gives him a sense of elevation. It is a quality of the inner man which 'enthuses into harmony' the jarring, warring, contentiousness which expresses man's will to live. That harmony would only be gained through an attitude of mind which Voysey called Love and Aldred called Understanding (Empathy). There are foreshadowings here of Aldred's secular *Word* and *Vision*.

After his day's work at the National Press Agency, Guy usually spent some time with the Lamb and Flag Mission seeking out and ministering to the city's social derelicts, or helping the Rev. George Martin to dispense sixpences. In the evening there was a growing pile of books to study, and every day more new ideas crowded into his mind.

> 'It is strange,' (he wrote in his autobiography), 'how my vision of life expanded and developed under contradictory influences. When I was struggling with my doubts concerning the truth of Christianity, George Martin sought me out....He believed fervently in the divinity of Jesus. His argument drove me to a strong belief in the humanity of Jesus....'(N.T.G. p. 64)

Guy felt that he had moved beyond the range of the Christian Social Mission and that now they must part company.   He finished a series of lectures on the Parables, then on January 25th, 1903, after just over three months, he delivered his last lecture for the Mission.   It was on 'Jesus and God', and was Guy's last Christian sermon.   He concluded:

> 'Christianity is not the property of a sect.   It is the wealth, — the common-wealth — of humanity.   It cannot be shut up in the few lines of an abstract and ridiculous creed, or compressed into a few dull propositions.   Christianity is a declaration of fire, light, freedom: the proclamation of the integral soul of man....'

So after three perplexing months the Holloway Boy Preacher retired from the rostrum — or the pulpit.   There could have been few sighs of regret from Mr. Willoughby Masters.   It may be that the girl who played the harmonium shed a few chaste tears into her pillow that night.

6: THE TRUTH SEEKER

Guy Aldred had the soul of a missionary, and he had a message. The message had been Christianity: now it was Theism.   He went to Voysey's church in Swallow Street, but rejected the ritual of prayer and its belief in immortality.   There was only one thing to do.   He must found his own Mission.

'It seemed natural,' he later wrote in his autobiography (p. 75), 'that I should seek to convert the world to my ideas.   Lance in hand I set out to find a "defender of the faith" worthy of my steel.   This was heresy in an audacious mood.'

At that time the Christian Evidence Society held meetings on Clerkenwell Green every Sunday morning.   Guy attended those meetings and asked questions 'with unnecesary timidity.'   He later described the speakers as an ill-informed, ignorant lot; but he accepted the suggestion that he attend the Sunday Morning Adult School meetings in the Peel Institute.   He was assured that there he would re-find Christ.   He did not rediscover Christ at the Institute: he lost God instead.

The Peel Institute was a local Quaker Christian Brotherhood, situated in 1903 in Woodbridge Street.   It later moved to Clerkenwell Green.   The purpose of the Peel Institute was to supply an alternative to the public house for married men in particular, but all males were welcome.   Guy's objection to the exclusion of women was met by the explanation that the wife who had to stay at home with the children would rather have her husband, who would go out in any case, go to the Institute and come back sober, than go to the pub and arrive home drunk.   She knew where he was, and her mind could be at ease.   But her mind would not be so easy if she knew he was mixing with women, probably younger and in several ways freer than herself.   So the Institute remained a male preserve.

There wasn't much piety in the place.   When the free-thinkers withdrew from the Bible Class it had to close.   And it was a hot-bed of political argument, with the predominance of *Daily News*-style Liberalism.   The Director of the Institute was George Gillett, a local Borough Councillor, anxious to become a London County Councillor on the Progressive (Liberal) ticket. Councillor Gillett did not scruple to use the amenities of the Institute or the energies of its members for the furtherance of his political ambitions. He ended his days as Commissioner for Special Areas in the Labour Government, and had become Sir George Masterton Gillett.

Aldred stayed with the Peel Institute for three years, but it was only three months before he was on the platform, lecturing for the Brotherhood. The subject was *'Total Abstinence: Tomorrow's citizens and their Present Environment.* He had the help of magic lantern slides which showed the alleged effects of alcoholism on the victim's inside. It was not, sadly, a purely academic subject for young Guy. His step-father was unable to work through drink-addiction, and his grand-father, an abstainer during all his married years, was now trying to drink himself to death. He did not succeed, but found the answer to old age and loneliness in corrosive poison a few years later.

Then, for a year, while he still had Martin and Voysey for his mentors, Guy lectured at the Institute on Theism.

'I insisted that a man was truly religious only in so far as his outwardly expressed view concurred with his inward view of life and his beliefs were trained scientifically and cultivated....Despite the brave words I had uttered as Boy Preacher, and despite my very real belief that faith involved works, my thought was coloured by a great deal of metaphysics....I had not reached a real sense of material values. I had not translated righteousness into a concrete reality. True, I had no inhibitions, and believed in reading of all kinds....Radical ideas did not alarm me....'

It is as well they didn't, for at the Institute he encountered many off-beat ideas. He became a reader of *The Clarion*, edited by Robert Blatchford (1851—1943),author of many books on atheism and socialism, founder of the Clarion Clubs, and probably, as John Maclean said, responsible for more socialist conversions than Karl Marx, A jingoist and word-eater in 1914, he nevertheless was a great force in the popularising of socialism.

Young Aldred met John Burns, founder-member of the Social Democratic Federation, at the Peel Institute. In 1903, Burns was at the height of his radical heyday. John Burns was born in 1858; he became an engineer and a member of The Amalgamated Society of Engineers. At an early age he was deeply involved in socialist activities, and in 1886 was charged with sedition, but acquitted. The following year he was sentenced to six months imprisonment for his part in the Trafalgar Square demonstration on 'Bloody Sunday'. He was the hero of the great London Dock Strike which won the dockers sixpence (an increase of one penny) per hour, with eightpence for overtime, and a minimum of two shillings per day wages for any man engaged, except for short periods in the afternoon. Those staggering concessions were won as a result of intensive agitation involving daily demonstrations of as many as 120,000 men, and Burns was the hero of the hour. When Guy heard him speak, and accompanied him to his out-door meetings, Burns was on his way from socialism through Radicalism to Liberalism. Young Aldred was headed in the opposite direction.

After a year (April 1903 to April 1904) addressing the Brotherhood on Theism, and being himself half-converted to agnosticism, Guy decided that it was time he had his own organisation. It would be called *The Theistic Mission.* Guy's grandfather accompanied him to all his meetings, and stood on the fringe of the crowd till the meeting was nearly over, then he vanished, most likely to obtain liquid refreshment, catching up with Guy as he got home.

Aldred had little support from his ecclesiastical friends. He had told them of his conversion to Theism earlier. They suspected he was playing with hell-fire. He had been warned that he would be no match for a man like Voysey. George Martin was mildly surprised, but continued to talk on Hellenic Christianity. Charles Voysey wrote: 'My dear Guy, I never expected you to be suddenly converted to Theism, nor do I think such a change desirable. Go on in your own way, earnest, sincere, zealous, conscientious and prayerful, and you will then be surely in the best way of learning the truth which God would have you learn....'

The meetings of The Theistic Mission were held as arranged, morning and evening every Sunday. The crowd gathered easily, because Guy Aldred was becoming known as a youthful orator. The audience was a mixture of the curious and the hostile. The offended persons were Christians, annoyed at the repudiation of Christ the Saviour.

The view Guy was putting forward was that there was a God, but that He did not have a son, and if He did, He could have derived no satisfaction from his crucifixion. It was illogical and absurd to suppose that this wicked act of God would atone for the wickedness of Man, particularly when the son had been put on earth as an example to all men in the way of gentleness, forgiveness and love. But young Guy was in a difficult situation, and the crowd sensed it. He was beginning to doubt his own contention. He was removing the human Jesus from the theological scene, and rehabilitating God. This was opposed to reason and his feelings. He was really in sympathy with the Son and hostile to the Father. He was gaining Christ and losing God. Guy never gave up the idea that man was basically virtuous. There was no virtue in the world that did not come from man's nature. It had no transcendental source.

Grandfather Holdsworth did not oppose Guy's views publicly, but told him privately that he could not remain hanging in midair between Christianity and atheism. Guy knew this himself. God, without Christ, had nothing so say; but Jesus, without God, had a message of hope for mankind.

The Theistic Mission lasted from April to August 1904, then one week the audience found that the banner had changed. It now read *The Clerkenwell Freethought Mission*. Its object was clearly stated: 'For the promotion of Religious, Scientific and Secular Truth, and the advocacy of the right and duty of every man to think for himself in all matters relating to his own welfare and his duty to his Brother Men.' The leader was Guy Aldred, 133 Goswell Road, and he undertook to be of any help he could to strangers in mental or domestic distress. Meetings would be held on Sundays on Clerkenwell Green, and on Tuesdays at Garnault Place. The first lecture would be entitled: *The Perfection of God,* and the second *The Mission of Freethought.* Guy, coming up for eighteen, was moving at his own pace in his own direction, helped a little by grandfather, and by Blatchford's *God and my Neighbour*, which had recently been published. He had also discovered *The Agnostic Journal*, and from that arose his friendship with its editor, Saladin.

7: THE YOUNG ICONOCLAST

Saladin — self-styled master of the rapier of words — was the pen-name of William Stewart Ross. 'Acquaintance with Ross,' Aldred wrote in *No Traitor's Gait* p.91, (his autobiography) 'was my first acquaintance with things Scottish.' Ross was born in Scotland in 1844. His father was a farm servant, but Ross was able to go to Glasgow University when he was twenty-one to study for the Church. He soon found this was not his vocation. He did not find the subject agreeable, and the professors found *him* rather disagreeable. He was quick with his tongue, which got him into much trouble, and fluent with his pen, which got him a living. He became a freelance writer. Eventually he settled in London as editor of *The Agnostic Journal*, with premises at 41 Farringdon Street.

Friendship between the professional agnostic editor and the ex-boy preacher was instant and sustained. Among the references to Guy in the *The Agnostic Journal* is one of special interest to this biography. In the issue of 28th October 1905, Saladin wrote: 'This Guy, born on Guy Fawkes' Day, and intent on an argumentative blowing up of the House of Priestcraft, has done so much at eighteen that I am sure the readers of A.J. would all like to see what he will have done by the time he is eighty.' Saladin died a year later, and Guy Aldred was one of those who spoke in tribute at his graveside.

Guy met several interesting people at the Journal office. They were an argumentative lot, and it is unlikely that young Aldred was left out of the discussions. We may mention one of those characters, John Morrison Davidson. He was a *Reynold's News* columnist, a Republican, an anti-authoritarian, a Tolstoyan, a Scots Nationalist, a Scots historian, and an authority on Scottish folklore. He was the author of *The Annals of the Poor, The New Book of Kings, Scots Rediviva, the Book of Erin,* and several other volumes. Aldred later wrote in *N.T.G.:*

> 'When I sought out *The Agnostic Journal* offices and bearded Saladin in his den, I did not think that destiny would treat me to a Scots digression. Despite his anarchism, Davidson gloried in the traditions and folklore of Lowland Scotland.

At that time I had not crossed the border....I felt no desire to wander far from Clerkenwell. It was my fairyland of rebellion and revolt. Indeed I loved the history of Clerkenwell. Its very environment was an education in itself. Morrison Davidson insisted on my mind roving the glens of Scotland. He imposed his strong patriotic provincialism on me in the heart of London, not a stone's throw away from Fleet Street, and about the same length from the Cockney tenement in which I had been born.'

Morrison Davidson was born at Fetterangus, in the parish of Old Deer, Aberdeenshire, in 1843. When he was sixteen he obtained a scholarship which enabled him to enter Aberdeen University. A difference of opinion with one of the professors forced him to leave the University. He was attracted to national causes, and at the age of twenty tried to join the Poles in their nationalist insurrection. Rejected by the Poles, he returned to Scotland, married, and became a school teacher in Glasgow, and then a school headmaster in Berwick, ending his teaching career as a master of the famous Circus Place school in London. Davidson's heart was not in teaching, so he resolved to qualify for the Scottish Bar. He became a distinguished law student, but, at the age of twenty-six, settled into a career of journalism, becoming leader-writer for the *Peterhead Sentinel* and the Edinburgh *Daily Review*. Then, moving back to London, he entered the Middle Temple and was called to the English Bar in 1877.

Davidson was a grey-bearded man of sixty-one when Guy got to know him. He carried a heavy walking-stick, and he would sit with his chin resting on his hands on top of the stick, eyes fixed on young Guy while he told him endless stories of the Scottish countryside. During his daily visits to the office, Aldred was transfixed by Davidson about three times a week. 'His assault on me was continuous and lasted for nearly two years.' (*N.T.G.* p. 97.)

It was not all romantic history and folk-lore. Davidson claimed to be a vigorous champion of the oppressed peasants and labourers. 'The most important lesson I learned from the strange scholarly musings of John Morrison Davidson was the need for integrity in life. Actually, the *Agnostic Journal* office was my college. From Saladin came the learning, and from Davidson's ramblings came the inspiration. Davidson taught better then he knew. Yet he had made of himself a character rather than a man who had developed character.' (*N.T.G.* p.107)

That year — 1904 — was a very full year for the seventeen-year-old Guy Aldred. In January he broke from the Christian Social

Mission, and started speaking for the Peel Institute. In April he founded the Theistic Mission and in August the Clerkenwell Freethought Mission. He kept up a corespondence with Voysey, visited George Martin, and attended his 'college' in the *Agnostic Journal* office. A Christian Boy Preacher at the beginning of the year, he was an atheist socialist at the end of it.

They spoke a great deal in the *Agnostic Journal* office about Spencer's 'First Principles' and the 'Unknowable'. It is not a subject we can explore here, but we may say that Aldred rejected the concept of the 'Unknowable' when it was postulated with a capital letter. That made it an absolute: an Unknowable underlying the phenomenon of existence. This became a substitute superstition, a watered-down, formless God. He believed that it was indisputable that there was that which was unknowable (no capital) since all persons were relative beings. The riddle of the universe was beyond finite apprehension. Much later he wrote in *N.T.G.*:

'Early in 1904, discussions in Hyde Park and at the Peel Institute, references to Professor Huxley at the *Agnostic Journal* office, my own dis-satisfaction with mere metaphysics, caused me to study Thomas Huxley. As he was noted for his popularising of science and of Darwin, his Romanes address of 1893 on *Evolution and Ethics* had a special appeal to me. It made me into a complete socialist....In his Romanes lecture, Huxley insisted that "the influence of the cosmic process on society is the greater the more rudimentary its civilisation." He spoke of social progress checking the cosmic process at every step, and substituting it for the ethical process. It thus repudiated the gladitorial theory of existence, and permitted Huxley to rebuke "the fanatical individualism of our time" for attempting to apply the analogy of cosmic nature to society.'

This was an attack on the Darwinian theory of nature being red in tooth and claw, a theory which justified the ruthless competition of capitalism, and the invasion of imperialism.

'Social life, and the ethical process in virtue of which it advances towards perfection Huxley defines as being, strictly speaking, "part and parcel of the general process of evolution." Readers of Kropotkin will see in this a support of the latter's view of "mutual aid" as a "factor in evolution". It must be remembered, however, that Huxley's "Ethical process" is developed by its author into a plea for sentimentalism and loyalty to the interests of an abstraction termed "the community". I believe in the community — in a different social order

— but I see only two classes today. Huxley sees no classes, only a "community". And Kropotkin's mutual aid tends to create faith in the same paralysing and fatal abstraction....All this was not clear to me at the time. Huxley has pleaded powerfully the grandeur of the anarchist ideal....I became emancipated from Neo-Darwinian fears. Capitalism and the struggle for existence were not the last words in social evolution. Equity, mutual aid, freedom, justice, etc. *did* represent realisable ideals....This vision of the coming social harmony, this conviction that the new era *would* dawn, filled me with new energy. I knew that I had to leave the capitalist parties and enter the real movement; that of socialism and working-class emancipation. So I turned my back on compromise and radicalism, on liberal labourism, and pure-and-simple secularism, and joined the *Social Democratic Federation.'*

In 1904, Guy Aldred heard Daniel De Leon speak on Clerkenwell Green. De Leon had been to the International Socialist Congress in Amsterdam, and had taken the opportunity, to visit Britain. De Leon was born on December 14th 1852 on the island of Curacao off the coast of Venezuala, and educated in Europe. He returned to America in 1872, and graduated from Columbia Law School in New York City in 1878, and held a post as lecturer in that college for six years. In 1880 he joined the American Socialist Labour Party, and four years later he became editor of the Party's organ, *The People.*

De Leon believed that the workers should be organised into Branches according to the tools used by them. '....The workers whose tool is the typecase or setting-machine belong to the compositors' branch;....the workers whose tool is the pen belong to the editorial or writers' branch....' The various branches are organised into a Local Industrial Union. 'The further stage in the ascending line: Industrial Councils, and Industrial Departments, are obvious. Their structure, hence their method of organisation flows from the structure and reason for the structure of the Local Industrial Unions.' (*Industrial Unionism*, De Leon.)

Guy Aldred wrote:

'De Leon saw and taught that the system of government based on territorial lines has outlived its function: that economic development has reached a point where the Political State cannot even appear to serve the workers as an instrument of industrial emancipation. Accumulated wealth, concentrated in a few hands, controls all political governments.' (N.T.G. p.147)

37

Aldred may not have been impressed by De Leon as a speaker, but he was sufficiently interested to find his way to the London branch of the Socialist Labour Party — referred to by the locals as the 'Scotch Group' — in the old Communist Club (officially known as *Der Kommunistischen Arbeiter Bildungsverein.*) Here the walls, then draped with portraits of Marx, Lassalle, Mazzini, Garibaldi and others, had once reverberated to the great voice of the mighty Bakunin. Guy, in 1904 a youthful member of the audience, later spoke in this hall with Guy Bowman, editor of *The Syndicalist*, who was jailed for twelve months in 1912 for publishing an appeal to soldiers not to shoot at demonstrating workers.

Aldred was learning, but he did not yet feel impelled to enter the political sphere of thought. He was still struggling from agnosticism to atheism. The meetings of the Clerkenwell Freethought Mission were not tame affairs. Sometimes there was much riotous opposition. The first meeting was held on Tuesday August 2nd in Garnault Place, and the second on Sunday 7th on Clerkenwell Green, and so alternately for two years. The first subject was 'The Perfection of God', then 'The Mission of Freethought', next 'Calvary's Lesson'. It was at the fourth meeting, held at Garnault Place on the 16th, and entitled 'What Constitutes Freethought' that Guy met trouble. Aldred became noted for his ability to control an unruly crowd, even during the stormy war years. But on this occasion he was still a lightweight, and for the only time in his life the meeting got out of hand.

It started with an argument on the outside of the meeting, spread to the fringe of the crowd, then involved the speaker himself. The verbal abuse resolved itself into a chant of 'Infidel: Infidel'. Guy managed to restore a semblance of order and continue his address. But the trouble started up again, and Guy did not pour on soothing oil when he called the interrupters 'My Fidel Friends'. They charged the platform and knocked him off, then proceeeded to beat the love of God into him, but he struggled free and tried to remount, only to be pulled off again. Finally a couple of policemen intervened, ordered the crowd to disperse, and told Guy to go home. The seventeen-year-old Guy gave them much back-chat before he complied. It was his first brush with the Law.

Grandfather Holdsworth had left the meeting when calm seemed to have have been restored, and was doubtless surprised when Guy arrived home in a distressed state. As a consolation he fetched from his private cupboard a collection of pamphlets by Richard Carlile and Charles Bradlaugh which had been published under the title *The Atheist Pulpit*. He advised Guy to study these and said that in the matter of religion it was more important for one to read John Bunyan's

Life and Death of Mr. Badman, than the more popular *Pilgrim's Progress.* Aldred tells the story. (N.T.G. p 23)

'My grandfather delighted in poetry, and in the evening when he introduced me to these atheist writings, he gave me a volume of Shelley. He told me the story of the Titan god, Prometheus. If I wished to serve mankind, he warned me, I must expect scorn and abuse....(But) I must not permit persecution or neglect to make me bitter....He pointed the moral by reciting the lines:

"To suffer woes which hope thinks infinite;
To forgive wrongs darker than death or night;
To defy power which seems omnipotent;
To love and bear; to hope till hope creates
From its own wreck, the thing it contemplates."

'My grandfather's parting injunction that night was that I should discover actual and symbolical truth in this story of the immortal pagan, and embody the lesson in my life.'

Evidently refreshed in mind and spirit he returned to the platform, never again to be mastered by his audience. With youthful defiance he advertised himself as 'The Rev. Guy Aldred, Minister of the Gospel of Freethought' (later changed to 'Revolt'). He wrote an article for the *Islington Gazette* on 'Islington's Ecclesiastical Memories' by the Rev. Guy A. Aldred. During the whole of 1906 the *Gazette* had reports of Aldred's meetings, letters from readers about those meetings, and replies from the young, aggravating Mr. Aldred. By that time he had joined the Social Democratic Federation.

8: THE SOCIAL DEMOCRATIC FEDERATION.

The meetings with John Burns and other persons of the left at the Peel Institute led Guy to *The Clarion* and to an office opposite The Clarion where the National Democratic League met in Chancery Lane. The president of the League was W.M. Thompson, a barrister, and editor of *Reynolds News*, a radical republican Sunday newspaper founded in 1850. Aldred's social convictions were firm enough by March 1905 for him to join The Social Democratic Federation.

The Federation was founded in 1883, an event which is regarded as the beginning of the modern socialist movement in Britain. From it sprang many other groups in the years that followed. The organ of the S.D.F. was *Justice*, with Henry Mayers Hyndman as its editor, and, in fact, the leading figure in the Federation. The S.D.F. claimed to be Marxist, without a very clear definition of the term, and there was no satisfactory agreement on the question of parliamentary representation. A faction, led by William Morris, broke away, and in January 1885 formed an anti-parliamentary group which they called The Socialist League. The League dissolved in 1892, but its anti-parliamentary message lingered on.

Aldred, opposed to 'careerism' in the Church, maintained the same attitude in the political field. So it was as a cynical young journalist that he became parliamentary correspondent for *Justice* in January 1906. An Education Bill was being debated in the Commons at the time, and he had the satisfaction of seeing his *Justice* article on the subject being quoted in *The Times*. But, he says (in *N.T.G.*), he had suspected that there was much that was farcical in parliamentary debates; now he knew they were all farce. In May 1906 he gave up the job of Commons reporter.

He was not very popular with his elders in the S.D.F. For a nineteen-year-old he knew too much and he had no under-estimation of his knowledge or his ability. He was a sensational new addition to the socialist platform, with the ebullience of youth and the experience of maturity. When rebuked by the bearded Hyndman on one occasion, and reminded of his scarcity of years, he retorted that 'Wisdom came before whiskers'. H.M. Hyndman was not amused.

Aldred's break with the S.D.F came over the propagation of atheism from the platform. The elders (except Belfort Bax, who defended Aldred) did not want the matter of religion, or anti-religion, to cloud the socialist issue. Guy Aldred, still conducting the Clerkenwell Freethought Mission, thought differently. Socialism, he argued, was founded on a materialism which explained all abstract ideas and institutions in terms of mother earth. To embrace its teachings was to war against every myth 'from God to captains of industry.' Socialism entailed a belief in natural law, conditioned by the principles of its own experience, not in a deity, influenced by the whims of man. This should be the view of the S.D.F.; but the Federation repudiated these principles, and practically avowed their conviction that socialism was but a reformist legislation. The political opportunism of the S.D.F. suggested that socialism was secular and mundane, rather than atheistic or anti-religion.

'Here was socialism,' Aldred wrote later in *N.T.G.* (p 112), 'a clear-cut philosophy of materialism, representing the revolt of mother earth against the sky, the social and economic maturity of man, being negated for votes by people who mouthed working-class watchwords today, only to eulogise the deeds of a capitalist Cabinet tomorrow....'

It was his contention that Marxism was basically anti-parliamentary. The fall of the Paris Commune in 1871, and the break-up of the International (1864—1876) destroyed the international character of socialism and drove it within the confines of national boundaries. From this arose Social Democracy, as a wing of the bourgeois parliamentary system. Hence the betrayals of socialist aspirations, the prolongation of capitalist economics, the acceptance of war. In *The Herald of Revolt* (1910) Aldred probed this matter a little deeper, and came to the conclusion that Marx had deliberately contrived the destruction of the anti-state faction in the International as early as 1866. The International was very much influenced by the Proudonhists of France. Pierre Joseph Proudhon, born in 1809, had just died (1865), but his spirit lingered on in substantial form. Proudhon was a non-violent anarchist. He also believed that man was moved by basic feelings of justice, and this was at variance with Marx's theory that ideals had their roots in material, specifically economic, conditions. Now that Proudhon was gone, Marx conspired to exorcise his spirit. There came an opportunity when the Franco-Prussian war became imminent. Marx wrote to Engels, July 20, 1870:

'The French need a thrashing. Is Prussia victorious, then State-power will be centralised, thus centralising the German working class. German preponderance will shift the centre of the West European Labour movement from France to Germany....Its preponderence over France would mean the preponderance of our theory over the one of Proudhon.' (John Spargo: *The Life of Karl Marx*).

Aldred wrote that this wish by Marx in 1870 was realised in 1871 when the Franco-Prussian war ended with the defeat of France. Engels wrote: 'As Marx predicted, the war of 1870-1871, and the fall of the Commune, shifted the gravity of the European Labour movement from France to Germany.' (1895 Preface to *Class Struggles in France.*) This, said Aldred, brought Engels to the ridiculous conclusion that:

'The successful employment of the parliamentary vote entailed the acceptance of an entirely new tactic by the proletariat, and this has undergone rapid development. It has been realised that the political institutions in which the domination of the bourgeoisie is incorporated offer a fulcrum whereby the proletariat can work for the overthrow of those very institutions. The social democrats have participated in the elections to the various diets, municipal councils, industrial courts....consequently the bourgeoisie and the government have become much more alarmed at the constitutional, rather than at the unconstitutional activities of the workers, dreading the results of the elections more than the results of rebellions.'

Thus, remarked Aldred, the leadership of the movement passed to Kautsky, notorious for his weary theorising, practical reaction, and renegadism.

Guy blamed Engels for fostering parliamentary socialism as opposed to 'Commune' socialism after the death of Marx. The early Social Democratic Federation was unsure on this point. Belfort Bax recalled that there was a feud between the 'believers in political action and those who were convinced that all political action — and indeed anything beyond propaganda tempered by occasional direct action in the way of riots — was of the — well, of the bourgeoisie.' Aldred saw in 1906 what was to become clear twenty years later, that to make socialism a matter of electoral power was to make it a power *within* the system, and part of the system. The object of socialists should be to overthrow the system.

In June 1906 Guy Aldred left the S.D.F., and looked around for a Group which would help him express his ideas. He was now a *non-parliamentarian,* believing that parliament was useless in the socialist cause, but that the ballot-box might serve a purpose other than that of presenting an easy job to careerists. He drew up a 'Revolutionary

Manifesto', which was published in the *Islington Gazette* for October 28, 1906. This was addressed to 'The Electors of Finsbury'. By the time the next election is held, he stated, he would be twenty-one years of age, and eligible for parliamentary representation. He therefore put himself forward as a prospective candidate for that constituency. He pledged a refusal to take the oath, to recognise that reforms cannot remove the 'gyves and fetters' from the masses, and to promote the realisation that economic determinism precludes the interference of any deity in the affairs of man.

He wrote to the Social Labour Party paper *Socialist* suggesting the endorsement of a 'very few' candidates selected from the Socialist groups, all of them pledged not to take the oath of allegiance, and to oppose all palliative policies. The editor, J. Carstairs Matheson, rejected this suggestion with some scorn; but when, in 1912, the Croydon Branch of the S.L.P. passed a resolution endorsing a motion that its members pledge themselves not to swear or affirm any allegiance to capitalist institutions, Matheson (by that time an ex-member), accused them of wearing Guy Aldred's old clothes.

Young Aldred was now well-known as a Socialist with extremist views, and his eloquence was drawing crowds around his platform in Hyde Park. He was also writing for several socialist and radical papers. John Turner of The Freedom Group asked him to contribute to a new paper *The Voice of Labour*, a journal which would stress the syndicalist aspect of anarchism. Aldred wrote for every one of the thirty issues which were published, either above his own name or as *Ajax Junior*. As a matter of course, this led him to the anarchist club in Jubilee Street where he met the leading figures (if we may be excused the term) of London anarchism.

9: WITH THE ANARCHISTS

In 1848 Karl Marx wrote 'A spectre is haunting Europe; the spectre of communism....' During the eighties and nineties of last century the spectre carried a bomb under its cloak. If the crowned heads of Europe did not tremble, they were at least forced to accept the possibility of personal disintegration as an occupational hazard. The shift of emphasis in socialist agitation from *internationalism* and *State opposition*, to *nationalism, patriotism* and *State socialism* had not yet worked its way through the movement, creating careerist opportunities as it went. Anarchism held the stage, while social democracy gathered its cast and learned its lines.

The violent anarchists received the publicity and formed the image, but in fact they were in a tiny minority: many more believed in spreading the word rather than in throwing the bomb, and there were those who believed that there was more dynamite in direct industrial action than in hurling a hand-grenade at a king. *The Voice of Labour* tried to exploit the potential of this vast industrial arsenal. It was not very effective. There were several anarchist journals in London at that time, or but recently dead. In German there were *Die Freheit, Die Autonomie, Der Lumpenproleterier;* In Yiddish *Der Arbeter Fraint;* and in English *The Anarchist, Commonwealth, The Torch,* and *Freedom.* Each stressed a different aspect of anarchism. *Freedom* was founded in 1886 to express the views of Peter Kropotkin, though it was never the mouthpiece of just one person. It concerned itself more with thought than action, and in 1893, a year of intense anarchist violence, the paper stated its opposition to this form of propaganda.

'The genuine anarchist looks with sheer horror upon every destruction, every mutilation, of a human being, physical or moral. He loathes wars, executions and imprisonments, the crippling and poisoning of human nature by the preventable cruelty and injustice of man to man in every shape and form....Every well-meant attempt of the men in power to better things tends to confirm people in the belief that to have men in

44

power is not, after all, a social evil....Not the Parliament, not the Government, but the organised workmen could, if they but knew it, put an end to capitalist monopoly, peacefully, by simply bringing the capitalist to the condition of workmen, not by paper money — dreamed of by Proudhon — but by a general strike.... The guilt of these homicides lies upon every man and woman who intentionally or by cold indifference helps to keep up social conditions that drive human beings to despair. The man who in ordinary circumstances and in cold blood would commit such deeds is simply a homicidal maniac; nor can we believe that they can be justified upon any mere ground of expediency. Least of all do we think that any human being has the right to egg on another person to such a course of action. We accept the phenomena of homicidal outrage as among the most terrible facts of human experience; we endeavour to look such facts in the face with the understanding of human justice, and we believe that we are doing our utmost to put an end to them by spreading anarchist ideas thoughout society.'

There were several anarchist clubs in London at that time. The *Club Autonomie* had closed. It had been a special meeting place for anarchist refugees. Peter Latouche describes it: '....a dingy, badly-furnished ramshackle place.....Apart from its dinginess, the *Autonomie* had a certain amount of Bohemian picturesqueness. Most of the men affected sombrero hats and red neckties; the women had their hair cut short, wore Trilby hats, short shabby skirts, red rosettes in mannish coats, and stout, business-like boots.'

It was at the *Autonomie* that the 'Red Virgin', Louise Michel, held forth to a crowd which on one occasion included King Humbert of Italy. His Majesty (incognito) was slumming in London. He was anxious to study the poor, and felt that there were more interesting specimens in Queen Victoria's capital than in his own. He found a special fascination in the agitation of the anarchists, and was killed by an anarchist's dagger at Monza on July 29, 1900. Latouche, writing in 1908, says: 'There are five anarchist clubs in the East End, the chief of which, in the Kingsland Road, has a membership of more than a thousand. It is run mainly on the lines of the old *Autonomie*. All the anarchist papers published on the Continent may be purchased there, and like all similar clubs, it is largely patronised by detectives.'

It was easy enough to infiltrate the anarchist movement, for there were no strict rules of membership, and Special Branch men were so numerous that they had to concoct their own plots on occasion, and sometimes carry them out themselves. In Chesterton's satire *The*

Man Who Was Thursday, the whole anarchist cabal are on detail from Scotland Yard.

It is not likely that any (well, not many) spies frequented the Jubilee Club, and there was no theatrical flamboyance. Aldred did not remember the Jubilee Club as a dingy place. There was a recreation room, a meeting hall and a tea and soft drinks bar. The comrades did not throw bombs at presidents, but hurled ideas, hard as bricks, at each other. There were partisans of Proudhon, of Bakunin, and of Kropotkin, and the latter were in the majority, for the old man was still alive and writing well. Sometimes he came to the club and delivered a lecture. On one occasion when he was unable to come, Rudolf Rocker, who in *London Years* refers to Aldred as one of the promising young men of the time, asked Guy to deputise for the great old man. Guy obliged, and the audience was treated to (or subjected to) a lecture quite different from that expected, for the speaker was opposed to the over-gentle views of Kropotkin, and even refused an invitation to visit him. When Kropotkin became pro-war in 1914, Aldred felt an added justification for his opposition.

As we have already noted, in the middle of last century Marx found the ideas of Proudhon an obstacle to the propagation of his own theories on scientific socialism. As a youth, Pierre Joseph Proudhon worked as a waiter in an inn, and spent much of his spare time in reading. At the age of nineteen he became a proof-reader and read so much theology that he was able to contribute articles to the *Encyclopedia Catholique*. So valued were these contributions that he was awarded a pension of 1,500 francs per annum by the *Academie de Besancon*. This freed him for further study, and his mind turned to Political Economy, with a sympathetic leaning towards socialism.

In 1840 he wrote his best-known book *What is Property?*. He answered the rhetorical question in a dogmatic assertion: Property is Theft. Marx later observed that the title does not define what property is, and the reply to the question implies a belief in property, because without property there cannot be theft. The next book of importance was written six years later and was entitled *The Philosophy of Poverty*. He was unwise enough to ask for Marx's opinion of this work,. This came as a devastating criticism in *The Poverty of Philosophy*. Proudhon contended that Justice and Legality were not values apprehended by religious revelation, nor discovered by philosophical reasoning, nor did they have transcendental existence. Man was a social animal; he desired an ideal society. Such a society must give absolute liberty. Any control of man by man is oppression. Justice and Legality were innate qualities of human existence. They

The Paris Commune and he State Idea (1871).

'Humanity has be n ruled and governed too long. Indeed, the source of the pec les' trouble lies not in this or that form of government, but in t existence and manifestation of government itself, whatever orm it may assume. This is the historic difference between the authoritarian commnunist ideas, scientifically developed through the German school and partly adopted by English and American socialists, and the anarchist communist ideas of Pierre Joseph Proudhon, which have educated the proletariat of the Latin countries....'

In a speech to the League of Peace and Liberty Congress held at Berne in 1869, Bakunin asserted that he was a communist but a collectivist. The distinction has disappeared, and the word 'communist' is used in both senses: as a federation of communes (collectivism), or as a 'proletarian' State (communism). Bakunin said:

'Communism I abhor because it is a negation of liberty, and without liberty I cannot imagine anything truly human. I detest communism because it concentrates the strength of society in the State, and squanders that strength in its service: because it places all property in the hands of the State, whereas my principle is the abolition of the State itself, the radical extirpation of the principle of authority and tutelage which has enslaved, oppressed and exploited and depraved mankind under the pretext of moralising and civilising men. I want the organisation of society and the distribution of property to proceed from below, by the free voice of society itself; not downwards from above, by the dictate of authority. In this sense, I am a collectivist and not a communist.'

Aldred agreed with this statement, except that he did not think that the State created property, but that property necessitates and decides the State.

Aldred was not uncritical of Bakunin — in fact he was not uncritical of anybody — but there was an attraction which caused him to call his printing shop, when he later established it, Bakunin Press, and the headquarters of his group Bakunin House. There was in Bakunin's 'spirit of revolt' a kinship with Aldred's 'indwelling urge', his 'divine discontent.' They both believed that authority weighs like leaden scales on the wings of liberty. *God* and the *State* must be abolished. Life is dynamic, it must challenge, change, reconcile, and challenge again. Only death conforms, and in conformity life dies. During that year (1906), when Aldred was making acquaintances at the Jubilee Street Club he wrote two articles for *Freedom* on the Philosophy of Anarchist Communism. These later became a pamphlet entitled *The Case for Anarchism.* We will discuss that at a later chapter, when we have Aldred confined in a cell at Glasgow's Barlinnie Prison.

The prevailing influence at the Freedom Group was that of Kropotkin. Prince Peter Alexeivch Kropotkin was born in Moscow in 1842. His family was of royal blood, more ancient than the Romanovs. Under the Czar his father was a country gentlemen owning three estates and twelve hundred male serfs, and their families. The town house in Moscow had fifty servants. Young Peter spent much of his childhood in the care of serfs and developed a sympathy for their thoughts and problems. He had two tutors, one of whom had served with the Grand Army of Napoleon. At the age of fifteen he became a member of the Corps of Pages at the Court of Alexander II This was a training ground for the sons of nobility, and Peter should have eventually attained high office. Military training was compulsory, and a privilege of the Pages was the right to choose their own regiment. Peter caused amazement and consternation by choosing the Mounted Cossacks of the Amur, a recently formed regiment from a region just annexed by Russia.

Kropotkin spent five years in Siberia, not, like most revolutionaries, in chains or exile, but in tasks to his own liking. He was secretary to two committees set up by the Governor, one to review the whole system of exile and prison reform, and another to prepare a system of municipal self-government. This caused him to reflect on the institution of government; it also brought him into contact with political exiles and 'so-called incorrigible criminals.'

Kropotkin was interested in people, and in the way in which they lived; also in the world in which they lived. In 1863 he led an expedition to the Amur. By a Treaty concluded in 1858 between the weak Chinese Government and Russia, represented by Bakunin's second cousin, Nicholas Muraviev, the territory north and west of that great river was ceded to the Russians. It had not yet been explored. It is probable that no European had ever set foot on that remote and sparsely populated land. Kropotkins' task was to make maps. That mission completed, he was sent on similar journeys into hitherto unknown parts of Manchuria. He later made geographic and geological surveys of Finland. Before he was thirty he had gained an international reputation for his work. Soon his reputation was to be of another kind.

Kropotkin's natural sympathies, his experiences in Siberia, his observations of primitive communities, his interest in history, all led him towards the convictions which ripened in his late twenties and became the best-known features of his personality. He became an anarchist. In 1872 he joined The International just when it was about to be wrecked by the Marx-Bakunin dispute.

Kropotkin identified himself with the Bakunin opposition. He never met Bakunin, but greatly admired that 'colossal figure.' After imbibing the ideas of the revolutionary exiles in Switzerland and relating them to his own, Kropotkin returned to Russia to spread the truth among his fellow-revolutionaries. In 1874 he was arrested and cast into the dungeons of the Peter and Paul Fortress. He describes his incarceration in *Memoirs of a Revolutionist.* Of the Fortress, he wrote: 'This, then, was the terrible fortress where so much of the strength of Russia had perished during the last two centuries, and the very name of which is uttered in St. Petersburg in a hushed voice.'

He reflects on some of the victims of this place of degradation and torture. Here Peter I tortured his son Alexis and killed him with his own hand; here the Princess Tarakonova was kept in a cell which filled with water during an inundation — the rats climbing on her to save themselves. He remembers the Decembrists and a list of rebels and poets who had suffered and died in the loneliness of the damp and dark dungeons. And he remembers Bakunin. 'All these shadows rose before my imagination. But my thoughts fixed especially on Bakunin, who, though he had been shut up in an Austrian fortress, after 1848, for two years chained to the wall, and then was handed over to Nicholas I who kept him in this fortress for six years longer, came out, when the Iron Czar's death released him after an eighteen years' imprisonment, fresher and fuller of vigour than his comrades who had remained at liberty. "He has lived through it," I said to myself, "and I must, too. I will *not* succumb here!"'

Kropotkin escaped from his dungeon, courageously and dramatically. Outside help supplied a carriage with a specially-bought swift horse between the shafts. He made for Sweden, then to England, and back to Switzerland. Bakunin had just died, but his *Jura Federation* was very active. Kropotkin joined in its work, becoming the editor of its journal *Le Revolte* in 1878.

In 1883 Kropotkin was back in prison again, a French jail this time, after a trial which lasted a fortnight and had a press coverage worth many pamphlets. Kropotkin was so well-known as a geographer, libertarian and man of science, that there was great agitation for his release, and so much concern for the conditions of his imprisonment that he was allowed to read and write while serving his sentence. After three years he was set free. It was then he came to England, in

March 1886, and remained there for the following thirty years, peaceful and respected, and writing continuously. *Mutual Aid* is the work most readily associated with his name. This title conveys the basic contention of his anarchist philosophy.

Mutual Aid was a challenge and a contradiction. It challenged the notion that nature was 'red in tooth and claw', and that it was a natural law that the evolutionary process involved mutual antagonism within a species. On the contrary, it was the element of mutual aid which helped many species to survive. Kropotkin was rich in ideas depicting the conditions of life in an anarchist society. There would be no need for compulsion, hence no need for the State, or for political government. Men and women would enter into voluntary associations to perform whatever tasks were necessary for the maintenance of society, finding, as far as possible, work most congenial. There would be no wages. All would take from the common store whatever was required for existence and enjoyment.

Guy Aldred was always opposed to Kropotkin. He felt that Kropotkin had abandoned his revolutionary Bakuninism and had adopted the position of a respectable suburban intellectual, propounding bland theories and becoming the patron of drawing-room anarchists. There was in his own thinking some of the ideas of mutual aid. The precept he had preached as a boy evangelist had been 'Bear ye one another's burdens' — which meant spontaneous, individual, self-willed service, free from institutional direction or conventional prompting. Aldred's atheist 'Word' and 'Vision' were more mystical, but blew from the same direction as Proudhon's and Godwin's innate sense of 'Justice'. Mutual aid was a preserving, binding force, essential in society; but equally essential, and complementary to it, was the seeming contradiction, the dynamism of rebellion, the explosive force of insurrection. This is what Bakunin had personalised; and this is what parliamentary place-seekers, and arm-chair anarchists had forgotten. Aldred felt there was no place for him in any existing group. He must form his own. And he did so, one group to educate, and one group to fight.

10: THE CORD OF DESTINY

We have reached the year 1907. Guy Aldred would be twenty-one on November 5th. It was a year of change for him in his domestic as well as his public life. His stepfather had fled to Canada to outwit his creditors: his grandfather had gone to live with an older daughter who had been widowed. Young Guy was the breadwinner for his mother and three stepbrothers. In his autobiography, Guy wrote:

> 'The years 1904 — 1907 were most interesting and important years of fruitful study and discussion. In London, at this time, I was in the very thick of much radical discussion. My mind responded like virigin soil. I rejoiced in this turnover of thought, this thrust and parry of theoretical conflict, and the attempt to visualise the practical consequences of the theories proclaimed.'

The parry and thrust of theoretical conflict was not a contest of purely intellectual quality. Sometimes heads were broken. Young Aldred spoke every night of the week in some part of London, and three times on Sunday in Hyde Park. The Hyde Park meetings were for the National Secular Society. As he did not get on well with Kropotkin of the anarchists, so he did not get on well with Foote of the Freethinkers — nor had he got on well with Hyndman of the Social Democrats. He never repented of this hostility towards his elders, even when maturity had revealed his own youthful faults. He maintained that they should have shown tolerance and unabrasive guidance to a youth of talent and sincerity.

R.M. Fox, the writer of Irish adoption, in his book *Drifting Men* gives a fictionalised account of Guy Aldred at that time:

> 'Among other rolling stones of the political underworld was a young Jewish agitator with the eyes of a dreamer who, within sight of the opulent mansions of Park Lane, spent his nights and days in vehemently attacking all that they represented. He had a rabbinical interest in theoretical disputations and dogmatic discussions. Sheer delight in controversy made him embrace many beliefs, and join many organisations of which he soon

grew tired.   He did not confine himself to the spoken word, but
wrote a new sort of *Pilgrim's Progress* under the title of
Dogmas Discarded, published for fourpence, with a photo of
the author.   It told....(how) he had come to accept his present
anarchist and atheist views.   Not yet did he despair of finding
new and still further advanced opinions....He added a preface to
the pamphlet announcing that he was far too intellectual ever to
want to bring children into the world.   "The mass of mankind
are slaves — slaves who beget slaves" he announced.   For
himself, he declared loftily, he did not care what happened to
posterity, or if the human race died out.

'Then came Milly Silverman — a tall, pale Jewess from
Poland, with an oval face and dark, wide, luminous eyes.   He
looked at her, and her eyes stroked him from head to foot.   She
went with him to meetings, listened to his theories, and agreed
with them, moving through the crowd in the violet dusk with a
grand romantic air like a Conrad revolutionary.   Within a year
the race suicide theorist was nursing his baby son by the Hyde
Park railings while Milly's dark eyes caressed them both.   Some
of his disciples jeered.   But he was indifferent.   Life had
triumphed over theory.   And he discovered that if he tore the
"race suicide" preface out of his pamphlet it was still saleable.'

There were imaginative liberties here, accepted good-naturedly by
Guy — he and Fox went to jail together in 1916, and were still good
friends when they were both old men.   Guy was not a Jew, although
one of his grandparents on his mother's side was.   The pamphlet was
not *Dogmas Discarded*, which was not written at that time.   Fox
was referring to Aldred's earlier pamphlet *The Religion and Economics of Sex Oppression.*   The preface was not removed, but later
printings deleted some obviously adolescent paragraphs, and reduced
the grand title to *Socialism and Marriage.*   The girl's name was
Rose Witcop.   She was Russian, not Polish.

In January 1907 Guy left the National Press Agency and joined the
Daily Chronicle.   Six months with the *Chronicle* and he quit
journalism to become a full-time progagandist, unpaid except for
collections and donations, which also had to pay for printing
advertisements and all expenses of his groups.   It was a hard road he
had set himself, but such was the call of the 'indwelling urge', the
'Inward *must*'.   He later wrote: 'During 1907 my tendency towards
heresy-within-heresy was shaping my destiny....'

Destiny was at young Guy's elbow on the night of the Jubilee Street
Club's Benefit Social on behalf of the *Voice of Labour*.   It had been

hoped that Kropotkin would grace the occasion with his presence, but the weather made the journey inadvisable. None of the older comrades felt inclined to bring forth on the spur of the moment the kind of speech required to open the proceedings: short, crisp, cheerful, yet serious and inspirational. So they asked young Aldred to oblige. He performed the duty so expertly that he was warmly applauded, and fussed over for a while. Then the dancing began.

Guy could not dance, he could not sing, and he had no small talk. Attention turned away from him. He bought a cup of tea and was sitting in isolation when John Turner noticed him and brought Rose Witcop over to meet him. Rose was much as Fox later described her, though her five feet ten inches stature was a trifle disconcerting in a seventeen-year old. She was the sister of Milly Witcop, the free-love partner of Rudolf Rocker, much-respected spokesman for Jewish immigrants. Born at Kiev in 1890, Rose had been brought to London by her family when she was five years of age.

Rose made the conversation. She asked Guy about his ideas, and about his meetings. She said she must attend some of them. Guy didn't think she would. She was just being polite. She was so stately and mature for her years, and she was so sad. He would have liked to ask her why she was so grave, but he felt that might not be a good question to ask.

It was a month before he heard of Rose again. This reminder came in the form of a letter to *The Voice of Labour*. It concerned votes for women, and was signed 'Rose Witcop'. It was a long letter, but it may be summarised as a criticism of the Suffragist movement on the ground that the vote meant little to working-class women. She would not qualify for it anyway, so why should a woman who slaved all week in an ill-conditioned factory for paltry wages care whether middle-class women had the vote or not? Even if she had the vote, how many working-class women would 'bother' to use it? And if they did use it, would it make any difference? What was required was the organisation of working women in an agitation for general emancipation; to make women understand that it is not the want of voting rights that creates bad conditions for her, but the social attitude which regards her as a slave, both in the factory and in the home. Guy was greatly impressed by the letter.

He saw her at several of his meetings after that. The next time he was near enough to talk to her was at the 1907 May Day Rally. The anarchists marched behind a lorry carrying many small children and a cargo of parcels of pamphlets. At the anarchist platform in Hyde Park Guy saw Rose with one of those parcels. As he approached her she asked him if he had a knife. Guy answered jauntily: 'No, I haven't. Being an anarchist, I never carry lethal weapons.' Rose affected not be amused. 'Well, maybe you can unravel a knot. When I saw you in Jubilee Street you seemed to be an intelligent person, so you ought to be able to undo a knot.' Guy witheld the observation that untying knots was not a test of intelligence. He leapt on to the lorry and obligingly undid the knot — and destiny threw a loop over both of them.

Rose started attending the Discussion Group which Guy conducted in the basement of his mother's house, and she wrote him letters giving an account of other meetings she had attended. Mrs. Aldred (we will call her Mrs. Aldred for convenience, though she lived as Mrs. Stray) felt badly the loss of grandfather's income when he left the house. She had three little sons to feed and clothe: Albert, Ernest and Reginald Stray, aged ten, eight and six. She took a four-month summer job, presumably in the parasol trade. Mrs. Aldred knew what was going on in her basement, but was more indifferent than tolerant — till Rose came along. She knew that Rose had her eyes on Guy before Guy knew it, and she did not like it.

Guy was working on the *Daily Chronicle* till July of that year. Sometimes he was on night work, sitting around for the news flash which would mean a quick write-up. On such occasions he was not at home when his mother left for work in in the morning, and she was not long at home in the evening when he had to leave for the office. How the little boys got to school is not recorded. They probably took a sandwich with them. Guy did not over-spend on food for himself. Every day he went to Pearce and Plenty's and had a plate of macaroni for two pence and a halfpenny cup of cocoa.

Some weeks after the May Day incident Rose was prompted by fate to pull the cord a little tighter. She told Guy that she wished him to invite her home for tea. She knew Mrs. Aldred did not like her, and though the suggestion may have been innocent, it is more likely, since she was an intelligent girl, that she was testing how far Guy would stand against his mother in her defence. And probably she would have welcomed a confrontation with Mrs. Aldred. Guy agreed, and invited her to call on the afternoon of the next day.

He was always at home in time to make a meal for the boys when they returned from school. Then he washed up and reset the table in readiness for his mother when she arrived later. Then of course he had to get some sleep. With luck, Rose would have had her tea and be gone before his mother arrived. If not, he would make introductions and hope for the best. But luck was not with him. It may be that Mrs. Aldred was early or that Rose's presence prolonged the meal. However it was, Mrs. Aldred arrived while they were still at table.

She must have been tired, for her health was not good, and her work long and tedious. She would consider that life had not been good to her. Her husband — Guy's father — had deserted her on the church steps; her bigamous husband had drunk himself into debt and absconded; her father had deserted her to support an older sister; her son was flirting around with atheists and anarchists. There was only one thing to be said, and she said it: *'Get that bloody Russian Jewess out of my house!'*

Guy was furious. He did not want to have a row in front of Rose and the children. He and Rose left the house. Guy did not return home to get any sleep, and he did not go to work that night. He walked the streets, all the circumstances of the incident churning around in his mind. *He* had more to complain of than his mother had. *He* had not deserted her. He gave her every penny he could, and he looked after his half-brothers better than their father had. His mother had not been mindful of him. She had not wanted him in the first place. He had been the result of a clandestine meeting with his father. He had been brought up mainly by his grandfather. His mother had deserted him to go off with the worthless Ernest Stray. Why should he not have whom he liked as a companion? It was also *his* house. He now paid the rent. It was the next day when he went home to lie awake in more unhappy thoughts. Surely he was not to blame. He loved his mother. His dream was that he stay with her and look after her while the boys grew up, and still be with her in her old age — she was then forty. But he wanted Rose to be there too. He would have intelligent discussions with her, and together they would conduct great propaganda campaigns for the emancipation of mankind from economic bondage and religious superstition.

There is no record of what went on in Mrs. Aldred's mind during the night. She may have regretted her angry words, and certainly she would hate to see Guy so upset. It was not that she minded him going around with girls with unusual opinions. There was a girl who was a freethinker. She called on Guy for copies of Bradlaugh's writings. This girl worked in a food shop, and always brought offerings of fruit, meat or fish. She was very nice, and Mrs. Aldred often invited her to tea. She would have been welcomed into the household — as Guy's wife. But she was not an over-sized Russian Jewess with immoral ideas about free love.

Next day and thereafter there was a sad atmosphere in the Aldred household. It would remain so until Guy stopped seeing *that woman*. When Guy left his job on the *Daily Chronicle*, causing even greater economic hardship, his mother knew that his action was due to the influence of that dreadful woman. And she was helpless in trying to save him.

11: Liverpool Campaign.

The group which John Turner, Guy Aldred and other associates of *The Voice Of Labour* formed in 1907 was the 'Industrial Union of Direct Action' (I.U.D.A.). Its object was to operate on the industrial field, not for reforms or alleviations, but for the promotion of social revolution. The first target was the decentralised organisation of the workers in a pattern which would emerge, on the advent of the revolution, as a federation of Communes. The weapon of the workers would be the General Strike, which would not accept the reformation of the capitalist system, but demand its abolition. Violence would not be used by the workers except in response to violence from the other side. Members of the I.U.D.A would contribute two pence per week for general expenses.

The organisation got off to a good start considering its slender resources. Within a few months there were six branches in London and one each in Dover, Leeds, Liverpool and Weston-super-Mare. Guy, who wrote the 'Notes' for the I.U.D.A. in the *Voice* was ecstatic in his enthusiasm. The beginning of the end of the old order of economic injustice was in sight. Soon traditional bargaining Trade Unions would crumple, political parties would be swept aside, and the true and natural form of social organisation would assert itself in a network of free Communes.

Some of the meetings were stormy, mostly disturbed by ecclesiastics who were still after Aldred. *Reynold's News* for July 21st reported:

'Owing to the bigotry and monopolising tendencies of an East End divine, the rights of free speech are being jeopardised at Leman Street East, near the railway arches. On Sunday last, Mr. Guy A. Aldred, a freethought and communist writer and lecturer, and General Secretary of the 'Industrial Union of Direct Actionists', convened a meeting there, but came in conflict with the local police. On his affirming his right to be heard, the intervention of eight policemen notwithstanding, a temporary truce was concluded, Mr. Aldred agreeing to give up his meeting on the condition the police at once closed down the Christian meeting. This was done. Mr. Aldred will organise a series of meetings at this spot, and thus challenge the right of the police to interrupt the right of free speech.'

In June 1907 the Liverpool branch of the I.U.D.A. invited Guy Aldred to conduct an anarchist campaign on Merseyside. This branch had fifteen members, the most active of whom was Mat Kavanagh. He was the most enduring. He was ten years older than Aldred, and he was still in the propaganda field during the Second World War, when he was detained under Regulation 18b as an anarchist, but released when it was realised that the Regulation was intended to intern fascists. Kavanagh was born in 1876 and died on Friday March 12th, 1954.

He came from Dublin and worked with Kropotkin, Malatesta and Rocker in the years before the First World War. In 1916, just before the Easter Uprising, he returned to Dublin to join up with Larkin and Connolly, but his views were not acceptable, and he returned to England where he spoke for many years in Hyde Park.

Rose accompanied Guy on this expedition to Liverpool, ignoring the disapproval of her mother. Mrs. Witcop had two daughters who were anarchists, one of them living with the respected Rudolf Rocker, but she was an orthodox person herself, and did not think it proper that a seventeen-year-old girl should travel unchaperoned with a twenty-year-old youth. She need not have worried. Rose was very well able to take care of herself. Mat Kavanagh, who took his anarchism seriously, assumed that Guy and Rose were 'companions' in the anarchist sense of the word, and as he was their host, showed them to a nice little room containing what could have been a very delightful double bed. Rose was as outraged as any convent maiden — maybe more so. Guy was disconcerted; Mat was embarrassed. Other arrangements had to be made.

The Liverpool meetings were very successful, though the *Voice of Labour* reporter introduced a note of criticism by disagreeing with the statement 'that it is put abroad that Aldred was unnecessarily boisterously antagonistic to the other schools of thought.' This boisterous antagonism was most vigorously expressed at the best meeting, which was held in the Clarion Club. Here foregathered extremists of every shade: adherents of Bakunin, Spencer, Morris, and Kropotkin. There were Irishmen who had left the Redmond Party and joined the recently formed *Sinn Fein* of Arthur Griffiths. Their ideals were not the same as those of James Connolly: that came later. There was something paradoxical about their membership of Clarion. They were Nationalists among Internationalists, religionists among atheists, and among free-lovers they believed in the sanctity of marriage. This traditional Irish contrariety was obscured by their insurrectionary attitude, their anti-parliamentarianism, and their opposition to the British Government. There is no suggestion that they attacked Aldred's extreme views. That came from Social Democrats who objected to his freethought. The theme of Guy's lecture at the Club was that all idols should be overthrown, political as well as religious, and this should be accompanied by economic revolt, for the synthesis which would form the new society must come from the destruction of the old in all its departments of expression. With his youthful love of long-winded titles, he billed his lecture as 'Socialism and Synthetical Iconoclasm.'

The Liverpool *Porcupine* for September 1907 noticed his activity in a sarcastic leading article:

'It is only a young man — a very young man — who could swallow all that (Free Love, Anarchism, Impossibilism, etc.) at once, and at the same time have the courage — we almost said audacity — to expound so profound a doctrine from the public platform. What it all means no-one — unless exceptionally gifted — can understand, but at all events it strikes at the very roots of organised society. So let the capitalists beware, Mr. Aldred is very much in earnest, and he....means to turn the world topsy-turvy, so it is just as well that he commenced young....He is in his person a fascinating study and his lectures are delivered with a gravity of style which is in singular contrast to his youthful appearance. He is by turns cynical, argument-ative and humorous, and he shows his ability by the manner in which he controls his audience — especially when antagonistic. Altogether one whose career will be watched with interest. But what a programme!'

When Aldred returned to London, a quarrel began between him and John Turner. He accused Turner of promoting ordinary Trade Union activity, and other associates of being hidebound by the concept of the General Strike as though it was an end in itself. The object of the I.U.D.A. was positive, not negative. The Strike was but a weapon, thought to be useful, but not sacred as an ideal to be achieved. His criticism broadened to embrace the whole *Freedom* group. Their anarchism, he said, was mere Trade Union activity which they miscalled Direct Action. This was largely due to the immigrant influence. Refugees from oppressive countries settling in Britain were apt to consider liberalism and industrial organisation as advanced extreme expressions of political philosophy, and to link them with the desperate struggle of anarchists in their own countries.

John Turner was not an immigrant. He was born on an Essex farm in 1864. As a young man he came to London and obtained work as a shop assistant. He became manager of a multiple tea firm. He certainly had a Trade Union outlook. The conditions of the shop assistants caused him to form the first Shop Assistants Union. He was influenced by the teachings of Morris and Kropotkin, and became an active worker in the Socialist League. When Kropotkin formed the *Freedom* group in 1886, he joined that. He was the responsible publisher of *Freedom* from 1895 to 1907, then he helped to launch *The Voice of Labour*. Maybe Aldred's charges are substantiated by the fact that Turner's subsequent career led him to the General Secretaryship of the Shop Assistants' Union. He died in 1934.

The other organisation promoted by Aldred at this time was more his own than the I.U.D.A. This was the Communist Propaganda Group — the first time the word 'communist' had been used in the name of a British organisation. Its purpose was to educate and propagate. It held public meetings, ran discussion groups, speakers' classes, and a library. The public meetings were held in the open air or in public halls; the private meetings were held in the basement of Guy's house at 133 Goswell Road. And h·re the first *Bakunin Press* was established.

This was a second-hand platen machine. It cost ten shillings, with a tin of ink and various accessories thrown in. This historic machine was trundled across London on a wheelbarrow pushed by Guy Aldred and a young German called Karl Lahr — but known for sixty years thereafter as Charlie Lahr, socialist bookseller and encyclopedist, and visited at some time or other by all radical visitors to London. He later became connected with the Independent Labour Party, but in 1907 he was secretary of the Whitechapel branch of the I.U.D.A. The Turner-Aldred difference may not have caused the demise of this organisation, or the end of *The Voice of Labour*, but it cannot have had a sustaining effect.

The London Communist Propaganda Group had branches in Clerkenwell, Islington, Brixton and West London. Later it spread to Wales, the north of England, then to Scotland, where it established groups in Glasgow, Paisley, several Lanarkshire towns, Fife, Dundee and Aberdeen. In 1921 the groups federated into the Anti-Parliamentary Communist Federation. There was a programme of Twenty-One Points. Point Seventeen is an anticipation of the Third International.

(17) This political struggle does involve the negation of parliamentary action, the boycott of the ballot-box, and the organisation of the workers in one
INTERNATIONAL COMMUNIST PARTY
within, but antagonistic to the Capitalist States.

12: THE VOICE OF LABOUR

The Voice of Labour described itself as a 'Weekly paper for all who work and think.' It cost one penny and usually had eight pages. Its first number appeared in February 1907 and, considering the speed of travel in those days, in a very short time it carried articles from correspondents in Japan, Australia, Egypt, Argentine, Russia, Italy, Spain, Portugal and the United States. These concerned conditions of labour, and the plight of the unemployed. Their details are no longer valid, but the problems of a society organised primarily for monetary gain still remain. Some of the articles in *The Voice* are unrealistically theoretical and naive in their faith in the intrinsic goodness of human nature; a virtue subverted by the evidently congenital wickedness of capitalists and authoritarians in general.

Kropotkin, writing to the *Voice* to apologise for not being able to attend the benefit night (he had a touch of influenza) went on to express his views on the function of the paper.

'....I wanted to tell you why my warmest greetings and hopes go to the new paper, founded by our English comrades.

'The free organisation of labour, independent of all parliamentary parties, and aiming at the *direct* solution — by the working men themselves and working through their Union — of the immense social problem which now stands before civilised mankind, such a Labour organisation, wide and powerful, has become the necessity of the moment.

'This is why the same idea which prevailed in 1830 at the foundation of the great Trades Union of Robert Owen, in The Working Men's Association of the early '40s (before the Chartist Movement), and in the International Workingmen's Association of the sixties, has again been revived in France, in Switzerland, in Spain (where it survived all prosecutions), and now it grows, even in Germany. The working men realise the great mistakes they committed when they substituted Parliamentary politics for Direct Action of the Labour organisations in enforcing their demands upon the land and capital owning classes....

'The English *Voice of Labour* is thus a sign of a movement which is going on all over Europe, and our English paper will take its place by the side of a series of French, Swiss, and Spanish Syndicalist and Labour papers bearing the same, or very similar names....'

One paper with a similar name was *La Voix du Peuple*, the organ of the Confederation General du Travail, a federation of federations comprising the syndicate of French workers. Briefly what had happened was that the Great Revolution had destroyed the medieval Craft Guilds, and when the Revolution was over the fear of a swing further to the Left had caused the passing of laws against workers' organisations. As the nineteenth century advanced, those laws had been ignored and small unobstrusive syndicates formed. Those had federated. If only a small number of delegates, representing a large number of members, assembled, the law was not so obviously flouted. At first those syndicates were simply trade union societies, then socialism crept in; then as political doors did not open, came anarchism and industrial action, and the doctrine of the general strike. Anarcho-syndicalism became the character of the Confederation General du Travail. Although Kropotkin was credited with having effectively replaced Darwin's struggle for power as a social motive force by the principle of Mutual Aid, he still believed, as in the days of his Bakunin discipleship, that the rule of authority would be over-turned by the workers, and that this would involve a struggle. As the power of the workers was in the factories, it was there that revolutionary direct action should generate.

The industrial proletariat was a comparatively new phenomenon in human history. There had been societies built on slavery, on serfdom, on peasantry, but never on a mass of landless, propertyless industrial workers. These had appeared with the advent of mercantile capitalism and had become more numerous with industrial capitalism, and all-pervading with finance capitalism; for all talent was up for sale. It was inevitable that these free, landless, unowned slaves of the factory system should generate a power, and that it should attempt to found that power in association. Two courses were indicated: the way of industrial power and the way of political power. (We will leave consumers' co-operatives out of this superficial examination.) During the nineteenth century there was much shifting from one course to the other. Robert Owen's unionism gave way to political Chartism, and when that failed there was a return to the industrial battleground. Socialism was not always the creed of working-class leaders, but it eventually became overwhelmingly so in some form or other.

In Britain compromise led to confusion. Both aspects of the issue, the industrial and the political, were supposed to be represented in the Labour Representation Committee, formed in 1900 as the voice of Labour. It was not committed to socialism: some thought it would blossom forth as syndicalism. As late as 1911 this hope still flickered. (Tom Mann was one of the hopefuls.) When the Committee changed its name in 1906 to The Labour Party, it became obvious to others besides young Guy Aldred that it was intent on becoming His Majesty's Opposition *en route* to becoming His Majesty's Government, administering capitalism and creating a whole new class of political careerists, living as parasites on the surplus value extracted from the workers.

John Turner did not have Kropotkin's European thought processes; syndicalism concerned him less than British Trade Unionism. He was building up the Shop Assistants Union. He believed other similar Unions should be formed, comprising the low-paid (what we would now call 'service') workers. The Unions should be federated and work in a common cause to overthrow the wages system. It was an insult to the intelligence of the workers to say that such organisation would be betrayed by its leaders in the interests of their own careers. To John Turner industrial organisation was enough, and he refused to enter politics as a Labour candidate when, later on, he had the opportunity; but in 1930 he drew upon himself the censure of former colleagues when he sent out a circular to members of the Shop Assistants' Union which said: '....Whilst not by any means looking to or waiting for legislation for all the reforms of shop life we are out to obtain, we ought to use every means in our power to bring them about, and the great extension of the Trades Union element in the House of Commons (in the Lobby, and on the Benches) which the establishment of the Political Fund makes possible, will put an edge on one of the most powerful weapons at the disposal of Labour, and will eventually enable us to determine our own conditions.....'

Guy Aldred's view was that any amelioration of working-class conditions as a whole was impossible under Capitalism. His argument was that what was gained as a wage was lost as a price, or what was won as a worker was lost as a consumer. He did not lack sympathy for the lowly paid. In his column in the *Voice* he exposed many cases of gross exploitation. There were the shirt makers, (those of whom Thomas Hood wrote so pathetically in his poem *Song of the Shirt*) who, working at home with their own machines, were paid six shillings and ninepence *per dozen* for shirts which sold at one shilling and threepence each. If those workers agitated for, and succeeded in getting one shilling per dozen extra, and the shirt were raised to one shilling and four pence (possibly to one shilling and sixpence) the general condition of the workers had not improved.

Aldred believed that the total amount paid in wages under capitalism was no more than what was needed to keep a worker alive and well as an instrument of labour. This well-being included his ability to maintain a wife and 'procreate his kind' as future grist to the capitalist mill. If we remember Aldred's missionary work in the still-Victorian slums, we will not be surprised that he held this view. He did not mean that some workers were not well paid and financially comfortable compared with others: he did mean that if the butter of affluence was evenly spread it would be little more than a smear. And he contended that in a trade union organisation the object would be — despite federation and brotherly greetings — for each section to strive for the greater share of the total wage expenditure. Thus trade unionism tended to be a scramble for the scraps of capitalism, not an organisation for the emancipation of the workers.

This line of argument would hardly appeal to the unemployed girls of Liverpool who, if they were between the ages of sixteen and eighteen, and could pass an educational examination, and could produce three testimonials of character, might be considered for a job in the tramways department at the attractive wage of eight shillings per week, less threepence for the superannuation fund. They might think that, however sparse the spread of butter on the workers' bread, they were getting a mere smear of margarine. In such conditions, despite the (disputed) iron law of wages, Aldred had to side with the workers. He was nevertheless of the opinion that strikes for better wages resulted only in the manipulation of money from one section of the workers to the other, and from worker (as worker) to worker (as consumer). He thought a more solid gain would be the strike which demanded better factory conditions, since these, not being a continuing expenditure, were less likely to be passed on to the consumer.

In any case, the quintessence of socialism should not be its bargaining power, but its non-mercenary nature. It should not inscribe on its banner 'A Fair Day's Wage For a Fair Day's Work', but 'The Abolition of the Wages System'. Goods and services should be offered for *use*, and not for profit. Commerce was an ancient feature of society, dating back to the days of barter, but only recently had it become the dominating function of society. Human relationships at every level were affected by a 'Cash Nexus'. Alleged socialists were abusing the language and debasing the concept when they interpreted socialism as a doctrine demanding more cash for labour sold.

Aldred's view of syndicalism was that it was, in many countries, just another name for trade unionism, perhaps a *red* unionism, or an industrial unionism, but always with this weakness: that it considered the human being as a producer, and as an adjunct to the factory. It was conceived for the industrial complex. It had little room for the unemployed, and it was not free from embarking on polital adventurism.

He agreed with the syndicalists' doctrine of the class struggle, and the tactic of the general strike, though on this he had some reservations. In the twenty-one points of his newly founded Communist Propaganda Group he advocated the *Stay-In Strike* — unusual in those days. This he considered a sound move in the direction of the take-over of factories. The form of social organisation which Aldred depicted as the goal was a system of local Communes of consumers (who were also workers), building up to regional Communes; and a system of Soviets of workers (who were also consumers) building up to regional Soviets. Money would cease to be a commodity, though it might be needed as a token for some time. Eventually it would not be required in a community where everyone gave according to his ability, and received according to his needs. This was not, however, the end, the consummation of human endeavour. This was only the next stage on man's journey into the unknown. There must always be change, for change is life. We can only strive for our own objective. Future generations will have their own.

The Voice of Labour was struggling to survive, not because its principle supporters were at variance in their theories, nor because the *Voice* was strong in airing wrongs but weak in asserting remedies. It was just that they could not charge more than a penny (sometimes they charged a halfpenny) for the paper, and only a mass circulation paper carrying advertisements could survive on such a budget. Donations were not generous.

Aldred began to give more time to his own organisation. Much of the work there must be educational, he believed, with a strong agitational bias. To extend the work of the discussion group he started a correspondence course. There was also a speakers' class. To say that these meetings, as well as considerable printing activity, took place in the basement of his mother's house is to give a wrong impression.

The premises at 133 Goswell Street was a shop, a boot shop. At the back it had a house, where presumably the shopkeeper had once lived, but which was now rented by Mrs. Aldred. It also had a basement, extending under both shop and house. This basement could be entered from either the house or the shop. The house could be entered either through the shop or by a private side entrance. So the basement was very large, and by the grace of the proprietor, who had known Guy since he was a schoolboy, Guy was able to use it via the shop for the gatherings of his comrades. Thus it was that Rose Witcop could still attend the classes of the Group and not fall foul of Mrs. Aldred.

13: COMING OF AGE.

When Guy Aldred was seventy-one years of age he sat in his office at the Strickland press in George St. Glasgow and cast his mind back fifty years to the eve of his twenty-first birthday. He wrote:

'There is no doubt that 1907 was a most important year in the development of my life and thought. It was a period of political and revolutionary research and stocktaking. Then I associated more intimately, wisely or unwisely, with Rose Witcop. A domestic crisis confronted me because I had stalked out of Fleet Street with all its promise, and decided on an independent life. This completed the breakdown with my mother, who knew nothing of free-lance activity and was horrified at the thought that I should refuse to work at the office of a great London newspaper. Such a terrible thing to do!

'There were moments when worry and study and even propaganda were forgotten. I recall one Saturday when I went out to Chingford Old Mount with Rose Witcop. It was a beautiful day. And there there was an old-world garden and house called Rose Cottage, quaint and very cottagey. There tea and cakes, and eggs boiled or fried, were served in the garden. It was completely old-world and away from everywhere. There one sat and drank tea and romanced. Rose Cottage was run by two old ladies whose charges were certainly not excessive. They exuded beauty in their attitude and their garden was a haven. Alas! they were quite old, and unless they are near one hundred and twenty years of age they must have passed away by now. So ruthless is time and destiny!'

The courtship of Guy and Rose was not without intensity, for they spent much time discussing deep social questions involving emancipation of the workers and women's rights. It was also an austere courtship, for much of it was passed sitting in coffee rooms and tea shops, making a little cash go a long way. They had nowhere else to go. To Rose's mother, Guy was a 'Goy' (derisively, a Christian youth), and to Guy's mother Rose was a 'bloody Jewess'. Grandfather sometimes received them, but they were not made to feel welcome by the aunt with whom the old man now lived.

There was one solution. If Guy could convert his mother——— She had never heard him speak. If he could persuade her to attend one of his meetings she would realise the importance of the task to which he had dedicated his life. She might even help him in his work. She might receive Rose into her house and they would all stay together and no heartbreaking parting in bitterness need be contemplated. He invited, coaxed her, to attend one of his indoor meetings, held for the Freedom Group in the Bath House, 96 Dean Street, off Oxford Street. Those gatherings took place every Wednesday. He probably did not tell his mother that Rose Witcop took the chair. Mrs. Aldred was not the least bit interested in the ills of society, the slavery of women, or the oratory of Guy.

He tried again when the great and notorious Emma Goldman arrived in London a few weeks later. She had been attending an Anarchist conference in Amsterdam and was taking advantage of the occasion to visit some of the capitals of Europe.

Emma Goldman, known as Red Emma, at first among her friends, because of her red hair, and later, internationally, because of her politics, was born in Russia in 1870. She went to the United States when she was fifteen, and in her involvement with the poor immigrants, became an anarchist. In 1893 she was sent to prison for saying publicly that if the unemployed were not given bread, they should take it. Such extravagent utterances made her notorious, and when she came to London in 1899 for a series of meetings, Boar War jingoism was at its height, and the comrades feared for her safety.

She spoke at the South Place Institute on 'Patriotism'. Tom Mann took the chair. The hall was packed and hundreds had to be turned away. Half the audience had come to make trouble, and there were catcalls and scuffles, but eventually she got a hearing and spoke to the end of her intended address. It was then that she met Rudolf Rocker.

Rudolf Rocker stood next to Kropotkin in the ranks of anarchist pre-eminence. He was a German book-binder who came to London in 1895 — when he was twenty-two years of age — looking for work. He was not a Jew, but had become interested in the libertarian Jewish movement in Paris. This interest continued in London. He taught himself English and Yiddish, and became an outstanding public speaker in both languages — as well as in German. He became editor of the monthly paper called *Germinal*, and of the weekly *Arbeter Fraint*, published in Yiddish.

This paper, anarchist in outlook, had a struggle to survive, as all such papers have, but by 1906 it was prosperous enough to open the

Jubilee Street Club, the proper name of which was the *Arbeter Fraint Club and Institute.* But it was, understandably, more often designated by the simpler title. It became an anarchist and radical centre in London.

Emma Goldman renewed her acquaintance with Rocker in 1907, and with his companion Milly Witcop, and with Milly's sister Polly, (who was also an anarchist) and so, of course, she also met young Rose and Guy. She would have heard of Guy in any case, for Rocker at that time had a high regard for his abilities as a young hopeful in the movement. She probably had ill reports of Guy as well, for not everybody loved him. In any case, she paid no attention on this occasion. It was several years later, when he came out of jail, that she took friendly notice and mentioned him in her paper *Mother Earth.*

Guy's mother was not the least thrilled at the prospect of hearing the notorious Emma. She was probably of the opinion, as all respectable women were, that Emma was a brazen bitch as well as a bloody Russian Jewess. That Guy should want to take his mother to hear such a woman showed how terribly he had been corrupted by the company he was keeping. Guy and Rose went to the meeting without her.

It took place in the Holborn Town Hall on October 7th. Emma's subject was 'The Labour Struggle in America'. The hall was filled. John Turner, as Chairman, led the speaker on to the platform amid enthusiastic applause. There was no opposition. Guy was not impressed. Emma Goldman lectured vigorously, but there was no depth to her understanding. She spoke like an inspired mediocrity on mundane things. There was no undertone of eternal verities, no proclaiming of *The Word*, no flashes of *Vision* — but then, Emma had never been a Boy Preacher. She did make ominous remarks about the Western Miners knowing how to use dynamite. Rose thought this a defiant pronouncement of direct action. Guy did not agree. He said it was a cry of desperation and weakness, not a proclamation of strength. They argued long on this point.

By this time the little Bakunin Press in the basement of the Aldred house could list three penny pamphlets in its catalogue. These were: *An Open Letter to a Constitutional Imbecile: The Logic and Economics of the Class Struggle: The Ethics and Economics of Historical and Traditional Christianity,* (also containing *An Agnostic's Xmas Sermon).* Ready for the little press was *The Religion and Economics of Sex Oppression.* Young Guy *did* like impressive titles, the longer the better.

The October days were wearing in.   Soon it would be November, the fifth of November, Guy Fawkes Day, and Guy Aldred's twenty-first birthday.   He recalled years later that he felt a rising excitement as the day approached; not because there would be any celebration or any presents, but because he felt the ascent of his boyhood years would reach the summit on that day and before him would lie exciting vistas of futurity.

The great day was on a Tuesday.   On the Monday afternoon he met Rose by arrangement near Stepney Green.   They walked along Whitechapel Road till they reached a cafe not far from Jubilee Street.   Here they pretended that the tea and buns were an advance celebration of the next day.   There was a thrill of anticipation like that of a childhood Christmas Eve.

When they left the cafe they walked together in the happiness of each other's company.   Then, as though on impulse, Rose excused herself and went into a shop.   When she came out she had a parcel which she gave to Guy.   She said it was a birthday present; he must promise not to open it till he reached home.   Guy promised.

We don't know with what difficulty, if any, he kept his promise.   He surely wondered what was in the parcel, and surely he guessed without straining his imagination.   Yet he carried the parcel all the way home after seeing Rose to her door.   He must have guessed it was (metaphorically) dynamite; that it would cause an explosion, and blow him out of his slough of uncertainty, and out of his mother's house.   Either his promise not to open the parcel was inviolate, or he willed his fate.   Any down-and-out would have relieved him of his burden, yet he carried it home and opened it right under his mother's nose — figuratively speaking.

Unless she was very innocent and a bit stupid, that is exactly what Rose had planned.   The contents of the parcel was not so much a present for Guy — for how could he make use of it? — as a slap in the face for Mrs. Aldred.   It was a shirt — and either by diabolical design or unfortunate coincidence was a *blue* shirt, a colour his mother had told him did not go well with his swarthy complexion.

In those days, before the advent of the affluent teenager, throwaway commodities and unisex, it was a mother's care to buy her son's underwear and shirts, to wash them and to mend them.   The usurpation of this duty by another woman — other than a wife — was an affront, and Mrs. Aldred was affronted.

'Where did you get that?' she asked in a tone which showed that she need not ask, and put Guy's wits into top gear to find a pacifying answer. She supplied the answer herself: 'I suppose you got it from that Jewess!'

'Yes,' said Guy, and remained silent while the storm raged over him. He wrote about it later. 'I listened in patience and said nothing. My mother was driving me away from home and bringing tragedy into her life, the lives of my half-brothers and myself. How foolish she was....At that time no great desire possessed me. I wanted to be dutiful to my mother. I wanted to conduct the propaganda to which I was devoting my life. But I *did* want to be able to bring my friend home.'

That was not to be. Next morning his mother uttered a cheerless 'Happy Birthday' and, knowing what was in Guy's mind told him that if he invited 'that woman' to her house *she* would walk out. He could go and spend the day with her if he liked. Guy had purposely *not* arranged to meet Rose that day. He wanted to spend it with his mother and half-brothers.

It was a day of gloom for Guy. He hated 'atmospheres' and tried to obliterate the brooding unfriendliness by making the tea and not allowing his mother to exert herself. Then he asked if he might read to her, and when she had agreed he read aloud a novelette of her own choosing. When he had finished it was near bedtime. 'Oh, Dady,' she exclaimed, giving him his childhood pet-name, 'that was wonderful!'

Her happiness gave Guy no pleasure, but rather increased his misery, for he knew he must plan the end of his boy-hood life and leave home.

'It was a day of tears, not one of joy.'

73

14: THE FREE-LOVER

We may surmise that Mrs. Aldred's happy mood continued as she went to bed and sank into sleep. Dady was not so bad after all. He still belonged to her; he still loved her. It was that awful woman —— Bloody Russian Jewess——.

Guy sat in his cold gaslit room and thought sad and angry thoughts. His pain was not assuaged by the reading of a novelette, or by his mother's gratitude. She had not relented. The victory had to be hers. His resentment mounted as he reviewed the situation. All he wanted was to bring Rose into the house as part of the household. His mother had nothing to lose. Rose would be a help to her in many ways. She would be a help to Guy also, in his printing and propaganda work. Her sister, Milly, had learned to set type when Rudolf Rocker's *Arbeter Fraint* was struggling to survive; and everyone respected Rudolf Rocker and his companion.

If he and Rose shared the same room in the house, or occasionally did, it was nobody's business. Certainly his mother had no claim to self-righteousness. None knew where she had met Alfred Aldred, or where Guy had been conceived. Ernest Stray she had met on top of a tramcar; and she had invited him to become a lodger in her parents' house without asking anyone. It was not an innocent arrangement. When she was three months pregnant they married, and had left Guy to stay where he pleased in complete indifference. There was no doubt about it: he must leave home. Justice was on his side.

He turned his attention to the paper he was writing for at at that time — *Freedom*. This was another twenty-first birthday celebration. The paper was one month older than Guy Aldred. The October issue reviewed the historical events of the past twenty-one years. It was a very long time to Guy, a whole lifetime, and an even longer time lay ahead of him before the wholeness of his lifetime was complete. What lay in store for him?

74

He felt a shadow of the future fall over him as he read that in Germany Karl Liebknecht had been imprisoned for writing an anti-militarist book, and the Berlin editor of *Freie Arbeiter* had followed him into incarceration for printing articles on the same subject. He also read that six German secret-service men had been sent to London to work with Scotland Yard in protecting 'The Little Kaiser' during his proposed visit to cousin Edward. The menace to the royal person came from the anarchists, who had 'dispatched' the United States President a few years back, and were still in business. Guy did not know that his public utterances had gained him a place on the list of suspected would-be assassins, and that a visitor from Scotland Yard would enlighten him.

If Aldred's writing table in his bedroom in 1907 was anything like his writing desk in the Strickland Press in 1957 — and it probably was — then it was a great mountain of books, papers, letters and pamphlets. Into this mountain a little inlet had been cleared to give him a place for further writing. The excavations from each clearing were thrown on top of the pile, and the mountain grew higher daily. By internal evidence we may determine the composition of the mountain.

There would be several back issues of the *Voice of Labour*, now temporarily suspended after thirty-three issues; *Freedom, Clarion, Agnostic Journal, Freethinker, Freewoman,* and *Islington Gazette.* There would be dozens of pamphlets, some by Blatchford, some by Bradlaugh, and some by Annie Besant. There would be tomes by Madame Blavatsky: *Asia Unveiled,* and *Key to Theosophy.* There would also be books by Madame Blavatsky's convert, Colonel Olcott: *Buddhist Catechism, Theosophy, Religion and Occult Studies,* and *Old Diary Leaves.* He was getting through those books as part of his continuing self-education. Much of what he read he rejected, but he felt he had to read it first.

Aldred had been introduced to Theosophy by 'Saladin', who had sent him to interview Annie Besant, probably as part of young Guy's journalistic training and intellectual development. He was eighteen at the time, which was July 16th 1905. Mrs Besant gave him much of her time, and evidently enjoyed talking to him. It is not for us to follow the interview here. A small taste only. Guy began by asking Mrs. Besant if Theosophy was the antithesis of agnosticism. Mrs. Besant replied that the meaning of the word 'agnostic' according to its coiner, Huxley, was 'without *gnosis*', that is, the faculty to know anything about the universal spirit (since the mind is finite), where Theosophy asserted the contrary, and offered the direct antithesis to that position. She talked a long time with Guy, but when the interview appeared in *The Agnostic Journal* for July 29th, Saladin had removed some political references, for he would not get involved in politics.

Among the pamphlets which Mrs. Besant gave Guy to take away and study were *Fruits of Philosophy* by Charles Knowlton, and *The Wife's Handbook* by H. Arthur Allbut. It was from those books that Guy derived much of his sex education, rather than from experience, for at twenty-one, he tells us, he was still innocent, and there is no evidence to the contrary.

Fruits of Philosophy was the booklet which Mrs. Besant and Charles Bradlaugh published in 1876 and for which they were prosecuted, sentenced to six months imprisonment and fined £200. This sentence was later quashed. The book advocated birth control. Its argument is that sex indulgence is a pleasure, but like all pleasures it is only morally justifiable if it adds to the sum total of human happiness. If it does not, then it is an evil, and should be repudiated.

Dr. Knowlton observes that the population is increasing much faster than the food supply, and thus life in the future is not going to be very pleasurable for posterity. Thus the pleasure of sex is a sin if it is over-indulged, resulting in irresponsible births. So he advocated the control of births, and gave advice on how this can be done. He also advised restraint in the practice of sex, particularly by men. He revealed from his medical knowledge the amount of blood (!) that is lost by the man on each occasion, and calculated the staggering amount this comes to in a year, and the dire consequences this can have on the health of the profligate.

Young men in their late teens cannot have found much comfort in Dr. Knowlton's book. Before the age of twenty the loss of energy by the sex act is particularly damaging. Twenty-two is the earliest safe age, particularly for a young man who has to use his mind. Involuntary nocturnal emissions he labels *Gonorrhaea Dormientium*, a dreadful nerve-shattering disease (but he is quoting from Dale Owen's *Moral Physiology*), while 'onanism' leads to insanity, and prolonged celibacy to 'spermattorrhoea'. Not a nice book for bedside reading, but, apart from its teaching of methods of birth control, quite typical of the sort of nonsense about sex widely taught in those days.

One thing Mrs. Besant had in common with Guy was that both had at some time in their lives come under the influence of Charles Voysey. They were both Christians who become theists on their way to atheism. Mrs. Besant went beyond that to Theosophy, becoming a convert to this belief when she read Madame Blavatsky's mighty tome *The Secret Doctrine* for review in *The Pall Mall Gazette*. When Madame Blavatsky died in 1891 (born 1831), Mrs. Besant took her place as high priestess of Theosophy. She was sixty years of age when she was interviewed by young Aldred, and she had another twenty-six active years ahead of her. She went to India where the international headquarters of the Theosophical Society was established at Adyar, seven miles from Madras. She was one of the founders of the *Indian Home Rule League*, and was interned for activities on behalf of that organisation in 1916. She died in 1933.

One little book which may have been on Aldred's desk that night was Edwin Arnold's *The Light of Asia*. He liked this poem, which tells the story of Buddha, and the book remained with him all his days (It is at his biographer's elbow as he writes these words.) Aldred has marked some lines of this book. At that part where the wealthy young Lord Buddha, half-asleep in the courtyard of his palace, hears the wind, like the breath of fate, play notes on a stringed instrument which is lying nearby, there is a marking at the verse which reads:

'We are the voices of the wandering wind,
Which moan for rest and rest can never find;
Lo! as the wind is so is mortal life,
A moan, a sigh, a sob, a storm, a strife.'

Perhaps those lines were marked on that sad night when Guy's twenty-first birthday faded with the chimes of midnight.

Towards morning he picked up the task which faced him and which he knew would cause further domestic trouble. This was the final proof reading of *The Religion and Economics of Sex Oppression*. The pamphlet would have forty-eight pages, and would cost threepence. The Foreword was the essay which R.M. Fox said Aldred deleted after the birth of his son Annesley. He did not literally tear it out, but as it advocated celibacy the advent of his son was incontrovertible evidence that he had violated its spirit — *de facto*.

The first part of the pamphlet shows the discrimation against women propounded by Holy Writ, despite the compassionate humanity of Jesus. The second part extends the examination to the commodity-society of Edwardian Britain. Woman is a commodity. Outside of marriage she is for sale. In marriage she is a osession. Young Aldred was of the opinion (not peculiar to him) that women have little, if any, desire for cohabitation, but are conditioned to submit, in humility or in kindness, to the sensuous desires of the male. Then the instincts of motherhood make secure the bonds of slavery.

There are many sensible utterances in the pamphlet, but it is not easy to grasp his conclusion. He attacks sexual association in every guise: in ecclesiastical marriage, in secular marriage, in the 'free marriage' of monogamous free love, and in promiscuity.

His conclusion is implied rather than stated. Sex is a male instinct, in its physical expression. It is a female instinct in its sublimations of gentleness and love. In its physical expression it is nasty and brutish. In this sense it is better for a man to burn than to marry. In its sublimation, man is carried beyond himself to the apprehension of a higher consciousness. But man in his brutishness dominates; woman in her humility submits. It is for the enlightened man to overcome this brutishness. Restraint is not only moral, it is an ethical duty. We have to end a society fashioned to accommodate the appetites of men, in their lust and in their possessiveness.

As the clock moved up to four in the morning, he re-read the Foreword. In this he explains that the pamphlet has its source in several articles he had written for various papers. One of these, appearing in the *Voice*, was 'The Ethics of Celibacy'. Aldred reached for his pen and on that morning of the first day of his twenty-second year he added a paragraph to that Foreword:

'As I take it, however, that the test of fidelity to one's principles lies in this willingness to practice what one preaches, I take this opportunity to affirm my intention to live up to the ideals and opinions outlined in this present brochure. For me, the terms 'wife' and 'husband' have no meaning, and the idea of a love founded on sexual-passion and necessitating intercourse of a physical character, no attractions. It only remains, therefore, for me in conclusion, to dedicate my present effort to my comrade and friend Rose Witcop, as a token of sincere friendship and affection, in the hope that by the example of our individual living up to the principles herein enunciated and described, others may be led to a greater purity of living, and clearness of comprehension.

'It is only fair, however, to add that it is dedicated without the permission of my comrade having been first sought or obtained.'

Altogether, it was a pamphlet which could only have been written by a young man like Aldred, and at that time. Today, it seems naive, and the idea of a youthful innocent venturing to tell all of humanity how to conduct its sexual and marital life rather touching and amusing. But it also indicates that he was seeking intellectual justification for attempting to keep his own passions in check — an attempt which was to fail.

It was half-past four on Tuesday morning 6th November 1907. Frozen, worn-out, Guy Aldred went to bed.

Next day, Guy had a visitor. He introduced himself as Detective-Inspector John McCarthy, and asked to see Guy privately. He said that, as was publicly known, of course, their Imperial Majesties the Emperor and Empress of Germany would be on a visit to Britain from 11th November to 13th November, and that he had been detailed to follow Guy Aldred during that time and report on his movements. He revealed that Aldred's speeches were reported to Scotland Yard, and that he was on a list of suspects should anything outrageous happen. The inspector said that he had listened to Aldred speak and had read his writings. He understood him to advocate direct action in the industrial sense. He did not think that he urged or defended assassination. He therefore was not going to trouble having him watched. He would call on Guy Aldred each day and ask where he had spent the previous day, and that would be enough for his report. He explained that there were still some Russians left over in London from the Fifth Congress of Russian Social Democrats which had met in London in July. They needed watching.

This was the Conference of 336 delegates, including Lenin, Trotsky, and Stalin, who met in the Brotherhood Church in the Southgate Road. An M.P. (Will Thorne) had asked the Home Secretary in the House of Commons in May if he was aware that these Russians were being shadowed and photographed. The Home Secretary, Herbert Gladstone (son of a more famous father), said that the persons in question were being neither shadowed nor photographed by the Metropolitan Police.

That was true enough, but was a typical evasion. The job was being done by the Special Branch. This had been formed as the Special Irish Branch in 1884 to deal with the Fenians, known as 'The Dynamiters'. When the violence of the Irish had (temporarily) subsided into the wordy battles of Home Rule Parliamentarianism, the term 'Irish' had been dropped. Then the Special Branch turned its attention to the Anarchists.

Detective Inspector McCarthy was very courteous on that first visit to Aldred, as he was on every other occasion, even when he was in charge of a raiding party, and even when he placed Guy under arrest. In the course of his Special Branch career, which extended from 1882 till 1918, he must have made many political arrests, including that of Savarkar, the Indian patriot. He also took part in the famous seige of Sydney Street, when the alleged anarchist Peter the Painter was either burned to a cinder or escaped to Russia — nobody knows which.

The *Sex Oppression* pamphlet was a best seller. Aldred was very persuasive when announcing his own pamphlets from the platform, but with such a title little persuasion would be required. Guy was known as an advocate of free love, and to most people at that time — and later — free love meant a glorious, or outrageous life-long orgy of bed-hopping and partner-swapping. To get forty-eight pages of this for threepence was not a chance to be missed, whether to be transported or outraged. There must have been many rueful customers, for young Aldred's serious dissertation in a style of commendable literacy cannot have raised a great volume of blood pressure.

It was not those who read it but those who had heard about it who were the real scandal-mongers. Whispers travelled into ears and out of mouths with astonishing rapidity and growing strength, till even Mrs. Aldred heard of it, and she declared that she was the last and only person in the neighbourhood who had not. The pamphlet had been circulating widely in Clerkenwell from the 12th November; it was late on Sunday 17th when, on returning from his meeting, his mother, waiting up for the purpose, demanded to know what he meant by it; what did he mean by Free Love?

Guy explained, and we will let him do so in his own words.

'I explained my attitude. I accepted the idea that marriage was a secular contract and not a church sacrament. Mating was a contract between two people. It need not be registered. There was nothing immoral in two people mating, and not promising to mate *for life*. The promise was void from the very start, for neither party knew if it would hold for life. Arising out of such mating there were obligations and duties that arose from ethics and self-respect, and had no necessary relation to love. Regard for children, if children resulted, was a duty of affection. Even without affection it remained a duty to be discharged. In current monogamic society, woman was denied equal status with man. Motherhood was not regarded as a service to the community, therefore the man ought to provide the means of support for his children.

'This brought me to other questions. In the first instance, I deemed woman the equal of man. Therefore she should retain her birth-name in marriage. In the second instance, I considered that 'born in wedlock' a male property disqualification of many children *not* so born. It was a stigma that some sensitive offspring felt for an alleged 'sin' of which they were innocent. It was opposed to sound law and every principle of equity. All children ought to be deemed legitimate. Other things being equal, the mother ought to rank, in every case, as the real deciding parent in law. The man should support *all* his children equally.

'I went further. I stated that it was said that sex relationship was necessary to the physical and mental well-being of every adult person; if this were so, since there were more women than men in society, *there must be sex association outside of legal mating.* (Mother was horrified.) This meant either some kind of promiscuity, or, even accepted without recognition, polygamy. Actually, legal marriage testified to the truth of this fact. Many women did not mind their husbands associating with prostitutes, or even having mistresses, as long as they could say *'Here is my wedding ring! Here are my lines! He belongs to me!'*

'To my mind all this was immoral, and merely a survival of chattel slavery. I did *not* believe that the love emotion was exclusive always. It might be better if it were. The fact was that marriage did not work. Hence the scandals in papist society, and the divorce laws in Protestant countries. In any case, neither church nor State could seal men and women in marriage. No woman should substitute her name nor attach a handle 'Mrs.' or 'Miss' to it because she had declared before a Registrar or Priest her intention of sharing her lot with a male companion. And if the male died first her name might change again. In short, her life, in time, would read like a house passing from person to person. A disgraceful state of affairs.' (N.T.G. p.372)

Guy's mother listened without hearing. He could tell that behind troubled eyes was a mind burning with resentment against Rose. *She* was the cause of all this nonsense. She had lured Guy into a circle of foreigners, shady people of loose morals and few scruples, like herself; and Guy was too innocent or too stubborn to see what she was doing to him.

When Guy had finished his explanation, his mother said she wished she had not brought him into existence. As she had had no intention of bringing him into existence, and had wished he had not happened before he was born, the remark was rather pointless. She said that Guy was defending 'paramours', and it was all because of that woman. Well, he could make up his mind; if he brought that Jewess into the house, *she* would walk out. Either he stayed at home and stopped seeing her, or he could take his belongings and go off with her, that was all she had to say. Guy considered that this ultimatum left him with no choice.

81

He went with Rose to see his grandfather, living with Aunt Helen and her daughter Gracie. Grandfather said he had no sympathy with Guy's mother in her reaction to the pamphlet. He had read it himself, and he approved. He thought its tone revealed the youthfulness of the author, but it proved that he had thought about the problems of life, and this was admirable. As for leaving home, Guy was making too much of an issue out of this. It was natural that he should leave home around his age. It was not a great tragedy. If he were getting married he would be leaving home. His mother would have to adjust; that was one of the circumstances of her life, and nobody should be expected to live her life for her. As for living with Rose without marriage, and each keeping his, or her, own name, well, if that was the way they wanted it, why not?

On another day they called on Charles Voysey. He was delighted to see them. Although Charles was a heretic and had blasted the 'doctrine of hell-fire' from his pulpit, declaiming that a God who believed in hell should be the first to be made to go and live in it, he was politically and socially orthodox: he was an old Tory. He was so conservative that he considered horseless carriages infernal machines, invented by the devil — in whom he didn't believe in less indignant moments. He would stand by the kerb, young Guy by his side, uttering execrations after spluttering exhaust pipes. He predicted that this thing would be the ruin of mankind. Yet for all his beliefs in past values and present respectability he gave not the least sound of disapproval when he heard his young visitors' intentions.

He was as excited and overjoyed as though he were a young man himself embarking on a like venture. There were no reservations: no 'ifs', no 'buts', no 'Are you both sure?'. Just happiness. He invited them to stay to tea. During the meal he said they must promise him one thing. The first child must be called Annesley, in memory of him. They promised.

As they left he asked if he might bless them. So Rose and Guy stood hand in hand while the old heretic reverently asked the God he had devised himself to bless the union of those two young people. It was love sanctifying love.

15: PENURY

It was now December. *The Voice of Labour* had suspended publication. The I.U.D.A. meetings had ceased. Guy's preoccupation with his pamphlet had prevented him from engaging in free lance work, so he had no money. Charles Voysey came to the rescue again. He found some research work for Guy. This brought £50, to which Voysey added another £50 as Christmas or wedding present. Guy had made up his mind about leaving home, but he would postpone it till after Christmas. He gave his mother £33 and treated the family to an extraordinarily fine Christmas dinner, with toys for the children. Then, a further excuse for delay, he could hardly leave them before New Year. On January 6th 1908 there were no further excuses: he gathered together his belongings, said a cheerless goodbye, and left home. He had entered a new phase of his life.

It had not been easy for this jobless, unwed young couple to find rooms. It would have been easier if the girl had not insisted on being called 'Miss', and had not refused to wear a ring. Then nobody would have known that the ceremony had been omitted. They eventually found a place at 102 Thorpebank Road, Shepherds Bush. Of course, there had been no honeymoon — that was bourgeois nonsense. There had naturally been a state of euphoria for the first week or so. They spent their days in such earnest and profound discussion that the unmoved breakfast dishes did for supper. There was so much to talk about, and on such a grand scale; they trailed clouds of glory over all the eternities of their minds. Whatever darkness and the night had to offer, it was the daytime platonic comradeship of the mingling of souls that raised Guy to his highest concept of love.

Reality waited outside in the chilling January rain where no meetings could be held because no audiences would gather. It seeped in draughts through the door, striving to drive love out of the window. Eventually it was there, inescapable; in the bare cupboard, the coal-less grate, the empty pockets — the reality of poverty.

One day there came to the door two men whose visit gave a short financial respite. One of them Aldred had known in his *Agnostic Journal* days. A bright-minded, dapper young man. He had then been Lieutenant Fuller of His Majesty's Armed Forces. Now he was Captain Fuller, and eventually he would be Major General Fuller, internationally known authority on tank warfare. By his side was *The Beast, Satan, 606, the Worst Man in the World* and any other horrific appellation which may occur to the reader. His name was Aleister Crowley, author, at that time, of thirty books, worldwide traveller in un-frequented places, and in amazing circumstances: mystic, practitioner of black magic and unholy cults. He had recently started a book which appeared in two volumes every year from 1909 to 1913. One of Crowley's biographers, P.R. Stephenson (*Legend of Aleister Crowley:* 1931) says of this book, *The Equinox:* 'There has never been anything at all comparable to it in the history of English literary journalism.'

In 1905 Crowley was climbing the Himalayas; in 1906 he was walking across China; in 1907 he was sojourning among the desert tribes of Morocco. During those three years his three volumes of collected poems was published. An essay competition was announced offering a prize of £100 for the best literary criticism of those collected poems. Captain J.F.C. Fuller of the Oxfordshire Light Infantry won the prize. His essay was called *The Star in the East*, and was published in 1907. Now he wanted it re-published, and it occurred to him that Guy Aldred was the man who would do it.

Aldred agreed. He had no printing press, but he was having his latest pamphlet printed, using his home address, Thorpebank Road, as printing and publishing imprint: *The Bakunin Press, 102 Thorpebank Road, Shepherds Bush.* He could do the same for Fuller's essay. As the Captain paid something in advance, and as the printer had not to be paid till the work was completed, Guy and Rose had a little money to use in the interval. Thus Aldred had Crowley for several months as an acquaintance. His opinion of Crowley was that he was a man of strange and wasted genius.

The landlady did not know that her address was used as headquarters of a dubious publishing firm. She was becoming disenchanted with young Guy and Rose. To begin with, it had been pleasant to view them with romantic eyes, all love and dreams, but familiarity dulls the imagination. Now it was evident that the young man did not go out to work like any respectable person, and that the girl had not the decency to wear a ring. The landlady became unfriendly and uncivil. When Guy reported that a plumbing repair was needed in the bathroom, she ignored him. This state of disrepair became so bad that Aldred refused to pay the rent till it was put right. The landlady probably thought that people of his sort should be grateful for a room without demanding a workable toilet. So she held out, and he held out. But as arrears grew, ability to pay shrank, and there was the possibility that the landlady would suddenly give way. So one night, when moonlight bathed the rooftops, Guy and Rose tiptoed from the house quietly, so as not to disturb the landlady's slumbers. They carried their belongings with them, but left the rent-book behind. Their new address was 35 Stanlake Road. There they stayed till Guy was arrested for sedition a year later.

Aldred's fortunes did not improve with the change of address. He did a little free-lance work, but had not left home and Fleet Street to become a hack writer. When the weather allowed, he held meetings. With his free-love reputation he was becoming regarded as less than respectable. His mother had said that she wouldn't be seen in the street with him for fear of what people might think of her. She wasn't just being abusive. She had refused his offer to meet her one day and carry the shopping basket. Former acquaintances looked in shop windows as he approached. What did the damned cad expect — living openly with a seventeen-year-old Jewess? It was not as though he already had a wife, and could plead legal impediment.

In May 1908, he heard the most devastating news of his life. Granddad was dead. Guy's little step-brother, Ernest, staying overnight with his aunt Helen, had rushed into his grandfather's bedroom to wish him goodmorning, and had been horrified to see the old man in a tangle of bedclothes, his eyes staring and his face distorted in agony. A writing pad was clutched in one hand and a pencil had fallen from the other. It was later found that the pad contained an account of his dying, till pain had overcome him. He had swallowed a quantity of carbolic acid. The coroner recorded a verdict of death by corrosive poisoning, self-administered whilst in a disturbed state of mind.

Grandfather had given no sign that his mind was disturbed, and indeed it probably was not unduly so. He just took the view that with Em gone and Dade grown up and himself considered an old nuisance in the household he had worked to support, life had no longer any attractions. He was in his seventy-fourth year; soon he would have to stop work, and as there was no State pension for the elderly, he, once the proud head of a happy family, would be an unwanted pauper. Why live merely to exist in misery?

Except for occasions of companionship with Dade there had been no real happiness since Em died. There had been periods of escape into an alcoholic haze with Ernest Stray, Ada's bigamous spouse. But when that poor incompetent creature had fled to Canada, the old man found no consolation in lonely indulgence. There was no joy now in watching Guy grow up, and his mind unfold. That was a pleasure of the past. There was nothing left. It was better to die now when he was strong and could pass from life without causing the trouble of nursing him in his feebleness. He took a poison which was available, and with some notion of being of service to medical science, he noted the progress of the symptoms of his own dissolution.

Guy Aldred never forgot his grandfather. He referred to him frequently during the rest of his life, and one had the impression that he would have said more, but he imposed on himself a certain reticence, so as to to keep some of his grandfather sacred to himself. He never mentioned the terrible day when the news of the death reached him; nor did he ever say a word about the inquest or the funeral. Here the doors of memory remained shut, for what was beyond was too awful to contemplate.

Fifty-five years later, when Aldred had just died, one old man remembered him as a companion of his youth at that time. He recollected that Guy was pale and thin, his usual exuberance dulled. When they went into a cafe after a meeting he was sad and preoccupied — and often very hungry. He had not been able to concentrate on earning money. The collections at the meetings went to the Group; he kept only the income from pamphlet sales. This would be required by Rose for a meagre housekeeping. His mid-day meal was reduced from macaroni and cocoa to four, sometimes two, halfpenny bananas. One afternoon he collapsed on the platform from the weakness of hunger.

There was a little easing of the situation after that. A few of his supporters gave him small personal donations. One man gave him a ten shilling note, or a pound, twice weekly. Then an admirer, who owned a chemist shop, (or shops), put a proposition to him. He believed it would boost the sales of his potions and toiletries if he gave away a little booklet with every sale over a certain amount. The little booklet would have a coloured cover and would contain sixteen pages, giving a gripping abridgement of one of the 'classics'. This meant the novels of Dickens, Dumas, Hugo and so on. It would also advertise the wares of the benevolent chemist.

It was not a bad idea; and it was a success. In those days children were taught to read in primary school, and by the time they were ten they had their little noses stuck in penny dreadfuls. This addiction to Deadwood Dick and his ilk was the cause, so it was said, of most of the juvenile crime of the age. It had to be — there were no movies, no television or horror comics, and something other than the evils of society had to be blamed. Guy Aldred himself would have been seen as a case in point. As late as the age of fifteen he balanced the Bible with Nick Carter. He had become an anarchist, surely as a result of the penny dreadfuls he consumed, and at twenty-two was heading for Brixton Prison.

The chemist who was benevolent to his own advantage offered Guy the task of making the abridgements of the classics. For this he would pay him a steady weekly wage of three pounds. One manuscript had to be delivered every month, and Aldred could choose his own novel for treatment. It was a job which suited Guy's peculiar gift of fast reading. Even in old age he was able to absorb the contents of a page very quickly. He did not seem to read every line, but rather to gaze steadily at the type for a minute or so, and thus absorb it. At the National Press Agency he had learned to condense and paraphrase. So a few evening's work each month produced the required copy.

Now with four or five pounds a week he felt he must do something which would be a pleasure for him, and show respect for his grandfather's memory. He made a point of arriving every Saturday morning on his mother's doorstep with his arms laden with groceries. Sometimes she welcomed him with smiles, and sometimes she let him know that he could not buy forgiveness from her as easily as that: if he was trying to give himself a clear conscience he had a long way to go.

Aldred had not ceased his studies and his pamphlet writing, even during his worst poverty. That little Bakunin Press (which cannot possibly have performed all the work attributed to it, and was probably often a convenient imprint for some frightened commercial printer) changed its address from the basement in Goswell Road to the rooms in Thorpebank Road, and then, silently by moonlight, insubstantial, but vital in spirit, from that address to Stanlake Road, where, considering its non-existence, it surprisingly fooled law officers.

Now that the weekly rent was assured, Guy was able to give more attention to developing his ideas, and making them public. He had three projects in mind. One was a book containing the biographies of ten radicals, among them such varied characters as Richard Carlile, Jonathan Swift, Theodore Parker, Robert Owen, Bishop Colenso, and Michael Bakunin. Some of these had already been written up as biographical essays in the *Agnostic Journal* in 1905-1906, and these would be extended and included in the proposed book. The advance subscription for the volume, in stiff covers, with art photographs of each subject, was ten shillings and six pence, or six shillings in paper covers. This would be the first of a series of books from the pen of

Guy Aldred under the general title of *The Library of Synthetical Iconoclasts.*

The term 'Synthetical' did not refer to the character of the biographical subjects, but to Aldred's theory that every aspect of dissension (iconoclasm) from right to left, whether in religion, politics, art or science, was the forward-urging of the first principle of change, of *becoming*. It was a manifestation of the *rebel-spirit* of Bakunin, or the *Word* of the Platonists. This dissenting articulation should be brought together, synthesised, in a general concept. So it was that he quarrelled with Hyndman on the logic of binding freethought to socialism.

This book was never published, though some of its chapters — that on Richard Carlile, for instance —were published separately.

Another work advertised and written, but never published in full, was entitled *Organisation*. The advertisement is worth quoting for the insight it gives us into the mind of the twenty-two-year-old Guy Aldred.

'ORGANISATION. This work is divided into ten chapters. The first is entitled "A fragment of Social History", being a summary of the life and teachings of Karl Marx and the History of the International. In the second chapter the reader is introduced to an account of the "Political Debacle" succeeding the fall of the International, expressing itself in the international supplanting of Marxist Communism by Lassallean Social Democracy. The third chapter deals with the development of Capitalist Imperialism, and the subsequent industrial development of the native races towards the stage of International Working Class Solidarity, the specific examples taken being India and Africa, whilst China and Oceania come in for less detailed treatment. The fourth chapter introduces us to the history of Working Class Industrial Organisation, and exposes the fallacious theory of the political economy which has hitherto proven its basis, concluding with an account of the *Industrial Union of Direct Action*. In the fifth chapter we are introduced to the reflex political struggle, whilst the sixth considers the reflex educational struggle; the seventh, the evolution and portent of bourgeois culture; and the eighth, Sexual Relationships and their development in relation to the class war. Chapter nine discusses and formulates proposals for the New Communist International; whilst Chapter Ten deals with the programme of the I.U.D.A, which the author puts forward as the most consistent embodiment of the requirements of proletarian organisation....Published by advance subscription of two

Shillings and Sixpence Cloth, and One Shilling Paper....'
Aready on the streets was *Anarchism, Socialism and the Social Revolution*, 84 pages, Sixpence.   The advertising copy said of this:
'This pamphlet is a reply, on the one hand, to those critics of his propaganda who maintain the necessity of political action, and the capturing of the parliamentary machine as a prelude to the Social Revolution, and, on the other hand, to the absurdities of those who contend for the necessity of syndicalist action, and maintain that sabotage, or machine-wrecking, etc., is, in itself, a revolutionary activity.   Maintaining the necessity of striving for nothing short of fully developed Communismn, or Socialism on other than the industrial plane, the author traces the reactionary tendencies of pure and simple direct action and negates the idea of Syndicalist or Trade Union palliative "anarchists" being more revolutionary than the ordinary political office-seeking "socialist."   Great space is given to the consideration of the Social General Stay-In Strike......'

From his latest address at Stanlake Road, Aldred issued an advertisement announcing a new series of *Pamphplets for the Proletarians.*   This was headed by the arresting question:

WAS MARX AN ANARCHIST?
A QUESTION FOR SOCIALISTS TO ANSWER.

Bourgeois society has proven itself so able to turn all agitations and philosophies to account in justification of its prostitution of principle, that revisionism and reaction under the magic of its pretentious hypocrisy have often assumed the role of revolutionary propaganda.   Of such pretensions, anarchism in its phase of pure and simple anti-statism must rank equally with socialism in its phase of state collectivism.   The former is a bourgeois counterfeit equally with the latter, viewed from the standpoint of the proletarian.   Amidst the confusion which such counterfeit coinage involves, it is as well for the worker to know where he stands.   This can come only from mastering the attitude of the father of scientific socialism, Karl Karx, and the relation of his caustic criticism of Capitalist production to the teachings of Proudhon, Warren and Bakunin.   In order to accomplish this, and to separate the teachings of Marxism from the bourgeois Social Democratic vapourings of Lassallianism, the Bakunin Press is publishing the following:
PAMPHLETS FOR THE PROLETARIANS
By Guy A. Aldred.'
A List of the pamphlets follows this announcement.

89

In N.T.G. (p. 415), Aldred observes: 'These advertisements were not issued in 1914, when the Great War demonstrated the debacle of the Second International. They were not issued in 1917, after the Soviet Revolution in Russia. They were not issued in 1921, after the Leeds Unity Conference of January 28th, when various persons who had never called themselves communists before began to describe themselves as communists because of the triumphs of the Bolsheviks in Russia. These announcements were made *in 1909*, when none of the founders of the Communist Party of Great Britain dared to call themselves communists....It is my claim that I have remained loyal to the communist ideals I defined and proclaimed in 1909. My vision was clear. My critics were without vision.'

Towards the end of 1908 it had become clear that Guy would have to delete that final paragraph of the Preface to *Sex Oppression*. Rose was pregnant. May Sunday, 1909, was on the 2nd of the month. Rose ought not to have ventured forth in the procession, but she did, and was surrounded by bands and banners, and raging orators, and the smell of springtime grass, when her labour pains began. She was taken to Queen Charlotte's Hospital where a baby boy was born. As she gave her name as Miss Rose Witcop she was treated with the disapproving brusqueness deserved by a fallen woman. She was an affront to the decent wives in the ward. Guy had been told to go home and fetch the articles needed for her stay in hospital. When he returned he was coldly received and not allowed to see her; nor was he allowed to see her or have any information about her till it was time for her to be discharged.

When Charles Voysey heard of this treatment he wrote angrily to the hospital authority pointing out that his church held special services to collect funds for the hospital, but he was sure the donors were unaware of this moral discrimination. The hospital then relented to the extent that they sent Guy the bill for the confinement. This was paid by Voysey, accompanied by more abuse for the hospital. The baby was, of course, called Annesley.

Neither Rose's mother nor her sisters came to see her, nor sent a kindly word. They were opposed to her 'running off' with Guy. They also seemed to object to her insisting on keeping her own name, though that was in accord with anarchist principle, to which the sisters themselves supposedly subscribed. Aldred declared that the sisters' 'free love' was false and hypocritical. They were only *companions* to their men because in both cases the men were in desertion from unwanted wives. Furthermore, they both used 'Mrs.' when it would have been awkward to do otherwise. Guy's mother had no congratulations to offer.

So now Guy was a father.   He had, in his own words, 'given a hostage to fortune.'   How well could he balance this responsibility with devotion to his Cause?   It was not long before he put himself to the test.

16: JAIL

We cannot lay down the law, or be dogmatic, in our reference to anarchists. They are not in agreement among themselves on the definition or the implication of the word. We may accept that they all believe in individual liberty, but are not all agreed as to what that means. They may demand *Rights* in their day-to-day propaganda, but they do not believe in *Rights* as a philosophical proposition — they do not believe in abstractions. Man has been befogged by the superstitions of abstractions since the beginning of history.

The Platonic notion of the Ideal, the Perfect and the Good, and the Judaic-Christian conception of the moral God, of Revelation, and the realm of the Spirit has caused a cleavage between mind and matter, body and soul, to the detriment of the material world, which was the battleground between the abstractions 'Good' and 'Evil': the one needed to complement the other. And this middle world, having fallen from Grace, was lower than heaven and on the brink of hell. This created a paradise for priests.

The deists had cleared the befogged mind of man, sweeping away old idols and holy ghosts, and demolishing the halls of the annointed. Then they had set up a few shibboleths themselves, for self-evident Truths, Rights, and Equality were also abstractions, and were paid the lip-service due to abstractions. But abstractions do not exist by themselves. There is no wetness, no hardness, no whiteness, except as qualities of something else. So there are no Rights, except as qualities required for the existence of man, features of his sentience, which, if suppressed, degrade life. The struggle was for a fullness of life; this would involve a realisation of Rights.

Aldred was not opposed to this line of thought. Later, when an orthodox Communism was taking shape, with a Kremlin-Vatican and Commissar-Cardinals, drawing all the logic-chewing intellectuals into its orbit, he said the dialectic had become a cloud, thrown high into the air, above reality, and on it sat Marx, deified and sacrosanct.

Yet Aldred had an umbilical link with the early Victorian Radicals. There was no father-influence in his up-bringing, only a grandfather-influence. His link was not with the 1880s, but with the 1860s, when his grandfather had quit the radical movement to settle in peace with Emma. At that time the working-mens' clubs were mostly free-thought and radical, which meant republican, rather than socialist, although socialism was emerging. This is brought out by Stan. Shipley in his *Club Life and Socialism in mid-Victorian London* (p. 40). He quotes Thomas Okey, *A Basketful of Memories* (1930):

'...during the seventies and eighties of last century, indications were obvious, both on the platform and in the audience of the Hall of Science, that the Marxian bible, or, rather, the earlier Communist Manifesto (1848) of Marx and Engels — the first volume of *Das Kapital* did not appear till 1867 — had begun to leaven English democratic thought. It quickly made a more potent appeal than mere republicanism and negative freethought to the working and labouring classes of East London.'

Shipley comments: 'The socialist turn was thus already well under way within Secularism in the later 1870s, and the process was a continuing one; down to the days of Guy Aldred and beyond, the Secularist movement served as the nursery of London socialists.'

That is sound observation, but Aldred was not typical of the young men of 1907. There was no parent generation between him and the 1870s. He was a continuation of his grandfather. Charles Holdsworth had stopped short of the transition from liberal-radical republicanism to socialism: his grandson had continued the development. This meant that young Aldred was strong in the liberal-radical tradition. More than other young men of his time he was aware of the struggles of the libertarians of the early nineteenth century for the bare freedom to organise, to speak, and to write in terms critical of the Establishment. His heroes were his grandfather's heroes — Tom Paine, Richard Carlile, Watson, Hone, Hunt, Shelley — to which were added his own, of the nature of Bakunin. Guy was busy on his researches for his 'Life' of Carlile when the event — the assassination — occurred which, in its sequel, led him to prison.

Richard Carlile was born in 1790 and died in 1843. He was apprenticed as a tin-smith, but left his trade to become fully engaged in selling the libertarian publications of the time, which were printed without payment of the Stamp Tax. Following the massacre of Peterloo he took over publication of a paper called the *Republican*, about to be closed by a frightened editor. He maintained it, despite its dangerous title, as a thirty-two page weekly for fourteen volumes, sometimes having to edit it from Dorchester Prison. He printed the banned *Age of Reason* of Tom Paine, and insisted on reading it in its entirety in Court as part of his evidence. He was an atheist, when even to be a deist (as was Paine) was socially outrageous. He was a pioneer of birth control, and of womens' rights. From his lecture hall — the Rotunda — and from his shop in Fleet Street, he uttered so much sedition and blasphemy that serious consideration was given to the revival of the old practice of public flogging especially for the good of his soul, and as a protection of public morals and ecclesiastical privilege. He spent twelve years in prison. His efforts, and those of others like him, gave Britain a free press. This freedom was wrenched from authority by courage, persecution and suffering. The struggle tended to be forgotten by a new generation. Guy, in the spirit of his grandfather, would relive its passion and turmoil to preserve its victory.

There was at that time (1909) in Highgate, London, an establishment called India House. It had been founded by a wealthy Indian named Shyamji Krishnavarma, who also gave grants to young Indians who were anxious to further their education in England, and who gathered at India House. As Krishnavarma was a nationalist, and most young Indians were nationalists to some degree, India House became a hotbed of Indian Nationalism.

One of those frequenting India House was Mohandas Karamchand Gandhi, then about forty. He was already well-known for his leadership of the Indian cause in South Africa, and was also noted for his pro-British sentiments, and for his style of dandified British dress. Of course, he became even better known many years later, as one of the architects of Indian independence. By then, he had long stopped wearing his Western clothes, and insisted on using his native dress, even to the most dignified and formal meetings, causing Winston Churchill to refer to him as the 'half-naked fakir'. At that time, in India House, Gandhi thought the British influence in India had not been altogether bad, and that there was much to be preserved. The Empire should be defended, but India should still work for her freedom.

A person with nationalist ideas in opposition to those of Gandhi was Vianyak Savarkar. Savarkar was a twenty-six-year-old graduate of Bombay University who had been recommended to Krishnavarma by Bal Gangadhar Tilak, a pro-Gandhi nationalist leader in India. Savarkar formed a *Free India Society*, and, being a person of lively intelligence and powerful personality, he soon dominated the minds of the other residents of India House. Krishnavarma approved his ideas, enthusiasm and administrative ability. He made him manager of the hostel which housed thirty students under the patronage of Krishnavarma.

There was nothing pro-British about Savarkar, nor did he take the soft approach. He believed that there was a Hindu culture older than the European, and that it should be revived and should obliterate the British experience entirely. He had written a history of the episode known in Britain as 'The Indian Mutiny'. He called it *The First War of Indian Independence'*. For its title alone it was banned in India. Savarkar believed that the second War of Independence was in progress, and it should be waged by every means. Political assassination was a justifiable weapon to be used by an oppressed people.

There was, at India House, a student named Madanlal Dhingra, who pined to serve the cause of Indian freedom. He listened to Savarkar and was fascinated. Fascination grew to inspiration, and inspiration urged self-immolation. The spirit of a martyr possessed him. He would kill for India, and he would die for India.

Savarkar supplied the revolver and circumstances provided the victim. The place was the Imperial Institute in South Kensington, on 2nd July, 1909. The victim was Sir Curson Wyllie, political secretary to the Secretary of State for India. Lady Wyllie was standing at the top of a staircase when she saw her husband shot down. She ran down the stair and knelt by the body of the dead man. He had died instantly. The assassin was arrested on the spot.

The Indian Sociologist, organ of the 'Free India Society' was suppressed and the printer sentenced to six months imprisonment on the day that Dhingra was sentenced to death. The Lord Chief Justice, in passing sentence on the printer, said that the publicity given to the case was ample warning to anyone else that printing this sort of matter was a serious breach of the law. *The Times* declared that no-one would dare to print this sheet in future. Young Guy Aldred was stirred into action. He said that he would do it, and he did. He did not believe in political assassination; he was not greatly interested in nationalism, and opposed the Statism it implied, but he was also opposed to suppression of opinion. He printed the August issue of *The Indian Sociologist*. On August 20th the authorities became aware of it, and Guy Alfred Aldred was arrested.

After the murder of Sir Curson Wyllie, Savarkar became a fugitive. He fled to Paris, then unaccountably returned to Britain where he was arrested under a telegraphic warrant from Bombay where five charges where laid against him, including 'Waging war, or the abetting of waging war, against His Majesty the King Emperor of India.' There was much excitement before Savarkar finally reached India to face trial. There was an attempted rescue by the Irish Republicans, and an almost successful escape by Savarkar when he climbed through a porthole on the ship that was taking him to India and swam ashore at Marseilles. He was five hundred yards on French soil when he was held by a policeman till his pursuers from the ship caught up and illegally detained him. This led to an international row between Britain and France, and finally an appeal to the International Court at The Hague.

At his trial in Bombay, Savarkar was sentenced to life imprisonment. This had to be served on the dreaded penal colony, the Andaman Islands. Guy Aldred, just out of prison himself in 1910, attempted to organise a 'Save Savarkar Committee', and devoted many columns of the *The Herald of Revolt* to this cause, but Savarkar's involvement with political assassination gained him little sympathy in Britain. Aldred had no approval for assassination either, but neither did he approve of distortions of justice to accommodate politics.

Savarkar served twenty-seven years in the Islands and in detention before he was able to take the field again. When he did so, he had an immediate army of support, but Gandhi, who had no chance against him when they stood face to face in 1909 had meantime established himself internationally as the leader of the movement for Indian Independence. Robert Payne, in *The Life and Death of Mahatma Gandhi*, says of Savarkar:

> 'He had it in his power, if the proper occasion arose, to let loose thunderbolts. An intense, tight-lipped fanatical man, commanding many secret stores of weapons and a devoted army of conspirators, he led the Hindu Mahasabha without ever daring to throw it into battle. Long before he died he knew that he had been like a man waiting in the wings for the call to occupy the centre of the stage, but the call never came. We shall meet him again in the last pages of this book, for his shadow hangs heavy over the death of Gandhi.'

But back to 1909. On August 25th, Detective Inspector McCarthy with his posse arrived at 53 Stanlake Road to arrest Guy Aldred. They found, beneath the name-plate, a strip of paper which read *Bakunin Press.* Inside they found no evidence of a press, only the living quarters of Aldred, Rose Witcop, and their baby son Annesley — and three hundred copies of a paper called *The Indian Sociologist.* This was part of the evidence they were looking for. But what of a press? Who printed this seditious material? Aldred said it was published by the Bakunin Press, and this was it. He would not tell the name of the printer, nor was a list of subscribers available. A search discovered a letter from Krishnavarma in Paris agreeing to Aldred's suggestion that he print 'portions of the prosecuted number.' That was enough.

Before he left with his prisoner, McCarthy paused, looked at Rose and the baby, then pressed a ten shilling note into Rose's hand. There was no such help or sympathy from the movement.

The Clarion said this was not a socialist matter. *Freedom*, with whose associates Guy had quarrelled in a mixture of principle and personalities, regarded the matter as a piece of bravado by a notoriety-seeking Guy Aldred. They were not to know how deeply Guy was immersed in the traditions of the radicals; how he walked in the steps of Carlile, and was willing to take the road Carlile had travelled, and how much, if only he could know it, his grandfather would have approved.

Rudolf Rocker, if he did not actually applaud, did not condemn. In the columns of *Arbiter Fraint* he defended Guy against imputations of unworthy motives. It was probably that which prompted Rose's sister to visit her, and her mother to write to Guy as 'My Dear Son, Guy'. After a week in custody, Aldred was committed for trial at the Central Criminal Court on September 10th. Bail of two hundred pounds was granted. When he arrived home, the landlady told him he had better spend the week at his disposal in finding somewhere else to live. Eventually he found a place at 64 Minford Gardens.

The trial came before Mr. Justice Coleridge. The indictment was for *'Printing and publishing a seditious libel in the form of a newspaper attempting to stir up and excite discontent and unrest among His Majesty's liege subjects, and to cause it to be believed that it was justifiable and commendable to resort to political assassination with a view to liberate India from the Government of the King.'*

Four officers of the Special Branch were called. These testified to having obtained copies of the *Indian Sociologist* through the post or by direct contact with Aldred. They had heard Aldred address meetings on general affairs, but never on India. They had never heard him suggest political assassination or violence of any immediate kind at those meetings.

As Aldred conducted his own defence, these points in his favour were brought out by his own questioning of the witnesses, which he did very skilfully. He then made a speech for the defence which turned on the definition of 'Sedition.' He spoke for fifty minutes and was frequently interrupted by the judge.

The Attorney-General then replied for the prosecution, after which the judge addressed his summing up to the jury, who returned a verdict of 'Guilty' without retiring. Justice Coleridge then asked Aldred if he had anything to say. Aldred replied: 'Nothing, my Lord, except that I desire no mitigation of sentence.'

Justice Coleridge was mildly surprised. 'Is that all?' he asked. 'Have you nothing more to say?'

'Nothing, except that I do not advocate political assassination.'

The judge then passed sentence: 'Guy Aldred, you are young, vain and foolish; you little know that others regard your sentiments far more seriously than they deserve. The sentence of this Court is twelve months in the First Division.'

The sentence was served in Brixton Prison. The term 'First Division' meant that he was not put to hard labour, could wear his own clothes, and received parcels, subject to prison regulations.

The press carried reports of the trial. Every paper remarked on the youthfulness of the defendant. *The Mirror* managed to obtain a courtroom photograph. *The News of the World* had to rely on the imagination of their sketch artist, who made Aldred look, according to one who saw it, 'like a cross betwen a bestial criminal and a sex pervert' — which was what they thought their readers would expect a free-lover to look like. The accompanying article hinted that Aldred was a professional arranger of assassinations in the regular employ of the Indian Nationalist Movement. Aldred did not know it, but in the same prison at the same time Savarkar was confined, awaiting his deportation to India, his trial and life sentence.

Aldred had two regular visitors during his imprisonment. One was Voysey, and the other was Rose. He nearly didn't have any. Voysey travelled all the way across London in his carriage without reference to visiting hours. This, he contended, was the privilege of a 'spiritual advisor.' He got his way finally by an appeal to the Home Secretary. The Governor would not admit Rose Witcop as a visitor. He said that a prisoner could not be visited by a criminal associate, and as Rose was of the same political persuasion as Aldred, she was an associate in his political crime, and so was barred by prison regulations. Voysey intervened. The Governor was prepared to make a special concession in this unusual case. If Rose would sign the Visitors' Form as Mrs. Aldred she would be allowed to see the prisoner.

Rose refused this condition. She would not use any name but her own. The Governor capitulated unconditionally. However, the warder on duty during visiting times was made of sterner stuff. He would not connnive at immorality. Only wives could see their men (and mothers their sons, of course), and as Rose was down to see an inmate, and was obviously not his mother, she must be his wife, no matter what name she put on the form. So he always called loudly into the waiting room 'Mrs. Aldred to see Guy Alfred Aldred.' He just looked through Rose when she protested, and to underline his disapproval he sometimes did not tell her in which of the visitors' cubicles Guy was seated.

Rose now had a four-months-old baby to look after, and no income. Again Voysey came to the rescue, despite his strong objections to revolting Indians and agitating anarchists. He gave Rose a regular £3 per week. Another sympathiser was George Davidson, a Director of the Kodak Camera Co., and also 'connected with' the Prudential Insurance Co. Davidson mixed with anarchists, and sent donations to several of their papers, responding to their special appeals, and for a time was the patron of the Glasgow anarchists.

Davidson got Rose a job, a lowly paid clerical job; and a lady from the Salvation Army came and looked after Annesley. She had been a fallen woman herself in her youth, and was now trying to get right with God. She developed an affection for Rose, who was only nineteen, to a degree that was unwelcome and embarrassing. Rose hated the job, but probably thought that since she was being helped she was obliged to stick at it to show she was willing to help herself.

She also hated George Davidson, maybe because he was responsible for her getting the job, or maybe he was a man whom women found easy to dislike. One day he and Rose quarrelled over a trifle. Davidson prided himself on his good taste in the art of house decoration and furnishing, and he was unwise enough to pass an unfavourable remark about the colour, or the drape, of Rose's room curtains. This brought forth such severe castigation that Davidson was dismayed. There was a break between him and Rose which he asked Guy, on his release, to attempt to heal. But Guy knew that Rose was set against reconciliation. Davidson then volunteered his support elsewhere — to the hostile Kropotkinists.

Rose also had a friend — though of no financial worth — in E.F. Mylius, a fellow-lodger. Mylius became notorious a few years later (1911) when he was sued by the newly-crowned King George V for criminal libel. Mylius wrote for publication an article which stated that George had contracted a morganatic marriage while in India, and had now abandoned this unofficial wife. Mylius was brought to trial on February 1st, 1911, and sentenced to twelve months imprisonment.   He was living with Guy and Rose at the time, and this fact was mentioned at the trial as evidence of his ill-disposition towards monarchy.   Aldred thought the libel foolish.

Aldred's prosecution had some mention in the international press because of its connection with the assassination of the British Government official, and the general situation in India.   The hanging of Dhingra had caused demonstrations in Ireland, where he was proclaimed a hero, probably on account of his last words (there is fair evidence they were written by Savarkar): '....I believe that a country held in subjection by foreign bayonets is in a perpetual state of war....I attacked by surprise....As guns were denied me I drew forth my pistol and fired.....'

In Paris Sir Walter Strickland heard of young Aldred's action and sent him a telegram of congratulation to the prison, declaring that Aldred had restored his faith in Englishmen, who at one time were noted for their stand for freedom.   He also sent a cheque for £10.   This was the beginning of a friendship which lasted till Strickland's death in 1938, when, as Sir Walter's beneficiary, Guy Aldred founded The Strickland Press in George Street, Glasgow.

Walter William Strickland was born at Westminster in 1851.   The family estate was in Yorkshire.   Walter was an eccentric.   He preferred books to the pursuits of normal young men of his class, and had no interest in sport, drink, gambling or women.   His father was disappointed and disgusted.   One day when he was having it out with Walter (probably not for the first time) about his unsatisfactory lifestyle, and the fact that he was nearing forty and still not married, Walter rose from the table and, so the story goes, proposed to the first girl he met, who happened to be the kitchen maid.   It is certain that he did not attempt to live in married bliss, but, on an allowance from his furious father, went abroad in the early 1890s and never set foot in Britain again.   The estate was entailed, so it remained intact, but when Walter inherited his father's money he withdrew it from Britain and invested it all abroad, from Brazil to Japan.   Most of this money was lost because he died as the Second World War broke out, but enough was saved to found the Press in his name.

Strickland wandered over the world, but finally settled in Java. Much of his energy was expended in denouncing imperialism and the White Man's Overlordship.   He knew personally most of the leaders of the subversive nationalist movements, particularly Tilak of India, Savarkar and Krisnavarma.   He lived for some time in Prague, long enough to learn the Czechoslovakian language and become an authority on Czech folk-tales, some of which he translated into

English. That was before 1914, when no Czech State existed. During the First World War he expressed his admiration for his friend Thomas Masaryk by donating £10,000 to his Czechoslovakian Independence Movement. For this service, after the 1914 war, when the State of Czechoslovakia was formed, he was made an honorary citizen. He was very proud of this distinction, and on the strength of it repudiated his British nationality, an act which caused great difficulty for Aldred when the Will had to be proved.

Aldred and Strickland met only once, and that was for a week in 1912. They visited several towns in France for hasty meetings with exiles, ending in Paris where they stayed with Krishnavarma. Strickland hoped that Guy would accompany him on his travels as companion-secretary, but it was not Aldred's nature to be *aide-de-camp* to any man. So Aldred returned to England. Over the years Strickland sent him contributions for the Cause, but they were irregular, so that there could be no forward-planning on the assumption of Sir Walter's help. It was not always a smooth friendship, for both men had minds of their own, and never trimmed a sail to catch the other's breeze.

During his time in prison Aldred dreamed of his release and what he would do when he was free. One thing he would do would be to produce a paper, a monthly journal. It would be called *The Herald of Revolt*. He recalled:

'I visioned this paper and its effect on human progress, always exaggerating its possible influence. This was a natural expression of my enthusiasm. I planned its appearance during the tortuous silent hours of the night. I played with the thought of becoming a great revolutionary editor. This was also a way of quietening my fears for Rose and Annesley. But for this dream, I believe my incarceration would have driven me to madness. I cared very much for them and was always wondering what was happening to them. This was a vanity of anxiety. I saw myself as Providence and imagined Rose and Annesley could not live without me. Events shows that my fears were ill-founded. I was not God. They survived quite well without any providing on my part. My worry was none-the-less very real.' (N.G.T. p.424)

The prison gates opened for Guy on 2nd July 1910. The governor and the chief warder were friendly that morning. They deplored the young man's ideas but were brightened by his cheerfulness. It was arranged that when Rose called she should not — as was the custom — be kept at the gates, but should be shown in and allowed to greet Guy inside. When she arrived she was accompanied by Mylius. She kissed Guy lightly — he noticed how lightly.   Mylius was the first to speak.

'Rose and I have had a good time together,' he said, then added, presumably facetiously, 'I'm sorry you're coming out!'

Guy reflected that there is many a true word spoken in jest.   'Rose heard, but was silent.   My joy at being free was damped.' (N.G.T. p.424)

17: THE HERALD OF REVOLT

When they arrived at Minford Gardens the landlady met Guy with an unsmiling reception. She did not, she said, mind giving accommodation to an unmarried mother, or even an unmarried couple, but she drew the line at giving houseroom to a street-corner anarchist. It was possibly the 'street-corner' and not the 'anarchist' which repelled her. She would hardly have refused to have Prince Peter Kropotkin as a tenant. So Guy and Rose had to shift again.

The new address was 17 Richmond Gardens. There they stayed until 1921, though after 1917 they also had an address in Glasgow.

One of the first things Guy did when he was released from prison was to go and see his mother. He had not heard from her for a year. It was likely that her silence foretold a cold reception, and that fear was confirmed. Mrs. Aldred kept her son standing on the doorstep. She could not, she declared, let a criminal into her house. Guy's protests only showed that he was prepared to excuse his criminal behaviour. In case he had forgotten, his mother outlined his degenerate progress from the day he refused to go to church; his denial of Christ; his meeting with *that woman*. She had known what would happen, and she had warned him. Now she never wanted to see him again. Guy was truly sorry.

Mrs. Aldred subsequently went to stay with a younger sister who had a large family and a husband who was 'connected with the stage', and usually down on his luck. Mrs. Aldred added her three children and herself to the large family, and they all moved from address to address, unsuccessfully dodging misfortune all over London. Guy's half-brothers grew up in time to fight in the 1914 war. One was killed. One was permanently incapacitated by gas, and with the other survivor settled in Canada. There they learned that their father, Guy's stepfather by bigamous association, had, some years before, faked his own death in order to be free from the matrimonial bond with Ada, which was illegal and not binding in any case. Then, under an assumed name this somewhat confused and inept man married a farmer's daughter, inherited the farm, and, one may hope, lived happily ever after.

Guy saw his mother only once after that doorstep meeting. That was in Hyde Park in 1911. She came specially to see him. She needed money desperately, and he records that he 'helped her a little', but conversation had hardly got under way before she began to abuse him for his views. The platform was set up, the audience was gathering, the Chairman was leading up to announcing Guy Aldred as the speaker. He had to leave her, but assumed she would wait till the end of the meeting, when they could have gone to a cafe for further discussion. He hoped to persuade her to accompany him back to Richmond Gardens. But when he dismounted the platform she had gone. He never saw her again. Often he spoke of her, with affection, sorrow, and a twinge of guilt. She died of heart disease in 1912, aged forty-five.

On the Saturday after he was released Guy went to Hyde Park, where a Secularist meeting was about to be held. They at once turned it into a Welcome Back Guy Aldred meeting, and he was the chief speaker. Charlie Lahr was at that meeting, and he and Guy got together again. One of them had a great idea for propaganda education. They would found an Adult School.... It would be called the *Ferrer Adult School* in memory of the Spanish anarchist educationalist Francis Ferrer, who had recently been shot by the Spanish Government. They drew up a large, full-worded handbill advertising the school. The handbill explained that the school had been founded to honour and perpetuate the name of Francis Ferrer, and therefore stands for free discussion. All are welcome: Christians, Freethinkers, Mohammedans, Buddhists, Confucians or Theologists. The opening day is Sunday, November 13th, 1910, at 9 a.m. The class leader will be Guy Aldred, and the secretary Karl Lahr. The school lasted for three months, then failed. It may be that 9 a.m. on a Sunday morning is a time of very low enthusiasm for self-improvement.

The surviving three branches of the Communist Propaganda Group were running in low gear, and Guy set about speeding them up. He re-issued a six point programme he had advertised in 1907. Point One asserted that the emancipation of the working class was the task of the working class, consciously educated and militantly antagonistic to the capitalist class on the economic plane. Point ·Four is interesting: 'That the overthrow of capitalism alone is worth while working for by the workers, who can only accomplish this result by economic Sinn Feinism.'

The interest here is in the reference to Sinn Feinism. Aldred found himself in jail again some years later partly because of such a reference. Guy Aldred was not concerned with the Irish question except in the general way of left-wing agitators. He was not an authority on the subject, and never spoke on it. His reference to Sinn Fein came from several motives. One was because the words meant a challenging 'Ourselves Alone', and conveyed what the workers' attitude should be towards politicians and self-emancipated leaders. Another reason for using the term was that it was shocking, and Guy liked to shock. Further, it stresses anti-parliamentarianism.

The Sinn Fein of Aldred's experience was that of 1907, when it had only been in existence for two years. Its published financial report showed that its total income for the past year had been £234: 10: 1. £32 had come from affiliation fees, and £39: 2: 8 from the sale of pamphlets. It had 57 branches. It was essentially anti-parliamentary, being a reaction against the parliamentary wranglings of the Parnellites and the Redmondites. It was not necessarily republican: its chief begetter, Arthur Griffiths, was not a republican. It intended to be non-violent, using the methods of non-co-operation and boycott of British goods. As Griffiths had worked in the mines in South Africa during the Boer War, he may have learned something of Gandhi's tactics in asserting the rights of the Indians in South Africa. It is probable that from the beginning some of its members, with a growing influence, were really *Fenians*, rather that Sinn Feinners, with thoughts of the bullet and the bomb never far from their minds. In 1917 a new Sinn Fein Constitution was drawn up, but by that time changes had taken place which we must not put in the context of 1907.

Two new pamphlets appeared, bearing the Bakunin Press imprint: *PAMPHLETS FOR THE PROLETARIANS, No. 10 'Representation and the State'*, and in the same series, No, 11, *'Trade Unionism and the Class War'*. The first of these described the author as 'Minister of the Gospel of Revolt, Late Prisoner for Sedition'.

The dream in the cold, tiled prison cell was not forgotten. In December 1910, six months after his release, the first issue of *The Herald of Revolt* appeared. Its masthead slogan was *'An Organ of the Coming Social Revolution'*. It must have given him enormous pleasure, for even at the end of his life Guy received each new issue of his journal from the press with youthful delight.

As part of his propaganda work, Aldred carried on a Postal Mission. He searched through newspapers and magazines for likely addresses and to these he sent bundles of pamphlets and a copy of the *Herald*. Most of this seed fell on stony ground, and it was a costly way to conduct propaganda, but occasionally fertile soil was sown, and a harvest reaped.

There could have been no more fertile soil than the Glasgow Clarion Scouts. They shot forth shoots and bore abundant fruit. They were running packed meetings every Sunday in Glasgow's Pavilion Theatre. One of these had booked Tom Mann as a speaker, but he couldn't make it. What about this young Londoner, Guy Aldred?.

The Glasgow section of the Scouts had been one of the first to be formed when, in 1894, Blatchford's *Clarion* call blazed forth in an orchestration of youthful enthusiasm for the new society. The notion of the *Clarion* manifested itself in many forms. There were Clarion vans pulled by sturdy horses along the lanes of England, providing sleeping quarters and propaganda centres for the distribution of the exulting message of socialism, and manned by dedicated missionaries. There were Clarion Cycling Clubs, pedalling the message o'er hill and dale. There were Clarion Glee Clubs to fill the murky evenings, and Clarion Photographic Clubs to capture beauty and memorable occasions.

The Glasgow corps of the Clarion Scouts was formed on September 13th, 1894. The Secretary was J.C. Reid, of 22 Water Row, Govan. They organised a great parade through the streets of the city, and so successful was it that the City Fathers appealed to Westminster for increased powers of civic protection. Slogan-bearing (horse-drawn) vans rumbled through the streets, laden with copies of Blatchford's *Merry England*, of which 10,000 copies were sold. The business (and they meant business) of the Scouts, was to make socialists. They were not doctrinaire; they had no heretics and no orthodoxy. They were at every socialist meeting, and active on every political occasion. They were always prominent at the demonstrations of the unemployed. Hearing that there was no socialist group in Greenock, the Scouts chartered a Clyde steamer and went forth to remedy that shortcoming. At the end of the expedition they were able to report a successful campaign with only one near-casualty, when a 'wild Orangeman' tried to rearrange the features of one of the speakers.

The Scouts were just as vigorous in 1912, if a little more mature. Aldred gladly accepted the invitation to address the meeting, and spoke to a packed Pavilion. His fellow-speaker was Madam Sorge, and Willie Gallacher was in the Chair. Years later, Gallacher discovered that he 'disdained' both speakers, but by that time he had forgotten his early socialism. Aldred continued his mission for the Scouts with nine open air meetings, ending with a final rally at Charing Cross, by the fountain which now stands dry and neglected. He spoke also for the Socialist Labour Party, at their hall in Renfrew

106

Street, where the organisation had been started by James Connolly in 1903.

Connolly was born in County Monaghan in 1870. His parents moved to Edinburgh, where young James started work at the age of eleven. He educated himself, and returned to Ireland as a socialist organiser, and became the editor of the first Irish Socialist paper, *The Workers' Republic*. Connolly spent seven years in America as an organiser for the Industrial Workers of the World, and as editor of *The Harp*. He returned to Ireland in 1910, and led the socialist movement there till his execution in 1916, following the Easter Uprising, to which he gave a socialist as distinct from a nationalist complexion. He is now a martyr of the Sinn Fein, as well as of the Irish Republic.

Some of Aldred's meetings in Glasgow were held at the gates of the Botanic Gardens. There, long after the meeting ended, he and other young men stood in groups, in the Spring evening, to midnight and beyond, talking of the great future which they foresaw as the enlightenment of socialism dawned over mens' minds.

The anarchists were particularly interested. They asked him to come back to speak for them at a series of meetings. Guy agreed. The Anarchist Group had emerged from the ruins of the William Morris Socialist League. At its inception in 1895 the Group had fifty members, and for the next ten years was very active, bringing to the city international notables like Peter Kropotkin, Emma Goldman, and Voltairine de Cleyre. From 1903 to 1909 the Glasgow Group gave way to the Paisley Group, but it revived when John Macara came from Edinburgh and stirred it back to life. It was Macara who fought for and won the right to hold public meetings without a permit on the Mound, Edinburgh.

In 1910 George Barrett arrived in Glasgow from London. He had been active in the Bristol Socialist Society in 1908, but had left for London and joined the Walthamstow Anarchist Group. Two years later he left for Glasgow, his reputation as an anarchist established. In October of 1910 he started indoor meetings in the city which drew crowds from outside districts. He and his comrades worked against considerable harassment from the police, socialists and trade unionists. Plainclothes police attended the meetings and took names, threatening to inform the employers of active members. In this way George Barrett lost his job, as he had in London. Among Barrett's admirers was George Davidson, of the Kodak Camera Company, who had helped Rose Witcop during Aldred's first jail term. Davidson gave the anarchists rooms in Buchanan Street and set up a printing press, on which, on May Day 1912, the first issue of a paper, *The Anarchist,* was published.

The paper, intended to strengthen the anarchists, instead weakened them. The secretary, Angus MacKay, a veteran among young men, resigned, because he said, a clique had formed round Barrett and *The Anarchist* which ignored the comrades of The Group, but held discussions with the Freedom Group in London. Meetings of the Press Committee were held without the local comrades being informed. This coterie became known, derisively, as The Paper Group. Such was the position when Guy Aldred arrived among the Glasgow anarchists.

Aldred's paper *The Herald of Revolt* now caried a double column of Scottish Notes above the signature 'Rob Roy (Jun.)'. From these we get glimpses of conditions in Scotland before the First World War. '....On cold winter mornings the pedestrian is confronted with the sight of starved-looking children going to school in their bare feet....' 'Two hundred Ardrossan strikers have entered the *eleventh week* of a strike in sympathy with twenty coal trimmers who are asking for a rise of sixpence a week. The Harbour Company say that they could not afford the £28 per year this would cost. The net profit of the Company over the past few years has been £223,000.....' Rob Roy (Jun.) comments that while expressing sympathy with these lowly-paid workers and starving strikers, the 'game is not worth the candle', for any increase in wages will be nullified by increases in prices. What is needed is 'class solidarity to give the workers victory in their struggle for freedom.'

Guy was acclaimed by the Glasgow anarchists for his platform skill and literary merit. He already had a great number of pamphlets to his credit. But he was not in favour with the London Freedom Group. They thought that for a twenty-six-year-old he had too much to say for himself, and not enough respect for his elders in the Movement. Certainly criticism, which he could express with devastating force, came more readily from him than did compromising sympathy. He thought the anarchists were too hidebound in their intellectual notions, and this made them ineffectual in action. The Freedom Group were too much cerebral Kropotkin and not enough rebel Bakunin. Aldred's idea, since the Industrial Union of Direct Action had not taken on, was the formation of Communist Propaganda Groups all over the country. In 1912 the Glasgow Comunist Group was started — largely out of anarchists disgruntled by the 'Paper Group' schism. They tended to return to the fold when Aldred was too long absent.

He was booked for another Clarion tour the following year (1913). He came six weeks earlier to speak for the anarchists. A record crowd gathered at George Square, Glasgow for the May Day march to the Green. But the dark sky opened in a torrential downpour which drove away all but the most dedicated. The soaked and steaming representatives of a hundred and twenty-five organisations left the Square to make their way to the Green an hour late. George Barrett, who was in Edinburgh speaking under the same foul weather conditions, caught a chill which developed into an illness which killed him four years later. At the time of his death he was only thirty-four years old.

The 1913 Clarion tour took Guy into Edinburgh, Leith, Kirkcaldy, Dundee, Aberdeen, Paisley and Dumfries. Then he spoke for his newly-formed Communist Group every night for a fortnight. He was becoming a familiar figure in Glasgow, and a familiar sound, his powerful young voice floating over the tree-tops at Botanic Gardens, Alexandra Park, Queen's Park and the Green; and over the rattling tramcar noise at a dozen street corners from Charing Cross to Dalmuir and beyond. Another tour took him through Lanarkshire, Ayrshire and Fife. During one of these visits he set in motion The Monklands Communist Club in Coatbridge. His lecture titles included: 'The Armed Forces', 'Where Trades Unionism Fails', and 'Industrial Unionism Explained'.

After three whirlwind Scottish tours he sped unabated southwards through Birmingham and Hull into the valleys of Wales, and back to London, where, when he was at home, he lived with Rose and their son Annesley.

In January 1914 the district London groups federated into the London Communist Propaganda Groups. Aldred had an able helper now, named Henry Sara, but, even so, the strain on his health was considerable. Every meeting outside London meant accepting the 'hospitality' of a local comrade, and placing his stomach at the mercy of his well-intentioned host. Most meetings were followed by a late-night discussion and strong tea, then the next day a dash for another venue. In February he became ill with appendicitis, but he was back in Glasgow to speak for the Anarchists on May Sunday.

Rain threatened again that year, but the sky cleared, and the procession of twenty thousand, representing a hundred and fifty organisations, set off for Glasgow Green. The most delightful section was that of the Socialist Sunday School children, who danced and sang their way from the Square to the Green. Dancing children, swaying banners, beating drums and blaring bands, and the smell of the damp pavement drying in the sun —— One joyous observer exclaimed 'Surely the Revolution cannot be far off!'   A spiritual ear might have heard satanic laughter in the springtime breeze.   Before another May many of those young men would be marching again — marching — and marching — but not to the Green where raindrops glistened on the leaves.

BOOK TWO:

THE STEEL-BOUND COFFIN

Mourne not your comrades who must dwell —
too strong to strive —
Within each steel-bound coffin of a cell,
Buried alive;

But rather mourne the apathetic throng —
The cowed, and the meek —
Who see the world's great anguish and its wrong
And dare not speak.

Ralph Chaplin

(Sentenced to 20 years imprisonment in the U.S. for war resistance.)

BOOK TWO
THE STEEL-BOUND COFFIN

CONTENTS

1: WAR

The war came, half expected, but still as a shock. Not altogether an unpleasant shock, but an excitement, an expectancy of adventure, and a break with life's dull routine. The horrors of war were yet to be revealed. A festive rejoicing filled the city streets. The present writer remembers standing disconsolate in a close-mouth with a little penny flag in his infant hand; sad — not because of foreboding of war's horror: he did not know what all the excitement was about, but his older brother had left him and had gone off to join other children in running and leaping at the side of marching men, with blaring bugles and beating drums. Soon after that, soldiers were billeted in the house, cheery young men who talked loudly and filled the place with cigarette smoke.

In high places financiers calculated, generals swelled with new importance, and politicians put their House in order. The last election had been held in 1910, and had resulted, not in a 'hung' Parliament, but in one already dead. The result had been a draw, with Liberals and Unionists (Conservatives) collecting 272 seats each. By August 1914, when the war broke out, the Unionists had increased their seats to 288 (via bye-elections) and the Liberals had decreased to 260, but were supported by 40 Labourites, and a number of Irish Nationalists and Independents. So a Coalition Government was formed, with Asquith as Prime Minister. The Labour Pary was invited to join.

It hesitated. The Executive called a conference to iron out uncertainties. The conference stormily decided that the Labour Party did not directly condemn the war. It 'deplored' the Balance of Power policy which had led to it. The day following the Declaration of War, the Labour Party issued a statement expressing these views, and adding that the 'duty' of the Labour Movement was to secure peace at the earliest possible moment.

This was a sentiment without substance. Within a few days a political truce was agreed. There would be no elections during the war. A seat falling vacant would be filled by the Party holding that seat. In tandem with the political truce came an industrial truce. There would be no strikes until hostilities ceased.

On October 15th 1914 a manifesto was jointly issued by the Labour Party and the Trades Unions 'to clear any misconceptions which may have arisen as to the attitude of the British Labour Movement to the war.' The outbreak of the conflict was attributed to 'the deliberate act of the ruler of the German Empire....The invasion of France and Belgium by the German Armies threatens the very existence of independent nationalities, and strikes a blow to all faith in treaties....'

On May 15th 1915 the Labour Party was rewarded by three Ministries in the Coalition Government: Education, War and Treasury. Thus established, the Party went recruiting for the Services, along with the Liberals and the Unionists. In January 1916 the Party had another pause on the matter of conscription, till it dawned upon it that conscription was an expression of equality of service. In 1916, when the second Coalition was formed, with Lloyd George replacing Asquith as Prime Minister, the Party's share of Ministries was increased to six; and so the Labour party was now deeply entrenched in the prosecution of the war. There were twenty-nine Members of Parliament who opposed the War as Independent Liberals or other Groups. In the Lords, there were at least four Peers who were opposed to the war, or conscription, or both.

When the lists of dead and maimed appeared and shocked the populace, the war fever cooled. Recruitment queues shortened despite the well-paid efforts of public-spirited orators to lengthen them. Every effort was made by Press, Pulpit, Platform, Music Hall and Patriotic old ladies handing out white feathers to young men, to encourage more volunteers. Lord Kitchener, national military hero, came forward himself to make an appeal to the youth of the nation to respond to the needs of 'Your King and Country'.

That appeal raised another one and a half million sacrificial lambs, but more were needed. Many more. How many could the country stand? The War Establishment had to know. So a National Register was called. All persons between the ages of 18 and 65 had to register, giving details of sex, age, occupation and disabilities. It was denied that it had anything to do with impending conscription, which was a foreign-type institution. Nevertheless a No Conscription Fellowship was formed, just in case.

The Register didn't yield anything in the way of recruits, and Kitchener's appeal was exhausted. Another way — short of conscription — must be devised. The Secretary for War, Lord Derby, devised it. Nobody would be conscripted, everybody should volunteer. All men aged between 18 and 41 should call at a recruiting office and attest willingness to be deemed a soldier. Particulars noted, he would be classified, and in due course, as the Armed Forces required, he would be called to the colours. Meantime he would be given an armband to wear, to satisfy wives, girl-friends, workmates and the public at large that he was not a war-dodger. The air was thick with sounds of music from the popular stage urging young men forward, and marching men onward, and for mothers and wives to keep the home fires burning. But even that was not enough. More and more men were needed, for elderly men with great maps and little flags on pins were planning the Somme offensive. Some offensive. The politicians gave way. But it would not be conscription. It would be compulsory military service. Every male between the ages of 18 and 41 would be compelled to join the Armed Services, much as people were required by law to get dog licenses. All decent people concerned would respond.

The Derby Scheme registration had begun in October 1915, and was extended from November to December because of poor response. It revealed that there were 5,011,441 men of military age in Britain. Only 2,829,263 had registered, and of that number only 850,000 were suitable additions to Kitchener's one and half million.

Spokesmen for the Generals, in Parliament, press and pulpit urged that men of military age should be deemed soldiers by general proclamation, and should receive calling-up notices according to their grades. This was not conscription, for conscription was abhorrent to the British democratic way of life. This was deemed compulsory military service, to be equated with compulsory registration of births, or compulsory vaccination, or compulsory payment of taxes.

On January 5th, 1916 the Prime Minister, Herbert Henry Asquith, introduced the first General Compulsion Bill, known as the Military Service (2) Bill. It applied to single men, and became law on January 28th 1916. It was extended to married men on May 25th. Provision was made for those who objected on religious grounds. Such objectors, if proved genuine, would be offered work of national importance, or non-combatant duties. An amendment by the I.L.P. faction to have inserted 'of a non-militarist nature' was defeated.

And so conscription, even if it was not called that, came to Britain. Tribunals had already been set up to consider pleas from employers who wanted their employees to be exempt from the Derby Scheme. Now those Tribunals had their functions extended to the consideration of claims for exemption from the terms of the Military Service Act. Those tribunals could grant exemption on the condition that the applicant did work of national importance, or non-combatant service.   Tribunals could also grant complete exemption, but some Tribunals did not seem to know this, and some, knowing it, 'did not believe in it.'   Objections had to be of a moral or religious nature.   Extreme hardship might be considered, but political objections were firmly disallowed.

These Tribunals were made up of local dignitaries of much self-importance and little vision.   Local civic busybodies of the committee-sitting variety, aided and abetted by a parson or two, and maybe (a worthy aquisition) a pro-war Labour Party man, and of course a military representative, who was there to see that few escaped the armed clutches.

The ignorance and bigotry of those worthies soon supplied a source of derisive humour and amusement.   It may not be true that one of them thought that a mine-sweeper was one who swept coal mines, though it is not impossible, considering the level of their understanding.   It was not their job to listen with humanity and understanding to the arguments of Conscientious Objectors.   They were there to get men into the Army, and that they did, delighting in the little brief power that they had attained.

By the end of August 1916 over two thousand young men had been rejected by those Tribunals, and, sticking by their principles, were in prison or detention barracks, subjected to whatever treatment their warders felt free to deal out to creatures devoid of all public sympathy, or human rights.   No ill-treatment was too harsh or violent for them, and no torture too degrading for the torturers.   The record of what was done to those young men, most of them inarticulate working class Christians, makes for hard reading, and makes clear also that the torturers' trade is not one foreign to the British people.   Some few of the Objectors were broken, and accepted their Army uniforms, but most were of the stuff of which Christian martyrs had been made. This was a challenge to their faith, and they arose to meet it.

In the meantime, the *Herald of Revolt* had changed its name, in May 1914, to *The Spur* —'Because the workers need a spur.'   Its assistant editor was Henry Sara.   During 1914 and 1915 he and Aldred and their colleagues carried on an extensive and intensive anti-war campaign the length of the country.   Aldred was still based in London, but in January 1916 he spent several days in Glasgow, discussing policies at the No Conscription Fellowship Conference, although he was not a member.   He held several open air meetings, as no hall was available, and he addressed a monster rally on Glasgow Green, sharing the platform with Harry Hopkins, John Maclean and James Maxton.

These were among the more prominent men leading the anti-war agitation in Glasgow. Harry Hopkins was a member of the Independent Labour Party. This party had been formed in 1893 to give the Labour Movement a voice in Parliament separate from the Liberals, to which, till that time, socialists tended to be attached as a Left-wing little brother. The Labour Party itself was not yet in existence — it took shape in 1906. The leader of the I.L.P. was Ramsey MacDonald, weak and uncertain. James Maxton was a rising star. Born in 1885, he became a school teacher and a young Tory, but was converted to socialism by John MacLean, who introduced him to the writings of Blatchford and Karl Marx. Elected to Parliament in 1922, for the Bridgeton Division of Glasgow, Maxton stayed there till his death in 1946, well regarded, and seen as the chief figure in the I.L.P. His slight figure, with long, lank hair falling over his eyes, was a cartoonist's delight, and as easily recognisable as the frequent caricatures of Aldred in his knickerbockers and boots.

John MacLean, now rightly a legend in Scottish socialist history, was born in 1879. He also became a school teacher, but there was never any doubt about his political affiliations. As a young man he joined the Social Democratic Federation, which at the outbreak of the war became the British Socialist Party. Although he, like all the front-line agitators of the time, engaged in reformist demands, unlike them his revolutionary principles were never in doubt. He spent five terms in prison. When he died in 1923, he had travelled far from his careerist colleagues. The people of Glasgow showed their love and appreciation of him by attending his funeral in their thousands.

It was a turbulent time in Glasgow. The Clyde Workers' Committee was creating a lot of trouble for the Government, and much embarrassment for Lloyd George, the Minister for Munitions. The Government wanted more munitions, the workers wanted more money — as much as twopence an hour more — and a curb on the dilution of skilled labour by the employment of women and unskilled men. The workers showed their power by withdrawing their labour: the Government showed theirs by arresting John Maclean, William Gallacher, Walter Bell and John Muir. Aldred did not agree with the aims of the Clyde Workers' Committee. To bargain over the production of weapons of destruction was to him a betrayal of working class solidarity. 'Every bullet you make to kill a German soldier is aimed at the heart of your conscript son,' he told his audiences. He advocated a policy of 'Down Tools'. From Glasgow he went on to Wales again, spreading his message of no compromise with militarism as he went.

2: ARREST

Guy arrived back at *The Spur* office to hear that Sara had been arrested on April 3rd.   He was locked in a police cell with a plank bed and no light till April 6th when he was charged before the West London Police Court with being an Army absentee.   He denied the charge, but made no defence.   He was fined forty shillings and handed over to the Army representative, who pushed him around in Court and had him led away roughly by an Army escort.   An attempt he made to hand Guy a note was rudely obstructed.

For several weeks nothing was heard of him, then two smuggled letters arrived at *The Spur* office.   He had been taken from the Court to White City Barracks where he was forcibly medically examined, and, despite defective eyesight, was passed as fit.   He had refused an order to strip and put on a uniform, and was taken to Harrow Road Barracks, headquarters of the 3rd London Rifles.   He was again ordered to put on a uniform, and again refused.   About a dozen jeering men then set upon him and pulled off his clothes, and forced on the uniform, punching his face in the process.   Sara was no cheek-turning Christian.   He had been an engineer before he became a full-time propagandist, and was a big man.   No doubt he could have altered a few of those grinning faces, but wisdom cautioned restraint.

His clothes were taken away, and, in dishevelled uniform he was dragged onto the parade ground and forced into line.   He refused to stay in line, and was ordered by the Captain to be dragged around the parade ground by relays of men who punched and kicked him as they went.   Finally the Captain ordered them to stop.   He told Sara he believed he was genuine, and apologised for the rough treatment.   He phoned for advice, and was instructed to send Sara to Hurdcott Camp.

Next morning Sara was ordered on parade and refused to go.   He was taken before the Colonel who asked him if he thought that he (Sara) was God Almighty.   A fine compliment to God for it meant he had come to earth to be a conscientious objector and defy arrogant colonels.   Or it may be that the Colonel feared a rival claim to Divinity, for he asked the question twice. Sara remaining silent, the Colonel's attitude eased.   He advised Sara to take things easy and

just do as he was told, or else — Hell.   Evidently he had an obsession
with things eternal, and infernal.   He sentenced Sara to 28 days
imprisonment in Parkhurst.   After being locked up over the weekend
at Hurdcott, Sara was taken to Parkhurst Prison, Isle of Wight, on
Monday, 10th April, 1916.

At Parkhurst a gun was thrust at him.   When he refused to touch it
he was informed that at Parkhurst they could break lions.   At the end
of the twenty-eight days, if he still resisted, they would put him in a
cage with his legs manacled to the floor and his hands fastened above
his head, and he would stay like that until he came to his senses.   Then
the soft approach was tried.   He was of officer material; it could be
arranged that he got a job in the rifle department.   The offer was an
insult.   At that point the letter ended.

Aldred knew that he would have to face a similar ordeal.   It could
not be certain what form the maltreatment would take.   The Army
officers had a free hand, and N.C.O.s and privates all shared in the
sadistic amusement afforded by the vulnerability of their victims.
Public opinion seemed to sanction any abuse, no matter how cruel or
degrading, and there is none so vicious, none so cruel, as the self-
righteous.

As he had signed as a married man, Aldred should have had till
after the 25th May before his notice arrived.   He had made speaking
dates accordingly.   He was therefore taken completely by surprise
when on the morning of April 14th a police sergeant called at his
house in Shepherds Bush, London, and asked him if he had received
notice to join the colours.   Aldred said he had not, and did not expect
such notice, as he was a married man.   The sergeant demanded
proof, ignoring the living evidence of Rose and Annesley.   Guy had
none to give, for Free Love needs no certificates.   So without
summons or warrant Guy Aldred was arrested.   Doubtless some
little soul with tiny mind in the Recruiting Office did not like his
speeches.

He was charged with failing to report for Military Service — which
he had not been asked to do.   It was quite certain that he would not
have reported, but authority had no right to make that assumption.

After being charged, he was thrust into a cell which had neither light
nor heat, and only a plank for a bed.   He had been suddenly taken
into custody without summons or warrant for not responding to
calling-up papers which he did not receive, nor was due to receive.
Allowed to see none but a lawyer, he sent for Scott Duckers.

Scott Duckers was a barrister, a conscientious objector, chairman
of the Stop The War Movement, and prospective Liberal candidate

119

for Brentford. He was on remand on a charge of having failed to comply with his calling-up notice. After Aldred's trial he was arrested, and spent the next three years in prison, stubbornly refusing to do any task which he considered a violation of his Christian faith.

Aldred appeared before the West London Police Court on April 14th, 1916, charged with not surrendering himself for military duty. Scott Duckers, acting on the accused's instructions, stated that his client had not responded to papers he had not received, nor was due to receive in the current batch of recruits, because he was a married man by the Scots Law of Habit and Repute. The magistrate expressed surprise at the informal nature of Aldred's arrest, but said that he 'was here anyway.' As for the marital status plea, he would have to take advice on that. He adjourned the case till 27th April.

Aldred made use of the respite to return to Wales, where he addressed anti-war audiences, and the proceedings were enlivened by a little occasional rowdiness. The resumed hearing in the police court was brief. Mr. Fordham, the magistrate, had still not been advised on the matter of Scots marriage law. The case was again adjourned.

The court convened again on May 4th. Aldred conducted his own defence, and the case lasted for two hours. Aldred called as witness a Scottish Advocate, Mr. Steadman, who said that he could say, *without hesitation,* that Guy Aldred was a married man in accord with Scottish law. Mr. Fordham, who had called for expert opinion, now repudiated it. 'Well,' he said, 'it rests with me to say whether he is a married man or not, and I say he is not.' He fined Aldred £5 and ordered that he be handed over to the military representative.

Aldred's political enemies said that he was hiding behind a woman's skirts in his defence. That was nonsense. By the time the third hearing took place, married men with one child were being called up anyway. Aldred's point was to assert the right of the Scots law, which by implication embraced common law wives in England, Wales and Ireland. A special enactment had to be passed before those women and their children could receive the marriage allowance from their service-men husbands, or, in so many cases, receive the widow's pension — and that was only for two years, it probably being assumed that such women would have found other support by that time.

Aldred was taken under escort to Davis Street Barracks. He refused to strip, submit to medical examination, or put on a uniform. From the barracks he was taken to the military camp at Fovant. There he was forcibly stripped and subjected to a cursory medical examination. He was forced into a uniform he refused to keep buttoned, and had a cap placed on his head which he promptly knocked off. He was charged with these offences and thrust into the guard room, where he 'received a friendly welcome' from other defaulters on a variety of charges.

On May 16th Aldred was given a sheet of paper on which to write out his defence. It is too long to quote in full, and one paragraph is enough to reflect his deeper philosophy, held from his Boy Preacher days. He believed we live in a world of sham abstractions. Virtue, and its off-shoot, morals, ethical values, and patriotism, are all fragile mental attitudes, cultivated over the years and dominating us as if they were eternal truths. In this sham world we live and die; but its falsehood, for which we are called to give our lives, suppresses the underworld of verity, the true reality, the *essence undefiled*.

'I have a sheet of paper on which to prepare my defence to the many charges standing against me before tomorrow's court martial. I intend to prepare no defence. I am thinking of good and bad, of persons virtuous and vicious. I want to indict the good, to deplore the bad, to denounce the virtuous, and to heal the vicious. For good and bad, virtue and vice, are not what they seem. I am thinking not of the good in essence, but the accepted good, the good in appearance. This good of fair speech, modish matters and pretty dresses has been the accepted good throughout the ages. And it is a lie. It is vice through and through: lust instead of love, adultery instead of integrity — sham upon sham. It is a business piety, a carnal wit, a stomach morality. Christ denounced it, Guatama exposed it, Socrates analysed it. And we must slay it.'

There is more, but that is enough to give us a glimpse of Guy's mind as he waited for his first Court Martial the following day, Wednesday 17th. The Court comprised three persons, one of whom insisted that an atheist could not have a conscience. Aldred objected at once to the jurisdiction of the Court. He was not a soldier. He had not been called up. He was a married man, and not, at the time of the irregular arrest, on the list of recruitment. The Court ordered the accused to withdraw while the legel competence of the Court was considered. They evidently found in their own favour, for Aldred was recalled, and the trial proceeded. The evidence concerned itself with proof that Aldred had disobeyed orders, without insolence. Several charges were dropped, but Guy was found guilty on others. In a closing statement, he said he was opposed to war and could not comply with the orders given.

He was kept in a cell for two days before sentence was pronounced. This was six months military detention, but the Colonel remitted four months of the sentence.

The following twelve days were spent in Fovant Camp, not in drilling, but in heavy labouring, digging and scrubbing. As Aldred had never handled anything heavier than a pen, they must have been exceedingly arduous. After twelve days he was transferred to Devizes military camp, where an abusive doctor, scornful of how lightly he had been treated, examined Aldred, and said that as far as he was concerned, they could do what they liked with him.

3: GALLOWS GRIM

That was the common attitude. The authorities could do what they liked with conscientious objectors. Colonel Reginald Brook, whom we shall meet again, said of the anti-militarist recruits who had the misfortune to be posted to his camp: 'I care nothing for Asquith or Parliament. I will do just just what I like with these men. I shall continue to act in my barracks according to my orders without regard for what any of the so-called public might think.'

The 'so-called public' were in several minds as to how the objectors should be treated. Probably the majority thought that refusal to fight for one's country should have unpleasant consequences, matching as far as possible the hardships of the front line. This, they thought, was but just and fair. And there was the vociferous minority who thought that hanging was too good for such creatures, and that a bullet fired in shooting them was a bullet that might have been more usefully employed in shooting a German. There was much support for this point of view from press and pulpit.

There was also a considerable number of Christian people in Britain who believed that their faith meant opposition to war. Probably the most active were the Quakers. And there were those whose opposition to war and military service was not based on religious conviction, but on moral enlightenment, and there were those who saw war as an exploit of the ruling class in the maintenance of its power and the protection of its profits. All had a voice raised against the hysteria of the orthodox. In this, the No Conscription Fellowship played the part of a mighty and irrepressible megaphone. And in the House of Commons a small — and not always reliable — pacifist minority played its part.

It is not surprising that there was public confusion about how to deal with conscientious objectors. There was much confusion about many aspects of the war, which could be summed up as a confusion about the war itself. A confusion glossed over by hollow sentimentality. The music halls were aflow with admonitions to keep the home fires burning, and assurances that the departing conscript was 'tickled to death to go — Goodbyeeee.' But the black cloud of

123

mutilation and death closed over ever more homes. And the incompetence and confusion of the generals were compounded into a virtue, an admirable trait in the British character — to 'muddle through'. At the point of reality that meant more men to be sent to their deaths, and the prominence of the type of mind which accepted this and gloried in it.

The war-fever had subsided into a trance-like acceptance of life as dictated by its own events, demanded by its own exigencies. Acceptance was its own justification. Pressures to accept were strong. There was the pressure caused by the human desire to be part of the herd. To have the comfort and assurance of belonging to a greater unit, to be approved of by friends, relatives and the community at large. The generating force of this attitude was fear. Fear fought the war and ignorance directed it.

On the first day of the Somme offensive there were 547,470 casualties, nineteen thousand of them fatal. During the first two months of 1916 fourteen soldiers met their deaths by firing squad. During the war, 346 died in that way. The war was only months under way — in September, 1914 — when the first soldier of the British Army was placed before a squad of his own comrades and shot to death by order of a General who had never seen him. He was only eighteen. In a panic he had run away and hidden in a stable. He passed his nineteenth birthday awaiting the court martial that would end his short life.

The present writer (a schoolboy during and after the First World War) heard an account of this execution from a member of the firing squad.

> 'The boy was put in a tent, with the chaplain to give what comfort he could. All night we heard him weeping and asking for his mother. In the morning at seven o'clock he was brought out and placed before a hedge, beside a newly-dug grave. Every one of the squad's rifles was loaded with a live bullet. The boy was blindfolded. A young captain drew his sword, raised it, paused, and lowered it. We fired. The impact of the bullets almost cut the youth in two across the chest. He was slid, still warm, into the grave while the chaplain muttered a few words. The captain in charge had to get sick leave. We never saw him again.'

It was argued that if young soldiers who had responded to the call of duty suffered death before a firing squad when their nerve failed in the face of dreadful battle conditions, why should those whose nerve failed them at the sight of an army uniform escape with a lesser penalty? The Government had made it clear, after all, that no-one with a genuine religious objection to taking part in the violence of war would, having satisfied a Tribunal, be required to violate his conscience.

What about the men who had not been granted exemption from all military service by the Tribunal, or those who were not covered explicitly by the Act? What would happen if a conscientious objector, despite his protests, and his endurance of penalties for disobedience, was sent to France, and there, in the theatre of war, refused to obey a military order? The Government spokesman would not be clear on that point.

Parliament discussed the point several times times, and on June 27th 1916, the Prime Minister said: 'As far as I am concerned, and as far as the War Office is concerned, no soldier will be sent to France whom we have good reason to believe is a conscientious objector.' But as the words were spoken, thirty-three conscientious objectors, of the most resistant kind, were on their way to France. The military commanders, endowed with a little brief authority, were ready to challenge Government, by ignoring it. The Government, made aware of the defiance, made bungling attempts to retrieve the balance. It was unsteady because it suffered from divided allegiance between the upright legalistic honest-to-God Britain of playground myth and the Britain that might lose all battles but would surely win the war. And it excelled in double-talk.

The Prime Minster was assuring the country that no objector would be sent to France, but the army commanders had been ignoring this assurance for three months, sending men from Harwich, Yorkshire, Abergele and Sussex. On June 1st, Mr. Tennant, Under-Secretary for War, read to the House a letter he had sent to Kimmel Park Barracks and to Richmond Camp, forbidding men being sent to France. He had been told, from both places, that the men had already been sent. The next day, despite this letter from a highly placed Government Minister, another batch of men was sent to France from Kimmel Park. But on the matter of the death penalty, Mr. Tennant was reassuring. If these men refused to obey an order in France they would be sentenced to a term of imprisonment which they would serve in Britain. It made no difference where they were sentenced.. This was not the view of Lord Derby, the Secretary of State for War, who said the men would probably be sentenced to be shot — and quite rightly, too.

While the Government looked both ways at once and moved with uncertain steps, the military commanders set about establishing precedents by having a few men shot. In the military prison at Fort Harwich, Essex, seventeen unwilling recruits of the Eastern Non-Combatant Corps were confined in dungeons built to house French prisoners, at a time when the vile French were our foes, and the gallant Prussians our allies. These men had refused to carry stones from the beach because they believed the stones were being used to build a military road. For this disobedience they were confined in the cold, damp cells, in darkness, on a diet of bread and water, their arms fastened in figure-of-eight irons. These irons were as much instruments of torture as means of restraint. The arms of the victims were placed high behind his back, one on top of the other. The iron was then placed in position and screwed down until the flesh was bruised. In this state the prisoner was kept at the mercy of his captors, most of the day and all night, having to endure the pressure of the screw, the weight of the iron and the cramp it induced in his arms, shoulders and back. It was impossible to lie at night, except on the face, and attention to personal needs was also impossible. These had to be met during the couple of hours in every twenty-four when the irons were removed, for the daily ration of bread and water.

The men had been placed in those ancient cells sometime in April 1916. On 6th May they were visited by an officer who told them they would leave for France the following morning, where disobedience would be met with the death sentence. At seven o'clock on the 7th May they were released from their irons and packed on a train with several hundred non-combatant men who had accepted this form of service. The irons were re-fastened and the train started its long slow journey to Southampton. The cruel treatment the prisoners had endured angered the other men, and as the train passed slowly through a London suburban station one of them wrote a note to the No Conscription Fellowship headquarters. This was thrown from a carriage window and picked up and posted (whether by someone sympathetic or by one ignorant of the significance of the address will never be known).

The letter arrived the same day — as letters did in those days. It sparked off immediate action. A representative of the N.C.F. set off at once for Harwich to investigate. Two days later, the Secretary of State for War, Lord Derby, was informed. 'Good,' he exclaimed. 'They will be shot, and rightly so.' This was in contravention of the Government's promise not to send C.O.s to France. The Prime Minister, Asquith, was told. 'Abominable' he exclaimed, and sent a telegram (telephones being still undeveloped) to Southampton, ordering the men to be retained there. Most of the non-combatant men had in fact been retained there because of an outbreak of measles, but so anxious were the military to make an example of those war-resisters that they hurried them on regardless of the measles.

The irons were again removed and they were free to mix with the others on the crowded ship. They made no secret of their convictions and their physical condition showed that they had suffered for them. The attitude of the others on board, all bound for the theatre of war, was one of great sympathy and generosity, pressing food and cigarettes on the resisters, and offering words of encouragement.

On arrival at Le Havre the objectors were told that they were now members of the British Expeditionary Force. Their sins were forgiven, their misdeeds expunged from the record. Now, with a fresh start the way was clear to serve their country like decent, sensible men. Having tasted freedom, the first day of food, the first night of untroubled sleep, it must have been a great temptation for those men to accept the situation and become willing members of the non-combatant corps. If their concern was to save their own skin, then this was obviously the time to give up protests, for severe punishment and even death were the alternatives.

On 10th May 1916 they were paraded as part of the British Expeditionary Force. When the order was given to quick march, the company moved off smartly — and left the seventeen standing, unmoved. Nothing like this had ever happened in the British (or any other) army. It was not a proud sight for the French spectators to behold, and blood pressure must have taken an upward surge in the red faces from corporal to colonel. But it *was* a proud sight. It was the beginning of a courageous stand against war on the stage of war itself.

The object of this account is not to thrill sadists. Yet the bravery of those non-soldiers should be remembered. They have little space in history books, and no monuments to them moulder in village squares. No Head of State bows in homage in annual ritual remembrance. Yet they were pioneers of the force that will save the world, if the world is to be saved — the inheritors of the Earth. Those men were scorned and rejected, yet by their stripes would they, and all of us, be healed.

They were subjected to all the penalties prescribed in the Regulations, and many other pains and indignities at the invention and the whim of the tormentors. There is no cruelty greater than that inflicted by the self-righteous acting with social approval, no viciousness as unrestrained as that of the virtuous. What an ecstacy of delight to scourge a man for his alleged cruelty, or hang him for the love of God!

127

Come Dungeons Dark......

The Jacket.

Those courageous and steadfast men were fastened in irons which were removed briefly every twenty-four hours, for eating bread and water, and attention to physical needs. Their diet was four biscuits a day for three days followed by one sparse meal daily for three days, then back to the biscuits and water again, and so on for twenty-eight days, when the order was renewed.

The punishments imposed along with this starvation diet were listed as Field Punishment No. 1, the severest form of torment allowed by Army Regulations, and designed for use by the Commanding Officer when the unit was on campaign or in a hostile situation, and places of confinement were not available. One of those tortures was called 'shot and shell'. In Victorian times a cannon ball was used; this had now been replaced by a bag of sand. This, by regulation, weighed 28lbs when dry, but more, much more, when it happened to get soaked in water. This bag was placed between the prisoner's feet. He had, on the blast of a whistle, to bend smartly, pick it up, hold it out on the palms of his hands, pause for the next whistle, take three steps forward, pause, on the next whistle lay the bag between the feet, pause, then bend again and pick up the bag. This would go on for an hour. It was often used on the same day that a man had been 'crucified'.

'Crucifixion' was the common name for another part of Field Punishment No 1, in which the victim was tied by wrists and ankles to a fixed object for two hours every day for three days out of four, for twenty-eight days. The fixed object the devisers of this torture had in mind was the huge wheel of a cannon. The victim's arms were tied firmly above his head to spokes, and his ankles to the lower spokes. An eye-witness to this barbarity told the present writer that the victim's spine was bent backwards over the great hub of the wheel which dug into his bare back till the skin was abraded and flesh wounds appeared. For two hours every three days out of four for twenty-eight days the poor wretch had the hub of the wheel press on the raw wound while he hung by the wrists. 'Was the cannon firing at the time?' 'Of course it was.' That sounds incredible till we see on record that, at a later day, W.G. Tyrell was 'crucified' so far in front of the firing line that his guard had to take cover a hundred yards behind him.

There were no cannon wheels convenient at the non-combatant camp, so other fixed objects were used, and to make up for the inadequacy of the binding post, an extra hour was sometimes added. On one occasion they were tied to a barbed wire fence so tightly, by wrists, waist and ankles that a movement of the face would have resulted in a nasty wound. A variation of this torture was devised when their wrists were tied to posts on either side, each five feet high. The knees and ankles were also bound, so that the prisoner was in a position where he could neither crouch nor stand upright. A few minutes of this brought pains to the arms, back and legs. It should be remembered that this was only part of the day's punishment those half-starved men had to endure. An added irritation was the mockery and abuse the victims had to take from the other soldiers. One Canadian expressed indignation at this treatment, although he had a great contempt for conscientious objectors.

There were others who took advantage of the vulnerability of the objectors to exercise their sadistic impulses, especially on men in solitary confinement. In the evening those creatures would go into the cell of a helpless wretch whose arms were still pinioned behind his back and twist the irons to increase the agony. They would, it hardly needs to be said, indecently torture him. On one occasion a sergeant-major joined in the fun. He invented a little game. They would think of some absurd 'crime' (probably of the 'You raped your mother' variety) and by torturing the helpless victim make him 'confess'.

The sergeant-major thought of a good way to deny his victim any relief he might gain by screaming. He wrapped a piece of soap in a rag and stuffed it into the victim's mouth. He doubtless glowed with the self-righeous emotion of a good man chastising a delinquent.

In London the Government was, of course, in a state of confusion. They were unable to locate those men. The press sent a team of journalists to France to investigate. They found a non-combatant camp where the men were willingly preparing road metal for military roads. They sent back a glowing account of this, showing that everybody was content and nobody in danger of the firing squad.

It eventually became evident beyond dispute that those men were not going to give way. The ultimate sanction must be applied. It was made known to them that they would be moved into the battle zone where disobedience was a capital offence. They were packed into a railway horse wagon with kitbags, provisions, and the accoutrements of their escort, and taken to Boulogne.

There they were taken to the Field Punishment Barracks, and, as a matter of ritual, given an order which they refused to obey. They were then handcuffed and placed in cells. Every afternoon they had their arms outstretched and their wrists fastened to a rope about five feet from the ground. Their knees and ankles were also bound. In that position they remained for the regulation two hours.

It was decided to pick four of the men and deal with them first as ring-leaders. They would be court-martialled and sentenced to death. That might make the others change their minds. There were no ring-leaders, so a sergeant was asked to name four men. He picked Howard C. Marten, Harry W. Scullard, John R. Ring and Jack Foster. Those four were placed in a separate cell. Cornelius Bettett asked permission to telegraph London for legal representation. This was refused. But the No Conscription Fellowship and the Friend's Service Committee had a network of information sources which convinced the government that it was impossible to escape publicity in any action against the objectors.

On the morning of June 2, 1916 the four were led out under escort with fixed bayonets to stand trial. The hearing was postponed, for technical reasons, and another hearing fixed for June 7th. The court martial went ahead then, but, unusually, it was eight days after that before sentence was pronounced.

On the morning of June 15th the four men were led out to hear their sentences. On three sides of a square men of the non-combatant corps and of the Labour Battalion were placed, with the fourth side being kept clear for the Court and the prisoners. It was not an entirely new experience for the four men, though their first time in the chief role. Some weeks before they had been forced to stand in irons and listen to the death sentence being passed on a young soldier, a youth condemned to die by comfortably-placed mass-criminals who were destroying a generation. Now those four who refused to take life had every reason to believe that their lives were at an end. Howard Martin was the first to be sentenced. After reading a long list of the accused's offences, the sentence was pronounced: *'To Suffer Death By Shooting.'*

There followed a long, silent pause. And then the President of the Court Martial added: 'Commuted to ten years' penal servitude.'

If there was determination in France to break those objectors, there was confusion in Parliament and Government about what was happening. At first the Minister denied that the men were even in France, and said that there was no question of their being sentenced to death. A little later he had to admit that indeed they were in France, and *had* been sentenced to death. He even thought that the sentences had already been carried out, and proceeded to defend what he had promised would never happen. Even the Prime Minister was involved, and was accused of deceiving the House. He promised to make a statement, and did so finally, undertaking that such a thing would never happen again.

Perhaps the Government would not have been so embarrassed had those particular men been socialists, and based their objections on political grounds. But they were Quakers, and never failed to let it be known. To shoot such men came very near to a revival of religious persecution, and that would raise a storm from the non-conformists, and place a question mark on Britain's liberal pretensions.

The militarists were fighting this war, and its chief end was victory for the generals, and that end justified all means, and contempt for those who thought otherwise. However, Britain was still under civilian government, and the Prime Minister's instruction to General Haig could not be ignored. So it was that, after a long silence, the Court President had continued: 'Commuted to ten years' penal servitude.'

So the men were transported in spirit from the awful prospect of death, through the relief of reprieve and renewed life to the realisation that the life offered was one of dark, diminished existence in the world of cold, damp cells, hunger, hard labour and abuse.

All the others were court martialled, sentenced, and, after an uncertain pause (for none could be sure he would not be an exception) reprieved, and the sentence of death commuted to ten years' penal servitude. Despite the Government's protestations and promises, conscientious objectors were being sent to France till the end of the war, and still being sentenced to death with the same uncertain pause before the commutation was pronounced. On at least one occasion the victim was placed before the firing post before he was told of his reprieve. This resulted in serious emotional disorder.

After the Court Martial and the contrived horror of the sentencing, conditions in the Punishment Barracks were easier for the men. They were allowed to mix together and a Quaker Chaplain was allowed to visit them and conduct a service. One of the men, Howard Martin, wrote: 'It is not easy to convey to others all the wonder and reality of this visitation. It was a tangible assurance of Heavenly Guidance.' To anyone not sharing his sublime faith, it might also have seemed that the Heavenly Guide was slow, sluggish, spasmodic, generally indifferent, and less attentive to his divine obligations than was his Diabolocal Colleague in his infernal misguidance.

A few days later the men were on their back to England. Their progress was heralded in advance. Stone-throwing crowds greeted them at Ostend. French soldiers hissed at them in Rouen, and rotten eggs and tomatoes showered on them in Southampton. In South-ampton they were separated and sent to various prisons. Later their sentences were reduced to two years' hard labour.

If Government Ministers were badly informed as to what was happening in France, there was no greater enlightenment among prison Governors or detention camp Commanders. Many of those persons had hoped the conscientious objectors sent to France would be shot. That was the reason for sending them. Now, whether they knew they hadn't been executed, or were unsure, or knew they had been reprieved, they spoke as though the men *had* been killed, and used this to frighten objectors in their charge.

The problem of the 'conchies' (they used the term themselves, and used it with pride) was new to Britain, and the phenomenon took the Government and the military authorities by surprise. If they had given it any thought at all it was in terms of a few religious fanatics or political cranks, easily dealt with. But two months after the passing of the conscription act, there were two thousand conchies crowding the cells, and the No Conscription Fellowship had a membership of fifteen thousand registered members and an untold number of supporters, all people of conviction and determination. And the Fellowship was well-organised, level-headed and efficient.

The conchies themselves were far from being the pallid weeds that might have ben expected. Their spiritual and physical endurance amazed and confounded their persecutors, and it had an eroding effect on authority. Obedience and subservience were the essentials of a brutal punitive institution. This was so accepted that it was considered self-evident and unchallengable. The conchies challenged it by ignoring it. Their disregard frayed the edges and distorted the whole pattern. By ignoring the whole vile process of torture and coercion, by refusing to co-operate with it in their own destruction, they made it impotent. But perhaps because it had been rendered impotent, the State and those who sought to carry out the will of the State, resorted to every possible sort of sadistic vileness in their efforts to impose themselves on that group of indomitable men. The State drew back only from the actual physical extermination of the conchies, although their minds and bodies were fair game.

Sixty-nine conchies died as a result of their treatment and conditions. Some died in prison, some in detention barracks, a few committed suicide, and some died shortly after release. It is a vile record, and one which had better not be forgotten, lest it, and worse, should happen again

The brutal treatment of conscientious objectors could not be hidden. It scandalised even the Army Council, who issued an Order on 25th May 1916 to the effect that conscientious objectors who disobeyed an order should be treated in the Regulation manner: that is, arrested, and confined to the Guard Room till tried and sentenced, not subjected to hours of torment at the whim of anybody so inclined. A later amendment to this Order decreed that objectors should serve their sentences in a civil prison. The reaction of the Colonels to this Order was to defy it. Only three of them were court martialled for their atrocious offences.

The treatment of nineteen-year-old Jack Gray was in blatant defiance of the Order. On 7th May 1917 he arrived at Hornsea Detention Camp. Refusing to put on the uniform he was abused and tormented for the rest of the day. Live ammunition was fired at his feet, his ankles were beaten with a cane, his mouth was split open by a heavy blow from a sergeant. Next day the process was continued. Then his hands were bound firmly behind his back and his ankles tied together. A rope was fastened to his wrists and pulled tight to the ankles. In this position he had to stand for several hours, then a bag of stones was fastened on his back and he was beaten round the training field till he collapsed. There were other brutalities inflicted on Jack which we will not detail, but of such a nature that eight of the soldiers refused to take part, leaving themselves liable to severe penalties.

The torture which broke the boy's resolve was when he was stripped naked and had a rope tied round his waist. He was then thrown into the camp cesspool and pulled around. After the second immersion the rope had so tightened round his waist that he was in great pain. Still the treatment continued 'for eight or nine times', said a witness at the subsequent court martial. Someone, transported into ecstacies of sadistic excitement at the sight of the lad's muddy, filth-encrusted body, got an old sack and making holes for arms and head, forced the youngster into it for further grotesque immersions. Then Jack Gray gave in, promising to fight for England and save the world from the barbarity of the Hun.

The local M.P. forced an Enquiry. The officers responsible were censured. Nobody was allowed to see the report of the Enquiry.

The case of James Brightmore was even more outrageous. It certainly got more publicity. Brightmore was a young solicitor's clerk from Manchester. After serving eight months of a twelve months sentence for refusing to put on the uniform, Brightmore was sent to Shore Camp, Cleethorpes. Still refusing, he was sentenced to twenty-eight days solitary confinement on bread and water. According to Army Order X, Brightmore should have been serving his sentence in prison, but the authorities pretended not to know. There was no solitary cell in the camp, so the Major had to improvise, like the efficient soldier he was. He had a deep hole dug in the parade ground, coffin shaped, and into this young Brightmore was inserted. For four days he stood ankle-deep in water, then a piece of wood was lowered for him to stand on, but that sank into the water, which now stank, and in which a dead mouse floated.

One day it rained heavily. Some of the soldiers took him from the hole and put him into a tent where he slept the night. He remained there all the next day, and then the Major became aware of it, and he was roughly wakened and thrust down the hole again, and a black tarpaulin pulled over it to keep out the rain. He was kept there for a week, the Major calling on him during the day to jeer, telling him on one occasion that his friends had been sent to France and shot, and that he would be in the next batch.

One of the soldiers who had been reprimanded for taking Brightmore out of the hole, realising that there was no intention of releasing the youth, tore open a cigarette packet and passed it down with a stub of pencil, suggesting that Brightmore write to his parents. He did so, and the soldier added a covering note, saying that the hole was twelve feet deep. They were under orders not to take any notice of the boy's complaints, but 'the torture is turning his head.' At that time Brightmore had been in the vertical grave for eleven days.

Brightmore's parents took the letter to the *Manchester Guardian*, which published it with a strongly worded editorial. Within forty minutes of the paper arriving at the camp, Brightmore had been taken from the hole, which was hastily filled in. The major and a fellow officer were dismissed from their posts for disobeying the Order.

The third case of Court Martial did not involve a young man, but the mature and articulate C.H. Norman, a writer on international politics and founder-member of the No Conscription Fellowship. He came up against the out-spoken sadist Lt. Col. Reginald Brooke, Commandant of Wandsworth Military Detention Camp, who declared that he didn't give a damn for Asquith and his treacherous Government. He would do what he liked with his prisoners.

C.H. Norman thought differently. When he went on hunger strike he was badly beaten, tied to a table and a tube forced up his nose and down into his stomach. Through this, liquid food was poured. Then he was forced into a strait jacket fastened so tightly that breathing was difficult, and he suffered a spell of unconsciousness. He was bound in the jacket for twenty-three hours, during which time the Col. called on him to jeer. Norman was not an inexperienced adolescent: he brought a civil action against the Col., who was court martialled and sentenced to be dismissed from his cherished position where his sadism (for it could have been no less) had free play. For some time thereafter he toured the country, lecturing to 'patriotic' groups on the secret agents of the Kaiser in the British Government!

4: WORMWOOD SCRUBS

On May 26th 1916 Guy Aldred drew up an appeal against his sentence of six months military detention. On the previous day an Army Order had been issued to the effect that a soldier charged with an offence against discipline who, at his trial, makes conscientious objection his defence, shall serve his sentence in a civil prison. Aldred's appeal was forwarded to the Commanding Officer, and was turned down.

Prisoners arriving at Devizes Military Detention barracks were warned that the treatment would be severe. Punishments would be harsh, including solitary confinement in irons on bread and water. Persistent trouble would lead to a prison court martial, which would be in secret and would award heavy penalties.

There were thirty conscientious objector prisoners in Devizes Detention Barracks while Aldred was there, and twenty of them were in the underground cells awaiting court martial. It was easy for the officers to put a man in this position, if he was a war objector. Just give a man an order he could not obey.

Guy Aldred and nine others were not given any military orders, but were employed in sweeping and scrubbing tasks. Later Guy staged a complete work and discipline strike, but not at this stage. He was waiting to see how his circumstances would develop. It will never be known why the Commandant did not force him into a court martial. Maybe he thought that twenty was enough to be going on with. It may be that Aldred's reputation as anti-war orator and his editorship of *The Spur* stayed the Colonel's hand, or maybe he had the fantastic notion that Aldred might be won over to the other side and use his oratory in the war effort, as some politicians, trade unionists, suffragettes and some-time radical journalists had done, to their considerable profit.

In fact, of course, there was no chance of this. Unlike many of the Christian objectors, he was not out for martyrdom to enrich his soul or gain credit in heaven. Nor was he a private person, who would go back to his trade or profession when the war was over. He was a soldier in the ranks of the new burgeoning humanity, challenging the old order of decrepit values. His course would be tactical to the best advantage of his cause.

During his imprisonment he met several people in the uniform of warder or guard who had heard him speak in the past, or who were readers of *The Spur*. They may not have have been able to make his path any smoother, but they were useful in smuggling out letters and supplying paper on which to write surreptitious articles.

Sometimes they wrote letters about him to Rose Witcop. From such a source it was learned that twice at Devizes he was in a state of nervous collapse, on one occasion for several hours in a condition of 'complete mental blank'. Nevertheless, his smuggled letters were strong and unflinching, although sometimes pensive.

After several weeks at Devizes, Aldred was returned to Fovant, where the Colonel told him he must make up his mind about obeying orders. As Guy was not in two minds about his course of action, there was no decision to make, but he accepted the Colonel's offer (he had no choice) to let the matter rest over the weekend. He was locked in a cell, undisturbed for the next three days.

On Monday June 16th, at 6.a.m. he was ordered on parade. He refused to go, and was taken before the Colonel, who remanded him for a court martial. This, his second, took place at Fovant Camp on Tuesday June 27th, 1916.

Guy argued that he was not in fact a soldier of the Territorial Force, as the charge described him, but was a civilian, and thus could not be tried for the alleged offence, since he could never have committed it. He explained that he had been arrested in an irregular manner and had been given no opportunity of having his reasons for opposing war heard before a Conscientious Objectors' tribunal. The argument was, naturally, over-ruled by the court. Aldred then pleaded not guilty. He had no witnesses but wished to make a statement. Permission to do this was refused, and after a period of discussion in the absence of the accused, the verdict of guilty was given.

Two days later, before a representative line of soldiers, the sentence of nine months hard labour was pronounced.

On July 4th 1916 Guy Aldred was taken to Winchester Prison to serve his sentence. On August 9th he was again forced into khaki and handcuffs and taken under military escort to Wormwood Scrubs Prison, London. On the train he was informed that he would be taken before the Committee of the Central Tribunal, for a formal hearing of his case as a formality before offering him open arrest. This was a scheme which would remove war resisters from prison and military camps, where they were proving to be a very disturbing influence. Those selected for open arrest would be housed in camps and do non-military work. They would be free to leave the camp outside working hours and within a nine o'clock curfew. But one had to be registered as a Conscientious Objector before those concessions were applicable, and that meant at least a token appearance.

Aldred considered this proposition involving open arrest. Prison conditions in 1917 were such as to make any alternative worth consideration. It was absurd to work at hard labour in prison and be locked up in a dimly lit (pre-electric) cell at 4.30 in the afternoon, with a final meal of bread, margarine and cocoa, and refuse to labour in a camp where the evenings and weekends were free, and where he could resume his speaking and writing. It was stated that the work would be non-military, otherwise the scheme would be turned down completely by the resisters. After five days in The Scrubs, the Central Tribunal members arrived to decide the future of Aldred.

It was a reasonable enough hearing, far removed from the farce of so many local Tribunals responsible for condemning young men to the hell of prisons and military detention camps. The transcript of the hearing shows an almost gentlemanly exchange between the Chairman and Aldred, who was given an opportunity of explaining his moral objection to participating in the war, and of explaining that his objection was in no way political, for he was not interested in politics, which he deemed mere electioneering.

A week later, Aldred was called to the Chief Warder's office and asked to sign an undertaking of the conditions of open arrest — and exile. If he refused to sign he would finish his sentence of hard labour and then be returned to the military. Aldred signed.

Britain had no Siberia, and transportation to Australia had ended, so the authorities were limited in choice. They made the most of what they had. Men from Scotland were sent to Dartmoor; and men from the south of England were sent to the north of Scotland. Guy left Winchester Prison on August 25th 1916 for the village of Dyce, near Aberdeen, where tents had been erected in the low ground of a granite quarry, on a lake of mud.

5: THE LABOUR CAMP

The Dyce Camp for Conscientious Objectors had been set up ten days before Guy Aldred arrived, with five others. They included Bonar Thompson, the 'Hyde Park Orator' of later years, and E.T. Jope, an anti-war activist. Other arrivals trooped in, and a week later, Aldred, Jope and Thompson formed the Mens' Committee (with ten members) to look after the interests of the inmates. The Brace Committee for the Employment of Conscientious Objectors accepted the Mens' Committee, in the hope that it would facilitate the running of the camp. (The Brace Committee was so-called after its Chairman, William Brace, Labour M.P.)

The camp was situated two and half miles north-west of Dyce, in a field immediately adjacent to stone quarries. The camp was made up of twenty-seven bell tents and three marquee tents. It 'housed' two hundred and fifty young men, who would not fight for King and Country. Thirty-four of them had been sent to France, as already related, and thirty of those had been sentenced to death and reprieved.

The three marquee tents were used as a store, a dining hall and a recreation centre. The men slept in the bell tents, eight to a tent. Each man was given a mattress, and three rough blankets — nothing else. There was only the tent and the muddy ground, covered at night by waterproof sheets.

The men had to work in the quarries, breaking stones, carrying them by hand to a wheel-barrow in which they were trundled through the clinging mud to a stone-crushing machine. The purpose of the task was allegedly the making of a road for a new Aberdeen suburb. The work started at seven a.m. after a meagre prison breakfast, and lasted for ten hours, with only one half-hour break for 'dinner'. The pay was eightpence per day, but only twopence for those with dependents — wife or mother — who received the sixpence, plus sixpence from the State.

One of the first actions of the Mens' Committee was to change the working hours. Seasoned labourers of navvy proportions could not have done their arduous work on such scanty rations, and such poor provisions for rest and sleep, and the conchies were for the most part

140

The Labour Camp, Dyce, Aberdeen, 1916.   The lad of 19, seated beside Guy Aldred, died a few weeks later from untreated pneumonia.

workers of mind rather than body. The camp had no supervisory staff: an Agent was in charge, with civilian foremen and machine operators. The Agent had no disciplinary power. He could only report defaulting inmates to the Brace Committee, which returned unsatisfactory men to jail, and, ultimately, after serving their prison sentence, to the military. So when the Mens' Committee decreed that the ten hours of labour should be divided into two shifts of five hours each, the Agent reported the matter to the Brace Committee whose representative arrived and reversed the decision. Aldred, Jope, Thompson and others refused to comply.

Only on the finest of days were the living conditions bearable for the fittest young men in the camp. On wet days the sixteen-year-old army tents leaked onto the bedding and the men slept in unheated tents on soaking mattresses. One of the inmates caught a cold which, in the conditions of neglect, developed into pneumonia. For five days he lay on a rain-soaked mattress, gravely ill. The Mens' Committee asked for medical attention, but none was given. His mates then moved him to a disused stable where, in in a worsening condition, he lay for a further five days, then he was moved to a ruined cottage, where he died. He was only nineteen, the first of the sixty-nine conchies who died in the camps. He was Walter Roberts, from Stockport.

The callous neglect of young Roberts caused great anger in the Camp. The Mens' Committee sent a statement of protest to the Home Office. This listed a number of requirements, among them a telephone link with the village for use in emergency, medical attention and hospital treatment for serious illness, and a building to be set aside near the Camp for the less seriously ill, with beds and medical facilities. They also demanded that the Committee should be able to discharge from the Camp men unable to bear its rigorous conditions.

The Home Office made no reply to this, but issued a Press Statement which appeared in the local newspapers, and completely denied the claims of the Mens' Committee. Its description of the conditions in the camp make it sound more like some idyllic rural retreat than what it in fact was — a penal camp designed to break the spirit and body of men who were defying the State.

Guy Aldred was an active member of the Mens' Committee. He was one of those who refused to work more than five hours a day, and he worked that long only because he had signed a document undertaking to work in camp as an alternative to prison. Now he was urging a general strike and a return to prison by all the camp inmates, with, for the Home Office, all the problems the camps were intended to overcome.

He had not forgotten the main reason for his acceptance of the Scheme — to resume his propaganda as much as possible. So despite the difficulties, within a few weeks the first issue of *The Granite Echo* appeared. It was in the same format as *The Spur*, and was published by the Bakunin Press as the 'Organ of the Dyce C.O.s.' It was sold in the camp, and in Aberdeen, Glasgow and London. Aldred explained the title:

'We are the corner stones which the builders have rejected. We have found a lodging in a granite quarry. That is appropriate. Dumped down in such fashion, in such circumstances, in such surroundings, we will send an echo throughout the length and breadth of the land. Stone has clashed against stone. The stony hardness of Government persecution; its supreme indifference to human suffering. There has ensued a war of stones and its noise and excitement will be recorded in *The Granite Echo*.'

Nor was his determination to hold meetings lessened by the difficulties of the situation. He and Bonar Thompson spoke at Broadhill, Castlegate I.L.P. rooms, and the Northern Socialist Hall, Mealmarket St. Aberdeen. Those meetings were reported in the *Aberdeen Journal, Free Press, Evening Press, Evening Express* and *Evening Gazette*, under sensational headlines: 'Allegiance to the Red Flag', 'Flaunting The Red Flag', 'Our Army in Exile'. *The Granite Echo* was noticed by all those papers, and even the *London Daily News* mentioned it.

In total disregard of the camp regulations Guy was in Glasgow on October 15th speaking in the Lithuanian Hall on 'Conscription and Compromise' under the auspices of the Herald League. He addressed the College School in an atmosphere of magnificent enthusiasm. The following Sunday he spoke in Aberdeen Adult School, then left for Glasgow and spoke there at 6.30. The next week Thompson made the trip to Glasgow. Guy also spoke at advertised meetings for the Northern Socialist Society on Sunday 17th.

Aldred continued his agitational activity in the Camp. When the Brace Committee rejected the Mens' Committee suggestion that work be reduced, Aldred called on the men to work only five hours. He said that the conditions and work at the camp did not constitute 'alternative service', as alleged in the agreement, but was rather alternative penal servitude without the cost of warders or confining walls.

When the the men did not respond, he decided to leave the camp and take the consequences.   After a weekend in Aberdeen he went to Glasgow and from there wrote a letter to the Home Office, dated 16th October, pointing out that he had received a certificate of discharge from the army dated September 21st.   He was no longer under military disccipline.   Apart from that, he he been declared a genuine objector by the Wormwood Scrubs Tribunal, and was entitled to absolute exemption.

The discharge certificate recorded that he had served 'no days' with the Army, and had 'no conduct', and that he had been discharged for misconduct.   It also had a warning stamped across in it in red, stating that persons so discharged would be liable to imprisonment if they tried to join the army.

He received a reply demanding to know if he had gone back on his promise to do civil work as an alternative to prison.   'Please let us know within four days'.

Aldred returned to Shepherds Bush.   Three members of the Mens' Committee from Dyce Camp, who lived in the district, called on him.   They told him that the Camp was closed.   They had been given a week's leave and ordered to report to Wakefield Prison where an 'open prison' had been set up for them.   On November 1st Guy was arrested and returned to Wormwood Scrubs.

Despite the Certificate of Discharge he would be court martialled another twice and spend a further two and a half years at hard labour.   This was outrageously in breach of statutory enactments and quite absurd, but that was the way the war was conducted in every department.   The war was in itself an outrageous absurdity.

6: DURANCE VILE

Prisons are not, by their nature, pleasant places. In 1916 they were even more unpleasant than they are today. The element of reformation of character or rehabilitation of person was minimal. Punishment of the trangressor was still the keynote, and unofficial punishment for the delectation of warders and guards was a widespread practice. If conchies had been the shivering cowards they were commonly perceived as being, their position would have been tragic indeed. But they were mostly men of courage, and they fought back.

There were three grades of imprisonment in those days: First Division, Hard Labour, and Penal Servitude. First Division was for first offenders and Top People. Penal Servitude was for long-term incarceration. The conditions there began with rigour but were relaxed by time and good conduct. The most severe form of imprisonment was Hard Labour. By 1916, the labour was not, perhaps, excessively hard, but the conditions of confinement were. A Hard Labour sentence could not exceed two years, for it was reckoned that no person could endure longer without grave risk to his mind. Conchies were often sentenced to two years, commuted to one hundred and twelve days, in the hope that a tasts of such imprisonment would do wonders for a sensitive conscience. This was true in a sense opposite from that intended. It strengthened resolve, for it acclimatised the objector to the consequences of his convictions. As sentence followed sentence, for what was essentially the same offence, most conchies spent about three years in Hard Labour conditions. We will look briefly at those conditions, under the guidance of John W. Graham, M.A., in his book *Conscience and Conscription* (1922).

He described the cell as being either eleven or fourteen feet by seven. The floor was usually of rough square tiles or black painted concrete. In a general Spring clean (and Spring was determined by the mood of the warder), the floor had to be scrubbed with the prisoner's hair brush. The window was narrow and of ribbed glass, too high for the prisoner to reach, unless he stood on a stool, and that was forbidden. The stool was three-legged and backless. It was an offence to sit on it and lean against the wall.

In some of the larger prisons the cells were lit by a dim electric bulb, but in most of them the light, such as it was, came from a gas jet in the corridor, shining through a frosted glass panel into the cell. As a black-out precaution against Zeppelin raids, in some prisons this glass panel was painted black, as was the narrow ribbed window, except for an inch along the bottom. In one corner was a fixed triangular table, and a triangular shelf above it. On this were three books: a Bible, a Prayer Book and a Hymn Book. After the first month, a library book, and after the second month, a second library book were added — although these were not of the prisoner's own choice. There was an enamel plate, a spoon and a blunt tin knife. No fork was allowed (perhaps these had been used in the past to chip away mortar between the glazed bricks in the wall). Normally there was a sanitary bucket which had to be kept clean and spotless.

The bed was a three-plank board. There was a tank provided in most prisons where those boards would be periodically soaked in disinfectant to rid them of the bugs which lived in the cracks. The bed-board was placed on the floor at night, for the first month without mattress or pillow. After that a mattress was supplied. During the day the blankets and bedboard had to be placed against the wall in a carefully prescribed position, the books on the shelf, the enamel plate, the knife and spoon set in an exact position. Any deviation, or anything which any warder cared to call a deviation, would bring absurdly severe punishment. In some prisons a slate and an inch of slate pencil were provided. The slate had to be wiped clean every day, so that no recording could be kept. Guy Aldred wrote pamphlets and even works of fiction on his slate, although of course, they disappeared each night as the slate was wiped clean. Getting a fresh piece of slate pencil was often extremely difficult.

In *Conscription and Conscience* John Graham wrote:

'In this place, alone, you spend twenty-three hours and ten minutes out of the twenty-four in the first month of your sentence, hungry most of the time. You get little exercise, and probably suffer from indigestion, headache or sleeplessness. The entire weekend is solitary until you attend chapel. After the first month you have thirty minutes exercise on Sunday. You would go mad but for the work. You sit and stitch canvas for mailbags. Your fingers begin by being sore and inflamed, but they become used to it. At first your daily task can hardly be finished in a day. You struggle hard to get the reward of a large mug of sugarless cocoa and a piece of bread at eight o'clock. It will save you from hunger all night, for your previous food — I cannot call it a meal — had been at

4.15. This extra ration, which varied, and was not universal, was a war-time incentive to produce work of national importance. It was cut off as a war economy in 1918.....

'Except on monthly visits (15 minutes), or if he has to speak to the Chaplain or doctor, or if he has to accost a warder, the prisoner is not allowed to speak for two years — the sentence usually given to a conscientious objector.'

After the first month the prisoner was allowed to work 'in association'. That meant that he must sit on his stool outside the cell door, with his fellow prisoners also sitting outside their cells, and sew his quota of mailbags, so many stitches to the inch. There, not only was the rule of silence imposed, but it was an offence to 'turn the head'. One must not even glance at one's fellow convicts. After the war the silence rule was amended to mean that it was not an offence to talk, but it was an offence not to stop talking when ordered. This led to a situation where one squad could talk, because the warder was in a good mood, and another squad had to work in silence because that was the whim of the warder.

The punishments inflicted on men who broke the most trivial rules were absurdly severe, especially as they were already living in punitive conditions. To quote John Graham again:

'The punishments for breaking a rule, for talking, for lying on your bed before bedtime, looking out of a window, having a pencil in your possession, not working, and many other such acts were savage. If those things were reported to the Governor, there would be, say, three days bread and water and in a gloomy basement cell, totally devoid of furniture during the daytime. This was famine. In addition, your exercise might be taken away, and your work in association, your letter or visit would be postponed, whilst your family were left wondering what had happened, and marks, with the effect of postponing your final release, would be taken off.'

Such were the conditions Guy Aldred found at Wormwood Scrubs when he was sent there again. It was two months before Aldred could get a letter out to the *The Spur*. It reveals, under a cover of cheerfulness, the mental agony of a thirty-year old man shut up for endless days in a tiny cell. '*....My brain throbs through my being the thought: "Time Flies! Death Urges". I feel myself responding, all my nerves concentrated to live my work, and I am compelled to patient sufference. But I do not wish the hours to fly. That would be folly. I just want to lay up a quiet store of energy; to watch my wasted moments turn to a reserve of future power....*'

On March 28th 1917 Aldred was ostensibly released from prison but was not allowed to go free.   He was taken under escort to Exeter Military Camp.   According to the Regulation of September 1916 he should have been taken to the military camp only to be discharged from the army.   But as he was already discharged, that formality was not required.   The regulation was ignored, the discharge certificate was ignored.   He was given another order which he refused to obey, and was confined in the Guard Room.

7: THE WORKHOUSE

The guardroom was very small for its purpose. It had no beds, and bed boards were not provided. It had a table on which six men could crowd at night. As there were twelve prisoners, six had to sleep on the filthy floor. There were no personal blankets or towels; each man grabbed what he could, and those were filthy. There were only nine tin plates and nine sets of tin cutlery. Three men had to wait for the first three empty plates, and eat their food from those unwashed utensils. There was only one small window, and that opened on to a urinal. The door, kept open during the day, opened on to the same urinal. At night the door was closed. There were no overnight toilet facilities. The conditions were ripe for contracting skin infection, and that is what happened to Guy Aldred. He contracted scabies. He was given no treatment for the complaint, but was sent to the City Workhouse, to keep him from infecting the others. It did not seem to matter much if he infected the paupers. The journey to the workhouse was made on foot. It was Aldred's first glimpse of the outside world for nine months.

The first Russian Revolution had just erupted. This was for the establishment of the democratic Republic, and was to be swept aside by the Bolshevik Revolution seven months later. This pale-pink Revolution was one of the main items of news. Aldred wrote, in the May 1917 issue of *The Spur* (he used the editorial 'we'):

'The other day we strolled from the Higher Barracks to our present residence, the City Workhouse, Hevitree Hill, Exeter. We were under military police escort, and were unable to take that interest in our surroundings that we would have liked. But we noticed a big flaming placard, announcing the convening of a meeting to celebrate the Russian Revolution. We smiled. In Wandsworth we had Lansbury's *Herald* announcing meetings in London to celebrate the same event. And we knew that throughout the country the great 'British Nation', whatever that entity might be, was rejoicing and waxing exceeding glad at the overthrow of Tsarism. The smile deepened, for we knew something of the celebrators and their antecedents.

'On Sunday, in the workhouse, we were able to get Northcliffe's *Weekly Dispatch* and read it in bed. It was (suitably) April 1st, All Fools' Day. On the front page a column was headed "Kropotkin's Advice to Russia: German Invaders Must be Driven Out. Frenzied Scenes in London." We wondered whether such headings in a conscriptionist, imperialist, antisocialist paper, evidenced the emancipation of the world's proletariat.......

'Northcliffe's reporter wrote: "With sweet music, with impassioned speeches, and amid delirious enthusiasm, the Russian colony in London celebrated the Revolution yesterday. From the white-haired revolutionary who has been an exile in England for twenty years, to the fiery young man who was a student in the uprising of 1905, every section of the Russian community was represented, and the roof of the Kingsway Hall, where they met, shook with the terrific roars of cheering. Russian women, many of striking beauty, were in attendance in large numbers and vied with the men in lusty applause. All present wore the red revolutionary colours....."

'One would conclude that Lord Northcliffe had toiled always for the Russian Revolution.'

There follows a long paragraph giving instances of anti-socialist propaganda in the Northcliffe Press, and a reference to interned Russian socialists, including Milly Witcop, Rose's sister. Then he comments on the letter sent to the meeting by Peter Kropotkin, who had ended his exile in England when he learned of the outbreak of the March Revolution in Russia. Aldred quoted passages from Kropotkin's letter, which supported the main resolution of the Kingsway Hall meeting, which was to renew the war effort against the Germans. That was, of course, the reason for the fullsome reporting in the *Sunday Dispatch*. Aldred reproved Kropotkin for allowing himself to be used by the reactionary press. Guy was out of favour with the No Conscription Fellowship for saying that they were specially concerned with the religious objector, who was in fact, a humbug because he was opposed to war without being opposed to the causes of war. Aldred was also out of favour with the anarchists (or they with him) because he denounced Peter Kropotkin's support of the war.

Now he made another criticism of anarchism's Grand Old Man for supporting a pale-pink republican revolution, and urged, not a revolutionary peace, but intensification of a capitalists' war, and for rejoicing in unison with the Tory war-mongers.

Aldred was returned to the Military Camp at Depcot at the

beginning of May.   He was on remand for refusing to obey a military order, but the Commandant seems to have decided to ignore that and start again.   On May 9th he was ordered to go on parade.   He refused, and was remanded for a court martial.   This legal irregularity was only petty compared with the more serious fact that Aldred had not been called up at all in the first place.   The magistrate tried to get round this by saying that the call-up was by general proclamation, and a call-up notice was not needed.   Then why were call-up papers sent to everybody else deemed to be soldiers?   And why was it that only the magistrate seemed to be aware of this general call-up?   Assuming that Aldred was covered by a not-too-evident general call-up, he had then been accepted by the Central Tribunal as a conscientious objector, and should, in accordance with the September 1916 Regulation have been returned to the army only to be discharged from the service.   He had, in fact, *been* discharged from the army on September 21st 1916, and had a certificate to prove it.   He had been transferred to the W Reserve over which the Army had no direct control.   Without even a formal recall to the army, he was again 'deemed' to be a soldier, and was about to face his third court martial.

This took place in Deepcut Military Barracks on 11th May 1917.   It was a short proceeding, for Guy refused to consider it a legal or a serious hearing, but it was serious enough to impose a sentence of eighteen months hard labour.

He found the opportunity, while waiting for the promulgation of his sentence, which followed a few days after the trial, to write a long essay for *The Spur*.   This was entitled 'The World as We Leave It.'   The opening paragraphs let us understand his frame of mind.   He was thirty years of age, and a person of boundless energy.   It must have been with a heavy heart that he faced another eighteen months of incarceration.   The article was subtitled '*A Farewell Essay*':

'We are commencing this essay on the eve of May 1917. Spring is with us at last and the mischievous vim of life is stirring in our blood.   But the Spring, and the Summer of which it is the promise, are not for us to enjoy.   This world of sunshine and activity must be put behind us.   Its temptations must be viewed as Christ viewed the offering of bread in the wilderness.   To nature, we must make the ungracious and insulting rebuke: "Get thee behind me, Satan."   For the world is at war.   The puny rulers of the world have coerced their subjects into dancing at the feast of death.   And whoever will not indulge in the orgy, the same shall not enjoy the kiss of nature's sun.'

151

Then Aldred touched upon a cardinal belief in his philosophy. That is, that we live in a reality which is a reflection of false concepts imposed on us from childhood in the interests of established authority: among these are Church and State, Religion and Patriotism, corrupt ethics, and War. Based on these myths, our reality is a sham, and we live in a fantasy of falsehood.

'Let us envision the world as it is....This chaos of falsehood out of which veracity must take its origin. This ignorance from which wisdom shall be begotten. This despotism whose aftermath shall be liberty. Let us understand and rejoice and be exceeding glad for great is the destiny of humanity. Where we see nothing but fate and mischance today, tomorrow shall be witnessed with purpose and well-being.

'Let us leave tomorrow to take care of its own visions and concern ourselves with the visions of today....to relieve the drab monotony of durance vile.'

Guy's view of man's potential and future in 1917 seems romantically optimistic today in this nuclear age, seventy and more years on, but he *had* to face incarceration in a spirit of optimism, otherwise despair would have crushed him.

So the court martial sentenced him to another spell of hard labour, and Aldred entered Wandsworth prison that May morning with optimism in his heart, but by mid-August he had fire in his belly. He led a prison revolt.

8: THE WORK CENTRE

With the break-up of the Labour Camps, Wakefield and Warwick prisons were turned into Work Centres to house the men prepared to do alternative service — the Alternativists. Locks were removed from cell doors, the cells re-named 'rooms', tables placed for working and eating in the corridors. Warders discarded their uniforms for ordinary dress and became 'Instructors'. The doctor became the head of the establishment. The work was the same as before — sewing mailbags — but the day ended at 5 o'clock and the men were free to leave the building till 9.30 p.m.

This was an acceptable situation for the six hundred men involved, provided no war work, or work releasing men for the war, was imposed. They had all been through the gamut of unjust persecution and illegal torments in detention camp and prison cell. Thirty-four of them had been 'crucified' and sentenced to death in France. All of them had faced the Central Tribunal in Wandsworth Prison for a re-assessment of their case, and all had been found to be genuine in their objection to participation in the war on moral or religious grounds. By the terms of the Military Service Act they should therefore have been granted absolute exemption, without penalty, but it was one of the confusions (or malevolencies) of administration that they weren't.

The Press, as the only means of the time for the spreading of information and the forming of opinion, worked up a campaign against the inmates of Wakefield, in the interests of high morality and increased circulation. Gruff-voiced old men and strident-voiced old women, and other good citizens of every degree, blazed their indignation at the coddling of those cowards while brave men died to protect them in their skin-saving comfort. Cartoons showed them lolling in easy chairs, carpet-slippered, side-tables piled with fruit and wine, cigarette in mouth, fag-ends scattered around, reading a paper, with a grin of self-satisfaction at the tragic headlines. Of course, angry young men who might in other circumstances have been

153

described as hooligans out for an excuse to beat-up and vandalise, but acting here in justifiable wrath, attacked the conchies in organised gangs. At Knutsford in Cheshire, eighteen conchies were sent to hospital. One man, lying battered and bleeding, was told by a policeman to 'Get back into your kennel'. Of course, no arrests were made.

Deliberately, following the example set by Knutsford, an attack was planned on Wakefield. This was organised to take place at Whitsun, 1918, when there was a holiday atmosphere. The joy and excitement extended from beating up the conchies to wrecking the houses of Quakers. So intense and violent was this hostility that a number of C.O.s including three of those who had been sent to France, wrote to the Home Office asking to be sent back to prison.

Ostensibly in response to popular demand, the conditions of the men in those Work Centres was made much more severe. Inmates were punished for the slightest offence, and punishment meant being sent back to prison, to hard labour.

In March 1917 the ninety convicts locked up in Dartmoor Prison were removed and it became the largest Work Centre in Britain. Between eight and nine hundred men, from many other camps, were confined there. They were not subject to the hard labour conditions of the Absolutists in prison. They had some social life amongst themselves, and they were able to go into Princetown.

In his *Conscription and Conscience*, John Graham said that:

'They fell into two well-marked groups — the religious group, taking either the Quaker, the Tolstoyan, or the more scriptural line, and the political or revolutionary group. Some of these were out for the Class War, and were not entirely disbelievers in all force; they would, on the contrary, have fought in a war against capitalism. There were, further, those who believed in immediate rebellion or escape — men who would break all rules and withstand a siege — scattered among a majority of more sensible men....The most difficult section were those who belonged to the Communist group, and who had little real sympathy with the pacifist position.'

When Dartmoor finally got organised as a Work Centre, it was found that other former penal tasks were being introduced again, and in conditions of increasing severity. It was soon obvious that the men were being overworked and underfed. Lydia Smith, of the Women's Committee of the No Conscription Fellowship, wrote to the editorially sympathetic *Manchester Guardian*:

'There are attached to the prison some two thousand acres of land....The agricultural work is penal in character, and it is organised on exactly the same lines as for the convicts....The crushing of oats is performed with antiquated machinery of the treadmill type, except that the hands are used instead of the feet. Sixteen men are required to work this machine, and the output is six bags per day....One of the men on this machine has been a research worker at the Royal College of Science....I saw a gang of eight men harnessed to a hand-roller engaged in rolling a field....The barrows and spades are prodigiously heavy, with a view to tiring the users, and all the appliances and methods are of the most antiquated nature. The coke for the gasworks is transported by teams of ten men harnessed to a cart....The food is poor, and the hours of labour (ten per day, with half an hour for food) are longer than those imposed on convicts.'

The Work Centres were a godsend to the sensation-seeking press. Newsmen were sent to find or invent outrageous stories about the repulsive creatures. Clever headlines appeared, probably written by the young men who were saved from the Army by the Press Lords, who needed them to write lies to order. Increased circulation was their aim: alliteration the extent of their wit. 'Princetown's Pampered Pets': 'Coddled Conscience Men': 'The C.O.s Cosy Club'. From platform and pulpit this outrage was denounced with fiery fervour.

There were attacks on the men by gangs of youths and women, and the treatment at Dartmoor, 'in response to public demand', became increasingly vicious. This was expressed in work conditions and discipline, and in medical attention — the lack of it, that is. The attitude 'You'd be worse off in the trenches', was more common than exceptional among the doctors, and was responsible for many of the sixty-nine who died.

One of those victims was Henry W. Firth of Norwich, who died at Dartmoor on February 6th 1918. He was diabetic. The doctor must have known it, but he let him suffer all the symptoms, and die. The men were so furious that they called a one-day strike in protest. As a result, C.H. Norman, whom the authorities decided was the leader, was taken under escort back to prison.

That could have been no great hardship for him. Some of the men were demanding to be sent back to prison, and some were absconding. Willie MacDougall got on his bike — or rather, the Centre's bike — and cycled back to Glasgow from whence he had come. There was no ambiguity about his position. He had been preaching anti-parliamentary communism and anti-militarism when he was arrested.

He simply went back and continued the good work — for the next sixty-six years, when he died, still in harness.

9: BRIXTON REVISITED

The hopes of the Allies had been raised by the Russian Revolution of March 1917. New men were in power in that vast country, capable men of the new generation: Western men. The outmoded princely caste had gone, and taken their Eighteenth Century obsessions with them. Now the war would be prosecuted with business-like efficiency, as befitted a business-like take-over from feudal romanticism. An organised and determined effort would be made to drive the Hun back to the centre of Europe where he would be crushed by the advancing West. It did not happen. Kerensky lasted one brief summer: with autumn came a new force —the Bolsheviks. They spoke of peace, and so did the soldiers, and they spoke with marching feet, homeward bound.

Panic swept over the Allies. The Germans moved battalions from the East and attacked the West with a fury that took them to within 45 miles of Paris and regained the Somme salient, so dearly won by the British. Something had to be done, whether or not it had any sense or relevance. A new Military Service Bill was introduced. This raised the conscription age to 51, and abolished occupational exemptions, except, of course, for politicians, policemen, priests and the Press. All exemptions on conscientious grounds for the new intake were also abolished, and the physical standard lowered. Belts had to be tightened, even in prison, where empty stomachs were already rubbing against weary spines. Bread rations were cut from 16 oz. per day to 11oz., and the porridge ration halved. The recent concession of an eight o'clock mug of cocoa and thick slice of bread was also removed from the menu, leaving the men with nothing to eat from 4.30 till the next morning.

These impositions, surely not essential to the object of defeating the Hun, were resented by the men: they added to the sense of injustice suffered by those who were undergoing the continuous sentences. Organised resistance took shape. A hunger strike was initiated in the prison at Newcastle on February 8th 1918, ostensibly against the inhumanity of the prison doctor, although that was but a peg on which to hang the general discontent. The constantly changing prison population was one reason why there was not more organised resistance. Fenner Brockway (later Lord Brockway, and a revered Elder Statesman) writing in *The New Leader* for September 18th, 1936, explained:

> 'During my three years I was in seven prisons (if one includes the Tower of London and Chester Castle). Until I got to Liverpool I was never in a place long enough to learn the ropes sufficiently to organise a revolt. There, a Prisoners' Committee practically ran the prison hall for ten days, though the revolt collapsed when the ringleaders were deported and segregated in isolation in other prisons.

> 'At Wandsworth the revolt led, I believe, by Guy Aldred, lasted longer. But under normal conditions such common action could be well-nigh impossible in local prisons with their changing and unrelated populations. We were organised political prisoners and most of us were doing sentences of two years.'

In Wandsworth, where the most serious disturbances took place, the men had been in a rebellious mood for some time before February 1918, when they refused to wash military uniforms. They would not wear them: was it considered they would wash them? The Governor conceded the point. A work and discipline strike was planned, but it was betrayed beforehand by one of the conchies who did not believe in making a disturbance.

The nine ringleaders of the alleged plot were brought before the Visiting Magistrates and sentenced to forty-two days No. 1 punishment. That meant seven weeks in solitary confinement with three days on and three days off bread and water, in unheated basement cells with no furniture, except bedboard, stool and sanitary bucket. Among the nine were Guy Aldred, Frederick Sellers, Ralph Morris and R.M. Fox.

When the nine had been on bread and water for three days, the Governor sent for them and told them he was transferring them to Brixton. This was good news, because punishments were not carried over to new prisons. It may have been the harshness of the sentences that moved him, but it is more likely that he resented the brisk, overbearing nature of the Visiting Body.

Guy had been in Brixton before, first in 1909 as a first offender in the Second Division. Brixton held convicts, remand prisoners, and detainees. Among the latter were I.R.A. men who, being there in restrictive rather than punitive role, were not locked in cells, nor were they subject to the silence rule or the cell task. They were, it is generally agreed, a lively and good-humoured crowd, who greatly relieved the prison gloom.

A special detainee was the Russian Tchitcherin, soon to be appointed Russian Representative in England while still in prison. It was he who explained to the socialist conchies that the Revolution was not, as they thought, an anarchist-communist uprising, but the work of an organisation called 'Bolsheviks' with a leader named Lenin.

The nine from Wandsworth made it clear to the Governor of Brixton that they did not intend to do any punitive work. They agreed to work in the kitchen, with minimal supervision and no silence rule. The Chief Warder asked if he could have the required number of mailbags put into their cells each morning and removed in the evening. Aldred, speaking for them all, said that the Chief Warder could do what he liked with his mailbags as long as he did not expect the men to sew them. So that was arranged.

The matter concerning visits entailed more insistence on the part of the C.O.s. One half-hour visit was allowed once a month. This took place under awkward and humiliating conditions. A two-foot passage separated two high partitions of wire mesh. The visitor stood behind one partition and the prisoner behind the other. Conversation was shouted across the passage from the row of prisoners to the row of visitors, in lighting so poor that they could not see each other properly. In those conditions, Rose Witcop was able to visit Guy after a month in Brixton. In *The Spur* she complained of the conditions, and of the unfeeling attitude of the warder who cut them short in the middle of a sentence.

The C.O.s also complained to the Governor, who said that shortage of staff prevented him from making any improvement. He suggested a compromise — two tables separated by a board with a hole in it. This would not do. The nine slowly removed their kitchen aprons. The Governor, rapidly thinking it over, thought he might be able to set a room apart for visits, without partitions.

The recalcitrant nine made full use of their relaxed silence rule. R.M. Fox describes the kitchen scene with Aldred standing behind a table holding forth in his great loud voice on some point of political philosophy, prodding the air with a bread knife. Off duty they held clandestine sessions for reading aloud, for studying and holding discussions on current affairs.

Guy Aldred found opportunity to write, and he made the most of it, supplying *The Spur* with essays, some as long as a sixteen-page pamphlet, smuggled out by sympathetic warders who read *The*

Spur. When the Governor questioned Guy about these articles, he said that they had been written between trials and sent to *The Spur* in anticipation of further imprisonment. The Governor said he had been instructed to explain the matter of these prolific appearances to the Home Office, and that the explanation offered was 'as good as any'.

On 20th August 1917, the current sentences being served by Aldred, Sellar and Morris ended. According to a Government ruling, the men should have been returned to their respective Army units for the formality of dismissal from the Forces. There does not seem to have been any occasion when this directive was observed.

The three men were conveyed to Blackdown Barracks, Farnborough, and given an order, knowing that they would not obey it, as a preliminary to further courts martial — in Aldred's case, for the fourth time. Guy spoke before the court for all three of them, making an unemotional legal defence, putting the point stated above, as well as several other points of legal relevance. He quoted the Army Act:

> 'An offender under this Act shall not be subject to imprisonment or detention for more than two consecutive years, whether by one or more sentences.'

He further pointed out that there must, by the Act, be a fortnight of freedom between sentences, when a series of sentences amounted to more than two years. In the past fifteeen months he had been awarded several sentences without that statutory break, therefore the command which he allegedly disobeyed was itself illegal. A further point was that imprisonment is regarded as a more rigorous and a more ignominious sentence than detention, and it is illegal to sentence a person to one form of punishment and impose another of greater severity or more socially damaging effect. Finally, he said that a person could not, in accordance with King's Regulations, be returned from prison 'to the Colours.'

The members of the court martial may as well have been asleep during Aldred's defence of himself and his three comrades. The procedure was a matter of course. A few days later they were sentenced to a further two years Hard Labour. In an article '*All for the Cause*' published in *The Spur* for September 1918, Aldred wrote:

> 'There is no need for elequence or passion. Facts speak louder than rhetoric. I must expect a sentence of two years....If released I shall refuse to follow any profession other than that of a revolutionary journalist....If convicted I shall refuse to work any further in prison....From now on I claim to be treated as a political prisoner. I claim the right to edit and write from

prison....I refuse tamely to acquiese in imposed silence....'

In the next issue of *The Spur*, the leading article was by Guy (written on the back of an envelope which our comrade handed over after his release from Brixton, explained Rose Witcop, in an editorial introduction). The essay, three columns long, is entitled: '*Shall we Deny?*':

'....Life is to me a serious and holy problem. I want to solve it sincerely, bravely, justly and honourably. I wish to do no harm either through being too respectable or for audacious unconventionalism....An indignation concerned with my present circumstances oppresses me; and I have lost my role of philosopher only to become that sorrowful creature, a man with a grievance....But, if you could, spare me the insult of your pity, flee from me as from a plague. For a man with a grievance is a plague, a veritable abomination unto himself, and all his kind......'

Guy Aldred was twenty-nine years of age when he was first arrested for opposing the war. He was kept in custody for three years — years of vigorous manhood, aggravated by the fact that he loved to be in the midst of things. He had a puritanical attitude to sex, although he believed in free love, but he was not indifferent to female presence, nor slow to give women normal attention. For those three years he was starved of this vital element in a young man's life. He had no female company, no touch of a hand, nor sound of a voice that would have meant so much to him. He saw Rose once a month only, at the most, and then for perhaps fifteen minutes behind a partition. It was the same, of course, for all the C.O.s in like confinement, and most of them must have suffered as reasonably good young men, constrained by religious conviction or political idealism. Frustrations and yearning sometimes expose themselves at this time in his prison writings.

In the same issue of *The Spur* as the article '*Shall I deny?*' there was another article by Guy, written in military detention, awaiting his fourth court martial. It is entitled '*Militarism and Woodland*'. A few excerpts will show its general drift:

'Since my release from prison I have been mentally and morally barren. The emptiness of life has weighed heavily upon me in this Deepcut Detention Barracks, and if I can succeed only in conveying to my readers some understanding of the soul-crushing monotony which now oppresses me, I shall be rendering a service, not only to my fellow C.O.s, but also to the soldiers, who, in one way or another and only to a little extent, travail through the slough of despond.

'I have normally small taste for the countryside. Yet I know somewhat of the joy of roaming through the woodlands. From the detention room window I can vision the despoliation which has been made to the countryside by militarism....Where birds should sing, only guns boom. Where men should love, males only lust. Where the mystery of sex should be wonderfully understood, only its sensualism is apprehended. Men understand the fact of sex only in a brutal, animal way. But the delicacy of sex, all the subtle tenderness which belongs to it, its tender charm and all the growing innocence which comes with deeper knowledge; all the wondrous realm of real comradeship is beyond the ken of those who dwell in a desert, which was once a happy woodland.

'From this window I watch the soldiers and girls go by. Sex attraction parades its vitality with impudence rather than with dignity. In some cases there may be tender feeling, but in many a conscious vulgarity obtrudes. Militarism destroys the woodland and degrades the mystery of life. It prostitutes all it touches.'

The November Revolution in Russia had set the socialist groups in a state of dissarray and ferment. This was aggravated by the imminent end of the war. There was a general feeling that they should sink their differences and unite in a single organisation, which would be a Section of the Third International. Much thought went into the structure and principles of that movement. *Unity* was the essential conception, but there was disagreement in defining it. Guy Aldred and those of like mind thought of unity as a working arrangement between federated Groups, while others saw unity in a mass organisation controlled from a 'democratic' centre. Those conflicting attitudes found their way through prison walls, and in February 1918 Guy Aldred wrote a long article 'under difficulties', and had it smuggled out.

The article was entitled '*Socialism, Unity, and Reality*'. It was read before the I.L.P. Brixton Branch on February 14th. It is a long essay, and we can quote only a short extract, in which Aldred defines what he means by 'Unity'.

'To define "unity" is a very simple achievement. The word means no more than "one-ness" or "at-one-ment". It implies identity of aim, or method, or both. To apply the definition is a different matter. Thus from time to time the apostles of every propaganda split into warring camps. Each calls the other "apostate", sometimes with justice. Suddenly a new movement arises. It is considered necessary by one, or by all, of the warring champions to end factional strife. "Unity" now becomes the watchword. Conferences are arranged. Sectarian speakers orate from the same platform. Acrimony gives way to mild platitude. "Unity" has been achieved!

'Unfortunately this is not true. Heresy is not exorcised so easily. Cleavages of ideas are *not* abolished by such mechanical window-dressing. All that has been secured is a temporary hush in the rivalry of bitter expressions. Sincerity has been given a State Funeral and the event is celebrated by a hypocritical parade of unity by those who still cherish secret antagonisms....'

Aldred then describes and analyses the six groups he thinks must come together as a federation, in the light of *reality*. But what is meant by *reality*? He touches on the metaphysical sense, the capitalists' sense, the reforming socialists' sense, campaigning for better conditions.

'But the absolute reasoner insists on the real principles in the background, the reality that negates transient fact, and holds that socialism alone is the immediate goal. It is between these two viewpoints that the struggle is waged. Until, therefore, a clear understanding of the reality that counts immediately to the wage-slave is recognised, socialism must remain an outcast theory of social organisation, and unity continue to be a dream.'

10: REVOLT

Every prison holding C.O.s was in a state of unrest immediately before and after the Armistice.   We must confine our account to Wandsworth, because that is where Guy Aldred was confined at the time.   It happened to be the scene of the most violent and sustained upheaval.

Wandsworth prison, in a borough of London, was built in 1851. During the war, it had been divided into two institutions, one a civil prison housing conscientious objectors, and the other a military wing for the detention of army defaulters from the Canadian, Australian and New Zealand armies.   Each of those prisons had its own Governor and administration.   In theory, they were quite separate, but in fact the military section overflowed into a part of the civil prison.   Sometimes the two factions of alleged delinquents came into contact.   This was stopped when the conchies, appalled at the brutal treatment meted out to the soldiers, made protest demonstrations. This reached a climax when R.M. Fox and others raised a vigorous protest when a youth was chased naked along a corridor by prison guards armed with sticks with which they proceeded to beat the young soldier.   But the windows of the civil cells overlooked the military parade ground and from there much abuse was hurled at the guards, and much incitement to revolt aimed at the soldiers.

The stirring of unrest among the C.O.s in Wandsworth began in the early months of 1918.   By June, the noise created in that establishment of deathly silence was such that it upset the subservient faction of the inmates, and harassed the warders.   In June, as we have already noted, a plot to launch an all-out work and discipline strike was uncovered, and the conspirators transferred to Brixton.

The first to return from Brixton, on September 4th, was Guy Aldred, with another two years added to his term.   He had openly stated at his court martial and in the columns of *The Spur* that he would neither work nor take orders while subjected to this illegal imprisonment.   He later maintained, not in self-defence, but as a matter of fact, that he was not the leader, but there is no doubt that his attitude would stir up the latent unrest, which had not been entirely inactive while he was away.

As the trouble got worse, sometime in October the Governor gathered the twenty most obstreperous men into his office and offered a truce. All punishments wiped out, several concessions granted, if the men would co-operate in running the prison properly. Aldred was among the twenty. It is not recorded who was their spokesman, but the reaction was unanimous. Their liberty was not up for bargaining. They were not objecting to the conditions of imprisonment but to the fact of imprisonment. So the peace bid failed.

The Governor retaliated by confining the worst offenders, including Aldred, to their cells, cancelling all visits, all letters and library books. Cell 'furniture' (bedboard and stool) were removed during the day.

By this time the men were on strike. The demands were for the release of the locked-up men, the resumption of letters, visitors and books (all of which had been cancelled), and one hour (increased to two hours, on second thoughts) of free talking every day. These demands seem to have been met, with the exception of the release of the locked-up men. They, it was said, would stay permanently under lock and key.

R.M. Fox (Dick, to his friends) returned to Brixton at that time. He had been kept in Brixton till the expiry of his two years' sentence, then on November 10th., the eve of the Armistice, he was released and taken back to the headquarters of his Army unit — which he was deemed to have joined — stationed at Mill Hill Military Barracks, not to be dismissed from the Army, as prescribed in the Regulations, but to face his fourth court martial.

The guard room at Mill Hill Barracks was packed with very drunk soldiers. They had been celebrating victory over the Germans by smashing up the West End. Now they were confined to barracks, and they were still celebrating. They sang the old war-time songs beloved of all soldiers: 'Take me back to dear old Blighty', 'If the sergeant drinks your rum, never mind!', and the parody on a hymn, 'Wash me in the water that you washed your dirty daughter, and I shall be whiter than the whitewash on the wall.'

A few days later Fox faced his fourth court martial. Fox was an engineer by trade, an author by preference, and a socialist by conviction. He had delivered many an anti-war speech at open-air meetings before hostile audiences. He took this opportunity to harangue the officers of the court, since they had probably never listened to an open-air meeting:

'Gentlemen, you think you are trying me. You are in error. It is you who are on trial. The havoc you have wrought in the past years is there to condemn you. It is not German militarism, nor English militarism, which is responsible for this. It is Militarism, without qualification, and the militarists are only the agents for the capitalists who coin money out of blood. I stand as spokesmen for that rising body of men and women who are about to condemn *you*. The war was a war of greed and plunder. Profiteers have plundered the people unmercifully since the war began....Thousands of honest poor people have been murdered and maimed to swell the money-bags of the vultures who made the war....Thousands of working men, sick to death of the horror, greed and hypocrisy of their present rulers are taking control of the world into their own hands....'

He could have saved his breath. The sentence of the court was automatic, as the members of the court were automatons, programmed to a War Office response. Two years' Hard Labour. A few days later Fox and five others were taken by an escort of ten soldiers to Wandsworth Prison.

The sergeant in charge halted his men outside a West End tearoom and proposed that they all meet again there in two hours' time. Fox looked up some friends and had tea and a chat. At the end of two hours, more or less, the prisoners had all assembled. Presently the sergeant arrived, but no escort. In some alarm the sergeant asked the prisoners to help find them. So, after an organised search of nearby pubs they were all together, the escort very merry, and some very unsteady. When they arrived at the gates of Wandsworth they were really being escorted by the prisoners.

Wandsworth, according to Fox, was like a cold damp scullery. 'My heart sank when I saw the grim entrance to Wandsworth again, and heard the key grate once more in the lock. A little band of pacifist women, led by Clara Cole, greeted us at the prison gate, where they were tireless in their demonstrations.'

Another of those women was Lady Clare Anneseley. Both were active in keeping a constant vigil outside Wandsworth, carrying placards in support of the C.O.s inside, and laying themselves open to much public abuse. Both Clara Cole and Lady Clare Annesley were associated with Guy Aldred in his opposition to the Second War, though in a quieter role. During the First War they also organised concerts of popular songs and music outside the walls of Wandsworth. Inmates were forbidden to listen. Seven men who gathered under a landing window to listen to one such Christmas Eve concert were seen, and promptly sentenced to one day on bread and water to see them over the Christmas celebrations.

Fox found that the prison was completely out of hand. Now that the Armistice was signed, long pent-up feelings demanded an outlet. One body of prisoners, who were known as the 'All-Out Strikers', had declared that they intended to disregard all prison rules. Those men were in permanent lock-up. They kept up a constant din all day, rattling their mugs along the doors of their cells and shouting abuse at the warders. Guy Aldred probably took part in this uproar,though it was quite out of character. He would rather have been reading or writing, or speaking. The din told on his nerves, and he was not the only sufferer. Only about a third of the C.O.s were in revolt. The others just wanted to finish their time and get out. They complained to the Governor that they could not read the extra book the concession had granted them, because of the din. The old lags — according to Fox there were still some in the prison — did not know what to make of it all. Jail had never been like this.

In the evenings the locked-up men held concerts, with songs and recitations echoing through the spy-holes, and Guy Aldred had his chance: he lectured. On at least one occasion the warders tried to drown his words by rattling on trays. On December 4th the Governor ordered the 'All-Out Strikers' to be taken down to the basement cells. R.M. Fox was not among them at that time: he was with them a few weeks later, so we can use his description:

'Those basement cells were appalling. They were half-underground dungeons. Not only were they gloomy, but everything in them was coated with an unbelieveable filth. Grimy cobwebs hung in the corners, the dirt of years was plastered on the small barred window through which I could just see the feet of men on exercise at ground level. Even the can of drinking water was festooned with dirt and grime. It was as if I had been thrust in among old forgotten lumber to die....

'The "All-Out Strikers" occupied similar basement cells. Nearly opposite my cell was a Scottish lad, Jack Hodgson, who had been down in this horible dungeon for months. He was not allowed out for exercise for he refused to obey the prison rules. He was nothing but a bag of bones, with a pale, hollow-cheeked face, and an indomitable spirit. I heard his thin treble voice singing revolutionary songs far into the night. His voice cut across the brooding silence of that terrible time.'

The furniture consisted of a bed-board, three blankets, a backless stool, a fixed table-bench, and a sanitary bucket, sometimes left for two days unemptied. Twice a week a convict barber came around and as each man in turn sat on his stool drew a torturously blunt old 'cut-throat' razor over his face.   There were no washing facilities and no exercise.   There was no heating — and this was mid-winter.   The light should have been supplied from the gas jet which shone through a frosted glass panel from the corridor.   This was not lit on the first night, and as a protest the men smashed the glass panels, an action for which they were awarded one day on bread and water.   The broken panels made a good opening for speaking to each other, and by that means the prisoners agreed to reject the punishment by throwing the bread back into the corridor.   The light was then restored, but withdrawn again when the unwisdom of giving desperate men access to a gas light was realised.   Therafter the 'Basement Men' spent their days in gloom and their nights in darkness for many weeks.

As a protest against the treatment of the Basement Men, the other conchies on strike decided to hold a meeting in the exercise yard on a Sunday, when most of the warders were off duty.   It was arranged that four men, Beacham, Knight, Spiller and Fox would speak in turn from a parapet: others would follow as each was dragged off.   So, instead of marching round in the prescribed manner, they gathered in a group round the speakers.   There was no interference, and the meeting proceeded.   There were only two warders on yard duty, and they probably felt the situation was beyond them, especially as these were not ordinary convicts, and the warders themselves were not quite immune from the radical tendencies that were gathering strength outside.   From that meeting a Prisoners' Committee of five members was elected.   This reported to the prisoners in the exercise yard.   A proposal of cell-furniture smashing was rejected, and a policy of 'massive deputation' was adopted.   If a grievance was not dealt with to their satisfaction, they would march to the centre of the prison and squat there till agreement was reached between them and the Governor.

Next morning fifty men made application to see the Governor.   He accepted only five.   The Chairman of the Visiting Magistrates was present.   The magistrates had arrived to hear charges against the basement strikers.   Fox read out a resolution passed at the meeting condemning the incarceration of the Basement Men, and demanding their release.   The Governor said those complaints had no personal bearing on the men making the complaints, and were therefore invalid.   He would run the prison as he thought fit.   Fox was permitted to speak to the magistrates, and did so with the satisfactory result that they took no action on the charges made, and so no further punishments were handed out.

Concerts were held in the evenings, both above ground and at basement level. The men above recited or sang from their windows, standing on their stools. Fox describes one such entertainment in which there were twenty items of song and recitation, ending with the 'Red Flag'. Prisoners from an opposite wing climbed on their stools to listen and applaud. So did the soldiers, some of whom joined in the singing of rebel songs. And so did the inhabitants of the nearby houses. They did not applaud or join in, but they listened, leaning on their elbows on the window sills.

The basement men held lectures. The most popular were delivered by Guy Aldred. Speaking through the still unrepaired corridor window, with his bed-board to act as sounding-board, he delivered on different occasions lectures on Karl Marx, Michael Bakunin, Jesus, Womens' Freedom, the Revolutionary Tradition in English Literature and Richard Carlile. On several occasions off-duty warders gathered at the foot of the stairs to listen.

News seeped into Wandsworth that a 'Hunger-strike policy' was being advocated in several other prisons. It was proposed that this should start with a wholesale refusal of work or eating on New Years Day. R.M. Fox was one of those who disagreed with the hunger-strike policy. There were those who were opposed to the whole campaign of objection. One such, named Leonard J. Simms, aquiring a plentiful supply of coarse brown toilet paper, wrote and circulated an attack on the 'Basement Oligarchy', whose infuence and noise kept the prison in a state of uproar. The Chief Warder did not help in the direction of calm and order when he jeered at several of the acquiescent men, calling them cowards who were prepared to accept all the concessions gained by the strikers, but were not prepared to participate in their protests. This led to a spate of cell smashing. One person, being particularly incensed at this accusation, reacted so violently that he was put into a strait jacket.

There had been hunger strikes for varying periods from the beginning of December. There is no way of knowing how many fell in with the Prisoners' Committee resolution to fast on New Years Day, but fourteen of those who did continued the strike, declaring that it would be maintained till they were released, which they were, on January 7th. Amongst them were Aldred and Ellison. Five who resumed the hunger strike after a break were not included in the release, nor were the non-strikers, that is, those who were non-participants in the All-Out Strike Campaign. These were men incensed at the jeers of the Chief Warder. Some of them were forcibly fed.

The release was not final. It was in terms of the Cat and Mouse

Act. They were out on licence for twenty-eight days, due to report back on the 6th of February.

11: THE CAT AND THE MOUSE

Guy had not seen Rose for four months.   He had not seen his nine-year-old son Annesley for over two and and half years.   He had not had a bath for three months, nor a decent meal for thirty-two months, nor anything to eat for seven days.   Coming home must have been a most traumatic experience.   A meal, a bath, a soft bed with a pillow.   And his family.   And his work.

His physical condition was poor, as must have been expected. Several newspapers commented on this when reporting his release. The London *Star* giving a description of the upheaval in Wandsworth, made it a matter for fun and ridicule at the expense of the C.O.s, implying that they were having a great time at the expense of the taxpayer — having a very happy time altogether.

Thomas Henry Ellison replied to that inaccurate and insulting screed in the columns of *The Spur* for February 1919.   Here is part of what he wrote:

'....The article gave no indication of the stern aspect of prison life as known to those who have served from two to three years imprisonment with hard labour — the most rigorous punishment known to English law.   It is true that there is a humorous side to prison life.   If there were not, most of us would have been transferred to an asylum long before now.   Nevertheless there is also a tragic side, which the *Star* did not touch upon.   It did not give the number of C.O.s who have been driven insane.   It did not tell of the hours of agony passed by those so-called cowards, during the years of silent torture in which they braved the world, braved it unfalteringly, with soul undaunted by the invective of the Prussianised press, and its lovely bride and supporter, the misled mob.'

171

The *Herald* had expressed concern over Aldred's health the previous August when he had faced his fourth court martial: 'We are informed that Aldred's state of health is such that another term of imprisonment would be highly dangerous; but, indeed, this endless torture would break the health of the strongest man. We call upon the Labour Movement to do something about these outrages.' Now the paper returned to the subject, and the *Daily News*, *West London Observer*, and *Forward* also mentioned Guy Aldred's temporary release, and the effect the long dungeon confinement had had. The editor of the Merthyr *Pioneer* declared that the sufferings imposed on Aldred and his fellows were not mob violence, but legal crimes. The Glasgow Anarchists in a manifesto demanding the release of all C.O.s, concluded: 'The condition of Guy Aldred is one of mental relapse. An active mental worker, a journalist by profession, the bare prison wall with its blank suggestion is fast bringing about in him a serious condition of mind.'

Aldred wrote to the *Manchester Guardian*:

'Sir, I am one of the many who have endured some two years and eight months persecution. I have suffered two-and-a-half years with hard labour; have received four sentences by court martial, and have one year and eight months still to serve. Beginning with my fourth court martial I went on a work and discipline strike as a protest against industrial conscription, and in order to emphasise the fact that I was a political prisoner. With several other comrades I have been denied for four months letters, visits and books. I have had only 24 hours open air exercise during that time. The last two months I spent in a cold basement, under disgusting conditions of filth. In January, after a six-day hunger strike, I and thirteen other comrades who had also been on work, discipline and hunger strike, were released under the Cat and Mouse Act till February 4th to recover our health. The conditions (which I and my comrades declined to accept) reduce us to the the position of constantly-supervised 'ticket-of-leave ' men.

'We are merely "enjoying" a temporary respite in the certain knowledge that a return to prison could mean our deaths. Every one of the released men thus menaced has been deemed a genuine conscientious objector by the Central Tribunal. I ask that this matter be taken up, and that the Government be called upon to put a stop to our persecution, and that of all other C.O.s. Let me add that I am dictating this letter with great effort from a sick bed — not so much on my own behalf as on behalf of the men whose constitution is being destroyed in prison, and who are already mental and physical wrecks.'

The *Manchester Guardian* commented on this letter in an editorial headed 'Principle or Crime?' The leader writer described treatment of the genuine conscientious objector as the most discreditable thing connected with the history of the war. He pointed out that several had died in prison from the prostration which made them ready victims to any infection. The writer added that the most elementary sense of equity, to say nothing of mercy, would appear to dictate that the limit placed by law on sentences of Hard Labour for single offences, should also apply to sentences for repeated offences when these are virtually the same offence, and a man is re-arrested as soon as he is released. Yet repeated sentences are imposed in defiance, or in sheer evasion, of the law. The article continued:

'We publish today a letter from the editor of *The Spur* who has been four times sentenced for the same offence and has already suffered two-and-and-half years hard labour, aggravated by extreme special punishment for what is regarded as contumacy.....And this is the way we give thanks for victory and approaching peace, and of encouraging men, who, however mistaken, prefer principle to life....'

Despite his poor state of health, Aldred used his weeks of recuperation in writing and in meeting other comrades. He wrote several articles for *The Spur*, of which Rose had been appointed temporary editor when Guy was first arrested, and who had carried out that task with great skill and courage. He wrote two articles for the Scottish *Daily Record*, one on Bolshevism, and one on Free Love. The editor of the *Record* said he published them to let his readers know how odious were the ideas of the communists. Guy also re-published three of his pamphlets: *The Case for Communism: Socialism and Marriage*: and *Trade Unionism and the Class War*. *Richard Carlile* and *At Grips with War* were already in circulation.

At the beginning of February, when he was expected to knock at the gates of Wandsworth and ask to be returned to his cell, with its long-familiar bedboard and sanitary bucket, Aldred boarded a train for Glasgow. He had first visited that city in 1912 to speak in its Pavilion Theatre under the auspices of the Clarion Scouts, then a very dynamic socialist propaganda group. He was attracted to the city, finding its citizens clear-headed, with a truculent attitude to authority, a rebellious spirit, and little respect for leaders.

In the March issue of *The Spur* he had an article headed *The Strike Issue*. In this he commented on various matters relating to his return

173

visit to Glasgow. He had not, of course, been a participant in the activities of the Clyde Workers Committee which had been working with great vigour and causing much ferment in the city on matters relating to working conditions in the munition factories and shipyards. It was not a line of action which drew much sympathy from Aldred. He would rather have seen this energy and endeavour exercised in a campaign to stop making the implements of destruction. He commented in his article that:

> 'A healthy sign in connection with the Glasgow strike is the rank and file contempt for orthodox leaders and the growing realisation of the fact that the economic interests of the bigger Union executives reconciles officials to the aims of the capitalist class, and oppose them to the strike....I am not much moved by the forty-hour-a-week cry, but I am concerned with the working class struggle and the revolutionary understanding that may emerge from the conflict.....
>
> 'An interesting feature of my visit to Glasgow has been a chat with William Duff. Comrades will remember that his companion was the friend of Voltartine de Claire and Emma Goldman at the time they visited this city 'way back in the nineties of the last century. It was a pleasure to run through our comrade's scrap book and note some of his news cuttings recording the development of anarchist propaganda in the city, since its first Anarchist Group was formed in 1903. This Group commanded a membership of 50, and was a product of the old Socialist League, whose inspiration and leader was William Morris.'

Aldred then comments that what struck him in looking over that history is the way the general is reflected in the particular. 'We are considering Marxism and Bakunin, then we leap to some old mining comrade who loves Bakunin fervently, and pledges his faith to anarchism, and dreams of its dawn, way down Burntisland way. Then we plunge back to Glasgow and the question of general principles.'

The last paragraph of the article is of particular interest, as it reveals the mood and aspirations of Guy Aldred, a revolutionary idealist, aged thirty-two, after suffering nearly three years of rigorous imprisonment, in the war-torn Britain of 1919:

> 'As I walk across the Glasgow streets again and reflect on the many hours I have spent in jail, I plan my revenge — a brave, bold, enlightening anarchist press. I plan the creation of a Pantheon of just appreciation in which Jesus, Marx, Bakunin

and Tolstoy shall all have their place, together with Socrates, Plato, Wilde, and Ibsen. I plan the papers which shall carry the stories of the men and their messages, and hope quickens my step and gives joyous spring to the rhythm of my body. I forget the Cat and Mouse. I forget my debts. I see the coming press achievements and immediately the world created anew there-bye. And I know that despite all failures the vision shall materialise.'

The Glasgow comrades were not lacking in their welcome of Guy Aldred. In 1912 he had formed a Communist Propaganda Group there. That was nine years before the formation of the Communist Party, and ideas of principle and organisation were different from what later became accepted and orthodox. During Guy's years in jail the members of his Group merged informally with anarchists. It was under the auspices of the Glasgow anarchists that Aldred's 'GREAT WELCOME MEETING' was held in St. Mungo's Hall in York Street on February 3rd, 1919. His subject was 'The Present Struggle for Liberty'.

The next Sunday he spoke in the Watson Street Hall, and left immediately after the meeting for Wales, where he spoke the next evening to a Welsh Welcome in the Tillery Institute. Then back to London to speak for the Clapham Labour Party (the Labour locals could be radical in those days before the inducements of governmental office weighed upon them). Aldred also spoke for the Walthamstow British Socialist party. Then up north again for a North of England and Scottish Tour. Sara accompanied him, having been released from Winchester Prison on February 27th. They visited Glasgow, of course, and from there carried their propaganda to Kirkcaldy, Lochgelly, Cowdenbeath and Aberdeen. The theme of their message was that the Groups, non-Parliamentary and left of the I.L.P., must unite to form a federated organisation which would be the British Communist Party, affiliated to The Third International. The tour worked its way back to London, and there Guy, speaking on Clapham Common, was arrested and returned to Wandsworth Prison on March 10th. He had enjoyed one month of glorious freedom, his heart pulsating with inspiration, his great voice pouring forth words of hope — encouragement to the disillusioned, and challenge to the State.

He let it be known that he would touch no food till he was released from this illegal and vindictive imprisonment.

12: THE FIERY MAJOR

The ferment had not abated in Wandsworth during Aldred's absence. It had perhaps even got worse. The non-strikers had taken to disobedience. They laughed and talked in the mornings as they were marched to the work-shed, and they sang on the way back at 4 p.m. If any one of them was reprimanded for talking at work they all burst into song. It was not just defiance and protest. Those men were being subjected without a break to a double term of what was considered the harshest sentence allowed by British law. Some of the laughter, coming from half-empty stomachs and torn nerves, was the release of hysteria.

On February 17th, 1919, some of the military prisoners confined on the civil side of the prison attacked their warders. The Prison Report issued later stated: 'There can be no doubt that the conduct of the disorderly section of the Conscientious Objectors and their direct incitements to their fellow-prisoners to set the prison authorities at defiance, was one of the main causes of this outbreak.'

Now it was the warders' turn to hold a meeting. They reached the conclusion that their lives were in danger, and petitioned the Home Office for support and protection. The result was that the Governor and the Chief Warder (the one who loved to provoke inoffensive prisoners) were each given a month's leave of absence. The Governor's place was taken by a Major Blake, who was a noted disciplinarian. He had served in several penal institutions, including Borstal, at a time when the rod was used more frequently than the pyschiatrist. The cowardly conchies gave him a rough ride, and a month later an enquiry was held into *his* conduct. He had overlooked the fact that conchies were more articulate, less overawed by authority, skilled in exposures, and righteously indignant. The common criminal or Borstal boy was beaten before he started, by his self-estimation of subservience and fear.

The enquiry into the Major's misconduct was held in Wandsworth Prison on 15th, 19th and 22nd March, 1919. The Report was issued as a White Paper on May 7th, and was available to the public at twopence a copy. Amongst other interesting observations, it said:

'By this time (the arrival of the major) all attempts to enforce discipline in the prison among the disorderly section of the Conscientious Objectors had been abandoned.

'While the promoters of the disorder in the prison belonged exclusively to the prisoners classed as conscientious objectors, it is right to point out that there is a considerable number of conscientious objectors who have from the first refused to take part in the disturbance, and have used their utmost effort to prevent it.

'The truth is that the prisoners in Wandsworth Prison classed as conscientious objectors belong to schools of thought which are widely separated. They may be divided into three classes: the first consisting of those who have a sincere objection to any form of military service, the second those who falsely pretend to hold religious views in order to escape from its perils, and the third composed of men who profess anarchical doctrines, who deny the validity of the law and right of the State to trench upon individual freedom. It was to the last class that the disorder in prison was mainly due.'

When he first arrived at the prison entrance, the Major was led by the new Chief Warder into the main hall. There they encountered a 'gang of men' drawn up and singing and making an awful noise such as the Major had never heard in any prison of his experience. The Major called out 'Silence!'. Somebody shouted out 'Get your hair cut!' (a popular catch-phrase at the time). Somebody else made an offensive and disgusting noise with his mouth and voices from the back called: 'Who is this bloody swine?' and 'Listen to the bloody swine!'

The Major said at the Inquiry that the most impertinent person in the crowd of unruly prisoners was a man who said nothing, but kept up an aggravating grinning and giggling. This was blatant dumb insolence. He ordered the warders to take that man to the basement and 'Iron him if necessary.' So the poor fellow was dragged to the basement and fastened into the cruel figure-of-eight irons, which were not normally in use in those enlightened times.

This was the first man to be punished by the Major, and the sad thing is that he was Ralph Frederick Harris, the one who, the previous June, had humbly petitioned the Home Office to protect him from the outrageous conchies. Now his deliverer had arrived, perhaps at last in reply to his petition — and not before time, for things had worsened. Doubtless the Home Secretary had mentioned the Petition and its author. What the Major crassly mistook for grins and giggles were intended as knowing smiles of welcome. But understanding did not shine from the irate Major's face. He thought the fellow a fool.

The tour of inspection proceeded to the workshop. About 450 men were sitting quietly getting on with their work. About 100 of them were conscientious objectors. 'I was not particularly interested in the conscientious objectors,' said the Major at the Enquiry. The officer in charge had just said 'All correct, Sir', when through the opposite door burst a gang of men singing The Red Flag. The flabbergasted Major had never seen anything like it in his life. Recalcitrant old lags, yes, obstreperous Borstal boys, certainly, but never a revolutionary tableau complete with vocal chorus in his own prison. He was outraged.

He ordered the warders to drive the mutinous swine back to their cells. He thought the leader was the notorious Guy Aldred, and called him a Bolshevik, with a few adjectival garnishes. Guy was, at that time, holding meetings not so far from Wandsworth, and planning his propaganda tour of Scotland. The conchie favoured with the Major's abuse was R.M. Fox.

'It is right,' read the Inquiry Report, 'to observe in connection with the last named man (that is, Guy Aldred) that he had been previously convicted and sentenced to a term of imprisonment for seditious libel, and in connection with a paper which propagates anarchical doctrines.'

The Inquiry also considered complaints of physical ill-treatment made by the prisoners. In one case, the doctor was reported as saying to a man-handled convict that it 'served him right.' The best the report could offer in the way of whitewash was that the reason the Major had transgressed on all counts was that he had failed to exercise reasonable restraint in his judgements.

The rowdy songsters were hustled back to their cells that first day, but some must have escaped the net, for that evening the Prisoners' Committee held a meeting in a secluded corner of the prison. Victor Beacham was speaker and chairman. They considered tactics to defeat the Major. Next morning at exercise it was discovered that all those who had taken part in the secret meeting had been confined to their cells indefinitely.

Leonard S. Simons, the man who had published the toilet paper manifesto denouncing the 'Basement Oligarchy', demanded that action should be taken on behalf of the locked-in comrades. A warder of the new regime seized him and dragged him inside. Fox called for an immediate return to the cells as a protest. Two men stepped out of the silent parading circle and joined him. The rest did not hear.

Next morning the three of them were marched, one at a time, into the Governor's office. Fox was first. The Governor banged the table and roared that Fox was guilty of mutiny, and that he had a good mind to order him a flogging. But he changed the good mind to a better one and ordered two days bread and water instead. The other two were awarded the same.

Everything was taken out of Fox's cell — bedboard, blankets, stool and table — and he was left standing in an echoing emptiness. Next morning he was given a tin mug of water and a hunk of bread. He heard through the whispered information of the landing cleaner that the other two were handing back their bread, so he did likewise. He did the same the next morning, but on the third morning he fell ravenously on the prison breakfast, and was told, when he had finished, that his friends along the landing had decided to continue their fast. Fox then resumed his fast. If he had not broken it, he may have been released after three more days, under the Cat and Mouse Act, as his companions were, along with nine others who had been on a prolonged hunger strike.

The Major's response to Fox's resumption of the strike was to have him taken down to the basement, which Fox described as damp, dark, filthy, and crawling with insects. Evidently he had a mattress, for he says the insects crawled over it. After four days Fox and others on hunger strike were taken into the exercise yard, supported by warders and marched around. A few were barely able to stand, but were dragged along.

Then they were forced into what a jolly warder called a 'Feeding Queue'. He also expressed the hope that they all had their life insurances fully paid up. At the head of the queue was a barber's chair. Into this each man was placed in turn, his arms held behind him by two warders. Into his mouth a wooden gag was forced — the same gag for everybody. This gag had a hole in the middle through which was passed a tube, all the way into the stomach. Fox, in his autobiographical work *Smoky Crusade* wrote:

'I had all the sensations of suffocation. Every choking breath I took drew the rubber tube further in. I felt it right down in the pit of my stomach. A funnel, as if for oil, was put over the tube and liquid food poured in. I choked again when the tube was withdrawn, and staggered, dazed and sick, back to my cell.

'Each morning we had a roll-call of hunger-strikers from cell

179

to cell, and we heard, day by day, the voices we knew growing fainter and fainter.'

On the eleventh day it was whispered that the conduct of the new Governor was to be the subject of a Home Office Inquiry, to be held in the prison.

Colonel Wedgewood had raised the matter of the inhuman treatment of C.O.s in Wandsworth in the House of Commons. The Major had only been on a temporary assignment to Wandsworth, and probably left there after the Inquiry. He did not leave the Prison Service, though, for in 1926 he was the subject of another Inquiry. He had revealed to the Press the personal confidences of a condemned murderer.

The hunger-strikers gave up their strike after the Inquiry. Guy Aldred arrived back in Wandsworth in the middle of the proceedings. He commenced his strike, as he had said he would, and determined to continue it indefinitely. But the authorities had had enough of hunger-strikes, and of Guy Aldred. After four days they released him. Fox had to wait a few more weeks, but on April 19th he was also set free.

This time Guy's only recuperation was a hearty breakfast of ham and eggs. Then a wash, a sleep, and that same evening he was back on Clapham Common taking up where he had left off.

BOOK THREE:

THE RED EVANGEL

The peoples' flag is deepest red:
It shrouded oft our martyred dead.
And ere their limbs grew stiff and cold
Their hearts' blood dyed its every fold.

It suits today the weak and base,
Whose minds are fixed on pelf and place,
To cringe before the rich man's frown
And haul the sacred emblem down.

BOOK THREE
THE RED EVANGEL

CONTENTS

Guy Aldred in full voice.

1: PARLIAMENT OR SOVIET?

The shooting war was over. Kings and countries had vanished.
A generation of young men had died. Now the greybeards gathered
round great tables and fought wordy battles over the ruins, compound-
ing muddle out of chaos, and in their stupidity preparing obituaries for
generations to come.

Over six thousand war objectors had registered in Britain. Several
thousand had not, but had been processed just the same. Over seven
thousand courts martial had been held. Now the gloomy cells and
dungeons lay empty for a while; but the irons would not rust, nor the
straps decay. Now the recent inmates had gone back to their former
mode of life, except for the sixty-nine who had died, and the thirty-
nine who had gone — been driven — insane.

In Britain, a General Election was over-due. The hero of the
House was Lloyd George. The trouble was that he was head of the
Coalition Government, but not head of the Party which was in public
favour. That was the Tories, or Conservatives, or Unionists. Bonar Law was their Leader. He was little known. His leadership in
an election might well produce bad results, because of his personal
lack of attraction — 'charisma' as we have been taught to say. Lloyd
George's leadership of the Liberals could equally well give a poor
result, because of the party's weakness on the question of the
undoubted public demand for Germany's blood. The best arrangement would undoubtedly be another Coalition, with the hero, Lloyd
George, at its head. The Liberals were appeased by a promise that
no Tory would oppose a Liberal where the standing Liberal candidate
agreed to accept the Coalition. The Labour Party was invited to join
the Coalition. After consideration, the Executive refused. They
saw the opportunity offered in working with those Liberals who had
not joined the Coalition to become the official Opposition. Obviously this would be a step in the direction of attaining governmental
power.

To do this, the party had to make changes in its Constitution and organisation. The Party had to become an organisation of individual members, not an amalgamation of Groups, Unions and Co-operative Societies. At a Nottingham Conference on 23rd January, 1918, the Object of the Party, which was defined as 'To organise and maintain in Parliament and the country, a political Labour Party.' was given a wider definition. The party became an organisation of 'the producers by hand or by brain', and was opened to individual membership, with Divisional Labour Parties being established.

This widened Labour party was not a happy band of brothers. In fact, none of the parties enjoyed fraternal harmony. The cries running round the country, and finding echoes in parliament, were expressed in fierce antagonisms. Those who cried 'Hang The Kaiser!' would gladly have hanged those who would not. A resolution moved by Ramsey MacDonald was ritualistically torn up without being read at a Party Conference, on the presumption (correct) that it would be moderate.

In some cases, there was a seam of agreement running through these fragments. This was shown in the support given to Russia. Among the Hang-The-Kaiser brigade there was strong opposition to the Government's proposed aid to counter-revolutionary forces in Poland. On June 3rd 1919 a conference was held under the asupices of the I.L.P. and the B.S.P with the avowed object of discussing policy now that the war had ended. Three hundred and seventy one Trade Union Delegates were present.

There was unanimous agreement on one point. There must be no invervention by the Allies in revolutionary Russia. A 'Hands Off Russia ' Committee was formed, and was very active in holding meetings all over the country. On this subject, Guy Aldred and Bertrand Russell spoke together. Attempts were made to establish Workers' and Soldiers' Soviets. The movement was strong enough to force the Government to withdraw a plan to send assistance to Poland, although nevertheless British Expeditionary Forces, and forces from other Allied nations, were sent into Russia to fight against the new regime there — an act which had great effects in the future, leading to a continuing mistrust of the West.

This was the mood of the socialist movement on the left of the I.L.P, and including many local Parties of that organisation. They repudiated the new-found role of the Labour party as a Parliamentary socialist Party, whose object was to nationalise industry and gain a bigger share of surplus value for the workers. This pallid apology for socialism was tailoring the workers' struggle into something which was a good fit for capitalism. In the betrayal by the Second International of the workers of Europe at the outbreak of war, the potential treachery of this form of socialism was made manifest. The mood was for Peoples' Power in Communes and Soviets. This was not something new. It went back to the great French Revolution when the Communes dominated the Convention, to the Paris Commune of 1871, to the aborted Russian Revolution of 1905, to the recent Bolshevik Revolution, where the slogan was against the Constituent Assembly :'All Power to the Soviets.' Parliament was an alien institution devised by history for the bourgeousie to debate their taxation with the Crown: it was not for wielding the power of the workers.

In his study *Anti-Parliamentarianism and Communism in Britain*, R.W. Jones writes:

> 'At the outset we should try and clarify what we mean by 'antiparliamentarianism. It is important to realise that for the Briitish comrades in 1921 anti-parliamentarianism was not merely a negative delineation of tactics — a rejection of socialists standing for and sitting in, Parliament — though this was obviously a key element in the Movement. Anti-parliamentarianism has, at this time, to be viewed in the context of a burgeoning commune movement. Indeed, till the formation of the Communist Party of Great Britain, which took upon itself the definition of all things "communist", it would not be too much of an exaggeration to say that the anti-parliamentary and communist movements were synonomous. To be a communist prior to 1920, even 1921, was to be an anti-parliamentarian. Only after 1921 was the prefix "anti-parliamentary" necesary.'

As we have already noted, Aldred was an anti-parliamentarian in 1906, stressing that definition because of the threat by the newly formed Labour Party. He was not speaking as a deviant, rather he was charging that the new Party was the deviant.

It was not antiparliamentarianism (which he took for granted), which concerned him when he came out of prison in January 1919, but unity. He had written from Brixton Prison on that urgent requirement. His hope was for the re-establishment of the Communist Propaganda Groups, which could then be federated into the Communist Federation which would represent Britain in the International. But when he found that the London Federation of the Socialist Labour Party advocated the establishment of a Communist League, he asociated himself with that. He became its Organiser, and editor of its paper *The Communist.* The League gained seventeen federated Groups, nine in England, one in Wales, and seven in Scotland, including the Glasgow Anarchist Group, which had also been trying to form a Federation of Communists.

A steering Committee met to work out the structure of the League. It was finally agreed that the Groups should have a central point of reference. This should be made up of delegates from branches proportionate to membership numbers. Those delegates should be recallable by the Group they represented, and should speak for that Group and not for themselves. The delegates should form a Local Delegates Committee.

The paper *The Communist* should be run by the Committee, to whom all contributions should be sent, but a comrade should be appointed to see the paper 'through the press'. The experienced Guy Aldred was the obvious choice. Aldred was appointed to, or simply slotted into, the post of Organiser. In *The Spur* he indicated his plan. He and Sara would have a roving commission over England, Scotland and Wales, holding meetings and explaining the ideas and objects of the League. To obtain maximum effect they would go separate ways. Aldred, perhaps with a memory from his Boy Preacher days, called this process through the country 'The Red Evangel'. Willie MacDougall of Glasgow, who was last encountered on a bicycle heading north from Dartmoor, and Alec Ross of Dundee, would take the Scottish fixtures, and Henry Bernard, the cartoonist, would cover London.

Aldred lived in London with Rose Witcop and their son Annesley, but he was seldom at home. He was constantly on the move, every evening in a different place, lecturing. From January to April the Communist League flourished, then it began to decline, probably affected by the efforts of other Groups to attain a communist unity in the formation of a Party which could stand for the United Kingdom in an affiliation to the Communist International. An organisational difficulty with the League was that its administrative council was so democratic that it required delegates from remote parts of Britain to attend. This was impossible for a penniless working-class organisation.

Aldred was working ever more closely with the Glasgow Anarchists, who were now very active, extending their propaganda into the Lanarkshire towns. They acquired an old Victorian terrace house in the west end of Glasgow, and made it their headquarters. It was initially 'Liberty Hall', but within a month or so had changed its name to Bakunin House, and the name of the Group became Glasgow Communist Group. This realised Guy's hope that his pre-war group would be revived. It also adapted the Group to the atmosphere of the time, setting the anti-parliamentary form of communism against the type that was striving to take over.

Another anti-parliamentary group was the Workers' Socialist Federation, centred round Sylvia Pankhurst. The Communist League had suggested a merger with the Federation, but Sylvia had replied that the two organisations were too similar for that to be necessary. The Federation then, without waiting for anybody else, declared itself to be The British Communist Party, and assumed affiliation to the International by adding in brackets (British Section of the International — BSTI). Lenin was not pleased. He considered that the Communist Parties of the world must be recognised by the International, and approved by himself. Besides, he did not approve of anti-parliamentarianism. He advised Sylvia to get in touch with other Groups and arrange a unity conference.

Unity conferences were already taking place, and had been doing so from shortly after the end of the war. We have no space to detail them all, but we should mention one that took place at the end of April, 1919. The main points concerned the question of parliamentary representation. Lenin's advice was sought, as acknowledged godfather. He replied, in part:

> I personally am in favour of participation in parliament and adhesion to the Labour Party, on condition of free and independent communist activity. This policy I intend to defend at the Second Congress of the Third International....I consider it most desirable that a Communist Party be speedily organised on the basis of the decisions and principles of the Third International and that the Party be brought into close contact with the Industrial Workers of the World, and the Shop Stewards' Movement in order to bring about their complete union.
> Moscow July 8th 1920   Lenin.

Lenin placed great importance on this question of parliamentary representation. He would like to have had the matter settled favourably before the Second Congress of the International and wrote a book thoroughly castigating the 'Infantile Sickness of the Left'. He did not pronounce the same diagnosis on his own attitude to the Duma in 1905 or the Constituent Assembly in 1918.

In *Left Wing Communism: An Infantile Disorder*, Lenin's examination of the position in Britain starts with Scotland, where lies the seat of the virus, and the first carrier of the disease he mentions is Willie Gallacher, later M.P. for West Fife for many years as representative of Stalinist communism. But at that time he was a member of the Scottish Workers' Council, whose function was to promote 'communes', not Party communism. Lenin quoted Gallacher:

> 'The Council is definitely anti-parliamentarian, and has behind it the Left Wing of the various political bodies....We represent the revolutionary movement in Scotland, striving continually to build up a revolutionary organisation within the industries, and a communist party based on social committees thoughout the country....'

With this accolade of Leninist recognition it is not surprising that Gallacher was chosen to represent the Scottish Workers' Councils at the Congress. Before he left, he called at Bakunin House, which had become (and remained for the next twelve years) an open-house political centre in Glasgow, to receive the good wishes of his comrades. Aldred praised him warmly. Tom Bell, in his *Short History of the Communist Party*, writes:

> 'Lenin, at the Second Congress, with his accustomed attention to human personality, engaged in many conversations and discussions with the anti-parliamentarians, and took great pains, endeavouring to persuade them as to the necessity for becoming identified with the formation of a Communist Party on their return to England. This pledge Gallacher and Ramsay faithfully fulfilled.'

When Guy Aldred heard that Lenin had sent a letter to the German Communist Party, advising them to repudiate syndicalism (a name covering 'Commune' communism), in favour of a strong centralised party, urging that the 'traitors to socialism' must be fought with utmost energy in the capitalist parliaments, he replied in the July 1920 issue of *The Spur*, giving a possible explanation for Lenin's surprising behaviour.

> 'But there are no workers in parliament....Workers never get any nearer parliament than the ballot box. They are influenced by the speeches made before and not after an election. The proper place to address and to influence the workers is at the street corner, or the socialist lecture hall, or at the workshop gate. As a practical revolutionist I accept the position that the communist must be everywhere where there are workers. But I draw a very different conclusion from that drawn by Lenin.'

Aldred then purports to explain why Lenin has taken this strange line of development.

> 'Circumstances are compelling him to give up his dream of an immediate world revolution, and to concentrate on conserving

and protecting the Russian Movement....In order to conserve the Russian Revolution, Lenin feels that he must offer no propaganda menace to the development of the ordinary everyday Labour Movement. He must not identify himself with minority extremists.'

That was an argument not likely to impress the minority movement. But Gallacher was impressed. He formed the Communist Labour Party, which promoted the formation of a Communist Party of Great Britain. It was four more months before that took shape, in Leeds on January 29th, 1921. So now there was a Communist Party of Great Britain, subject to strict central control and a rigid Party line. Into its vortex was drawn much of the minority movement. Henceforth it was considered that all things communist derived from it, and to it were all things communist referred.

In his pamphlet *Anti-parliamentarianism in Britain, 1917 — 1921'*, R.W. Jones observes:

'As a result of such retreats and the consolidation of the C.P.G.B., what was left of the evolving revolutionary and anti-parliamentary movement came to be centred around *The Spur* and Guy Aldred. Aldred and his associates were now almost alone in being both enthusiastic supporters of the Bolshevik revolution and yet not falling for the spurious unity line of the C.P.G.B. All that could be accomplished now was to bring together the few remaining communist and anarchist groups that still adhered to an anti-parliamentary programme.

'It was hoped to create a communist federation out of those remaining groups. The principle of federation — a federation of communist groups developed voluntarily from below, rather than an imposed centralism from above — was always an important and consistent part of the anti-parliamentary movement's proposals for unity. Aldred summarised the position in 1920: "I have no objection to an efficient and centralised party so long as the authority rests in the hands of the rank and file, and all officials can be sacked at a moment's notice. But I want the centralism to be wished for and evolved by the local groups, a slow merging of them into one party, from the bottom upwards, as distinct from this imposition from the top downwards."

'Aldred argued: "Lenin's task compels him to compromise with all the elect of bourgeous society, whereas our task demands no compromise. And so we take different paths, and are only on the most distant speaking terms".'

While the Unity Congress was forging the new Communist Party of

Great Britain, Aldred and his colleagues were consolidating the strength of the anti-parliamentarians, especially around the Glasgow Central Group.

2: THE 'RED COMMUNE'

The anti-parliamentary communism cause was certainly hard-pressed. Even the I.L.P., which at grass roots was indeed, as Gallacher put it, disgusted with parliamentary socialism, and active in the call for Soldiers' and Workers' Soviets, was nevertheless gradually grooming candidates for the coming General Election. In this vortex of scuttled dreams and sinking revolutionary hopes, Aldred felt it was not enough just to survive. Survival had to have a purpose and a direction.

There was no use adopting a purely negative stance. Meetings held to denounce parliamentarianism, the capitalist system, and the exploitation by bosses, would sink into a repetitious dogma. Action was needed. He proposed to counter 'revolutionary parliamentarianism', as the Leninists called it, with 'revolutionary anti-parliamentarianism'. He would have every 'revolutionary parliamentarian' challenged at the polls by a 'revolutionary anti-parliamentarian'. This would be a good way of spreading propaganda, for it would attract considerable attention. The anti-parliamentarian candidate would make a pledge in his election address not to take his or her seat in Westminster, but to remain outside Parliament, claiming the authority of an M.P. in dealing with the problems of his constituents, and forming a Council with other anti-parliamentary elected Representatives, challenging the parliamentary authority of the capitalist State.

He based this manoeuvre on the tactic employed by the Sinn Fein in Ireland at the 1918 General Election. They had used the election machinery to appoint their own candidates, who, when elected, did not go to Westminster, but assembled in Dublin, and declared themselves the first Parliament of the Irish Republic, electing a President and Cabinet, and declaring that the British troops on Irish soil were invaders. This Parliament was eventually broken up, and the struggle in Ireland continued, but in 1922 Aldred thought the idea was a good way of putting forward the case against capitalist parliamentarianisn.

He called it the 'Sinn Fein Tactic'. It may have been better if he had not mentioned the Sinn Fein, for the Group had no connection with Irish affairs, and it was not a good time to be connected even by analogy with the I.R.A. This was the time when the Anglo-Irish Treaty was being discussed, and the division of the country about to take place. The violence spilled over into the West of Scotland. Meetings were held, demonstrations broken up, Clubs and homes raided,and rowdy confrontations between youths of the opposing persuasions were taking place. It was not a good tactic to imply some connection with all that. The people in general and the authorities in particular are not perceptive in the appreciation of analagous subtlties.

The Group accepted the tactic of using the ballot box as a challenge to parliamentary socialism, on the terms stated: refusal to sit in the Commons: refusal to take the Oath of Loyalty to the Crown: determination to work as a Council with other Representatives so elected: and to be subject to recall on demand from Constituents. Guy Aldred was the obvious choice to pioneer this innovation. He was selected by the Group as candidate in the forthcoming General Election.

The Glasgow Communist Group had three branches: Central, Springburn and Shettleston, with fraternal association with Groups in the Lanarkshire towns. Those Groups, with others in Scotland, were moving towards an anti-parliamentary federation. As the revolutionary spirit was drained away down the conduits of I.L.P. parliamentarianism and Communist Party sloganising demonstrations, the anti-parliamentarians felt a growing strength. Now they would be really active: now Aldred was back. Contemporary opinion declared him 'a movement in himself', and, according to a much later obituary (in a very unfriendly newspaper), 'He bestrode the political platform like a colossus.' Some critics sneered at 'Aldred's one-man band.' There is no doubt that he was an outstanding personality, but that brought him more suffering than reward.

Despite the feeling of growing strength and eagerness for action, there were those in the Group who did not agree with Aldred's proposed tactics. One was Henry Sara, that old and valued associate. He went over to the Pankhurst faction, then to the Communist Party, then to the Trotskyists. Other dissenters were Willie MacDougall and Jane Hamilton Patrick. But those two, and others, stayed in the Group, to make their disagreement felt later on.

It was natural that the Group should want its own paper. *The Spur* was Aldred's own propaganda sheet, and reliance on it gave credence to the 'One-man band' traducers.   The new paper would be called *The Red Commune*.   It would be run by a five-person editorial board.   Aldred would have no say on it, except as a member of the group whose endorsement of contents would be required.   The 'Anti-Parliamentary Communist Federation' was in the process of being formed, but had not been finalised when the paper went to press, so the subtitle read 'Official Organ of the Glasgow Communist Group and affiliated Bodies.'   *The Red Commune* was not a wild revolutionary sheet,as might have been expected.   It was mild and level-headed, but it did contain a Statement of Sinn Fein Tactic, already published in *The Spur*, and quotations from an article by Colonel Cecil L'Estrange Malone, M.P., which described Parliament as the 'kept harlot of the capitalist press.'   For this, the Colonel got six months imprisonment for contempt of the House.

The new paper appeared on 1st February.   It took the powers-that-be a few weeks to decide what to do about it.   On 26th February the Glasgow Police wrote to the London Police to arrange a raid on 17 Richmond Gardens where Aldred lived, at four o'clock in the afternoon of March 2nd.

Aldred, Rose, and 11 year-old Annesley were quietly at home that afternoon when came the not-unfamiliar thump on the front door and in swarmed a squad of police and Special Branch men.   It was estimated by Aldred that as many as thirty were posted outside.   Nobody could say what they were looking for, as they did not know themselves.   They were obviously prepared for something more than a couple and their small son — probably a roomful of desperate men engaged in desperate conspiracy.   They spent four hours in the house, searching every corner, even breaking open Annesely's toys in the hope that some coded threat to the British Empire lurked there.   But there was nothing.   So they arrested Guy anyway.   Guy explained to the officer in charge that he was acting under a Glasgow magistrates' warrant, and that it was not valid in London.   He needed the signature of a London Magistrate.   They took him into custody, anyway, legalistic niceties or not, while they sorted it all out.   That took them three days.   On March 5th a sergeant came to his cell and formally arrested him.

In Glasgow the police got some notion that Guy was not in Glagow at 4 p m., March 2nd., the deadline for the planned raid.   A plainclothes man was sent round to Bakunin House to find out.   No, Aldred was not there.   Maybe they wired London and found that Aldred was already in the bag.   Whether or not, they decided to have their raid at eight o'clock.

So at that time, in the dark of the evening, police poured from police vans, flattened themselves against walls, straightened themselves behind lampposts, and stealthily advanced on Bakunin House. It had an ever-open door, so there was no problem of entry. Up the stairs in a rush: barge through a door showing a light, and there they found a small woman, Jane Patrick, secretary of the Group, brewing a pot of tea, and Douglas McLeish, a Group member, browsing through some pamphlets while the tea brewed. It was a cold confrontation. No pushing back of chairs, no scramble behind filing cabinets, no mad rush for the window, no upraising of hands, no pulling of revolvers, just the mixed aroma of infusing tea and ancient newsprint. This was a non-plussing anticlimax. Nobody has said so, but may we not suppose that the officer in charge, Superindent Keith, and his assistant were feeling a bit foolish?

The immediate cause of the raid was probably Aldred's use of the words 'Sinn Fein'. He had no connection with Sinn Fein. He regarded them at that time as nationalist republicans, not as socialists. It was only their *tactic* in the use of their enemy's electoral structure that he aimed to copy. But he did intend the words to be defiant and shocking, and they were. Irish troubles were not just on the boil, but had boiled over onto the mainland. Nineteen twenty had been the year of the Black And Tans, and their inflamatory effect was still being felt. And here was this man, self-avowed revolutionary anarchist, communist, leader of prison riots, now advocating a Sinn Fein tactic! He had, the authorities felt, to be taken seriously as a possible threat to public order.

A thorough search of the premises was made. This produced 'a number' of Communist Group membership cards, and fifty-one old cards of the Anarchist Group. There was also a list of *The Spur* subscribers, a few tradesmens' bills, and a letter from a Mr. Hunt, undermanager of Haunchwood Colliery at Nuneaton,, asking for some pamphlets which had been advertised in *The Freethinker*. Mr. Hunt was not a socialist: he was a freethinker. The pamphlets he ordered were by Sir Walter Strickland and by Guy Aldred. He also ordered a bound volume of *The Spur* back issues, presumably because of the freethought articles it contained. He did not order *The Red Commune*. A few days after the raid, Mr. Hunt was called into the colliery manager's office, shown the letter he had sent to Bakunin Press, and sacked.

Superindent Keith and his luckless men had been in Bakunin House for an hour, and had little to show for it when a ray of hope appeared. They had just decided that a dark stain on a basement wall had been caused by damp and not by the manufacture of explosives when the constable on door duty approached them with a housewife who had been intent on entering the building.

The woman said her name was Mrs. Macgill, and that she had come to collect a pair of boots from Miss Patrick, who worked in a shoe shop. Fair enough, but this alleged Mrs. Macgill had a foreign accent. Further questioning was obviously imperative.

Mrs. Macgill said she had come from Germany with her refugee parents when she was a child twenty-six years past, in 1894. Her father had been sent back to Germany in 1915, but she, having married a Glasgow policeman, William Macgill, in 1909, was allowed to stay in Britain. She was a qualified nurse, and probably, though this is not stated, worked in that capacity during the war. Being German, she met with much hostility and had few friends. But Miss Jane Patrick had been kind to her. A friendship developed. She, as a mark of that friendship, bought all her family's footware (she had two small boys) from the shop where Miss Patrick worked. And as a further mark of friendship she had taken out a subscription for *The Spur*, which cost one shilling and threepence (7½p.) postfree for the year. She had come to collect the March issue. That was all. She was not a member of the Group and took no part in its propaganda activities. It was easily confirmed that she was on the subscribers' list, and not on the membership list, but the Glasgow Chief Constable had to be told. He was informed on 7th March, and on the 16th informed Constable Macgill that he must resign. Macgill refused to do this, and wrote a defence of his position, and appealed to the Chief Constable. The Chief remained firm. As Macgill would not resign and thus admit some guilt, the Chief Constable dismissed him from the Force on 19th March, stating as a reason that he had ben guilty of misconduct in allowing his wife to be a member of a seditious and revolutionary society.

The case was fought all the way up to the Secretary of State, who endorsed the ruling of the Chief Constable. A man in public service is responsible, it was held, for his wife's convictions. After seventeen years of blameless conduct, and several awards, Constable Macgill was dismissed without pension.

So the swoop on Bakunin House and the Aldred home netted one colliery under-manager, one police constable, both thrown out of work, and Guy Aldred, Jane Patrick, Douglas McLeish and the printer Andrew Fleming, thrown into jail. It was like the war-time imprisonments, a muddled and legally suspect operation. If the Government wanted to silence Aldred, as they had already silenced John Maclean and Sylvia Pankhurst, they could have had him for the material that had already appeared in *The Spur*. There was nothing which could be construed as subversive in *The Red Commune* which had not already appeared in *The Spur*. In order to establish a connection, the Crown had to concoct a charge against Aldred of 'conspiring with' Patrick and McLeish to 'excite popular disaffection, commotion, and violence to popular authority.' Aldred maintained that he was prepared to take full responsibility. Patrick and McLeish rightly objected to that negation of their accountability.

On March 7th the four made a formal appearance before the Sheriff and were remanded in custody for a fortnight before appearing before the Lord Justice Clerk, who released the printer Fleming on £200 bail, and Jane Patrick and Douglas McLeish on bail of £150 each. Guy Aldred was remanded in custody, and there he remained for the next four months.

3: TRIAL AND IMPRISONMENT

The case against Guy Alfred Aldred, Jane Hamilton Patrick, Douglas McLeish and Andrew Fleming came up for hearing at the Glasgow High Court on Tuesday 21st June, 1921.   Aldred had been in custody for nearly four months — as he pointed out in Court, a period longer than the sentence usually pronounced in cases of this kind.   The indictment covered eight pages, and involved charges of urging anti-parliamentary action, employing a Sinn Fein tactic and of conspiracy to cause disaffection among the populace.   The trial lasted two days and was widely publicised.

The Evening News of Monday June 20th. wrote:

'A somewhat unusual calendar of cases was submitted at the sitting of the Glasgow High Court, which commenced at Justiciary Buildings, Jail Square, today.

'In all, there are 29 cases involving 74 persons.   Two capital charges are included in the list, but most interest will centre on trials in which a Sinn Fein element is introduced.   Several batches of individuals are charged with one or other of the following offences: sedition, illegal drilling, contravention of the Explosive Substances Act, mobbing and rioting.

'Unprecedented interest was taken in the Court proceedings. Hundreds of persons gathered outside the Court Buildings.... Demands for admission to the Court gallery were heavy, and the police took the precaution of seaching every person who entered the Court precincts.

'A long legal discussion heralded the commencement of the sedition charges against Guy Alfred Aldred....Mr. Aldred, who was undefended, held that there was nothing seditious in the statements....'

The Evening News continued with an account of the day's hearings, and next day resumed the report.

'Aldred, who last night spoke for over an hour, today occupied another hour in his resumed address to the jury. He recalled the speeches made eight years ago by Sir Edward Carson and Lord Birkenhead, speeches that were so well calculated to incite to violence and sedition that they prevented a constitutional solution to the Irish problem, and were responsible for the murders and outrages taking place in Ireland today. Those men were now honoured Judges in England, and what the workers felt was that if you preached sedition in a certain way you might be honoured by being required to fill the highest positions in the land; but the workers, who were without culture and University education, and said things bluntly, found that a different attitude was taken to everything they might say.'

The *Glasgow Evening Times* and the *Citizen*, the *Daily Record* and *Bulletin* all carried long reports. So did the Labour paper, *The Daily Herald*. Here the reporter was Patrick Dollan, later Lord Provost of Glasgow. He wrote:

'In continuation of his defence, Aldred spoke for a futher hour this forenoon, and in an eloquent plea for free speech said that Communism might be wrong, but a free Press was always right. He reminded the jury that the Liberals had threatened to destroy the House of Lords and were not prosecuted. If that was proper advocacy it was equally proper to urge the destruction of the House of Commons as an agency of government.'

Aldred referred to the exclusion of Catholics from the position of High Court Judge in the not-so-distant past, and to the inclusion of women (including the forewoman) in the jury at the present trial. It happened that the Judge was himself a Catholic. Only a few years ago it would have been an incitement to public disorder to advocate such an innovation. Now it was accepted. This was because the British Constitution was not written. It was not static, it grew with the changes in public attitude. The rebel of today was the orthodox of tomorrow. This maturing of the Constitution drew its sustenance from the roots of society, the common people. New values were conceived in the gatherings of the people, in listening and in speaking in back-street halls, and at street corners. He did not ask the people to do anything their informed nature did not urge them to do. His task, as that of every social teacher and preacher in history, was to inform the people. Not to incite them as an un-informed mob, but to move them as an enlightened factor in society. This was not sedition as he understood it.

Willie Gallacher wrote a very human and a very feeling account of the trial in the *Worker* for July 30th 1921, under the title 'The British White Terror.' He maintained that the country was run as much by the violence of Scotland Yard as by the peaceful processes of democratic government. Harry McShane's account of the trial filled several columns of *The Socialist*. The last paragraph read:

'After an absence of a few minutes the jury (which included eight women, one of whom was the chairman) returned a verdict of "Guilty". Aldred said that he took full responsibility, and suggested that he be given the heaviest sentence. Miss Patrick said that she was prepared to take her share of the responsibilty. McLeish said that he also took his share of the responsibility. He had no desire to hide behind Comrade Aldred. Lord Skerrington than passed sentences: Guy Aldred, one year: Douglas McLeish three months: Jane Patrick, three months, Andrew Fleming (the printer), three months and a fine of £50, or another three months.'

Aldred and McLeish were taken to Barlinnie Prison with Andrew Fleming; Jenny Patrick was taken to Duke Street Prison. Guy Aldred was taken out of circulation for a while. That was the main purpose of the trial.

It must have been with a sinking heart that Guy Aldred heard a cell door clang shut behind him again. He had already been in custody longer than the others' sentence. For fourteen weeks already he had been been in solitary confinement as prisoner-on-remand, and there was so much to do, so much going on outside. Social unrest, political upheaval, old forms destroyed, new concepts taking shape. He yearned to be part of it. He had been deprived of so much so often. And here he was, thirty-four years of age, at the very pinnacle of his confidence and energy, shut up again in a concrete coffin 14ft. by 7ft., in the loneliness which he loathed, and the silence which left his mind without the landscape of intercourse, a vast desert island where self-contemplation was inescapable, and thought had no release in action.

This time he was accorded political prisoner status. He could wear his own clothes, and he did not have to work. He was allowed books, approved of by the Governor. He had paper, pen and ink supplied, but he was not allowed to send any writing out of prison. What he wanted to preserve was kept in the Prison office till he was released.

This preferential treatment was not motivated by kindness or justice. It was a wise expedient on the part of the authorities. Aldred — like John Maclean — would have gone on hunger strike if convict conditions had been imposed, and that would have given them more publicity and stirred up their followers. But this 'humane' treatment was still exceptionally severe. It meant solitary confinement for 23¼ hours out of every twenty-four, and a silence rule they could not break. There was no workshop association. It was a lonely existence, which tested a man's internal fortitude and threw him onto his own mental and spiritual resources.

Aldred did not have the satisfaction of knowing that all was going well with his group. Jenny Patrick and Douglas McLeish were in jail. Sara had departed in the direction of the Pankhurst faction, while Willie Macdougall, like many others of the old anarchist persuasion, had not been greatly in favour of the ballot-box tactic anyway. There was no move to issue a second number of *The Red Commune*. Rose Witcop did not take over the editorship of *The Spur* as she had during Guy's former imprisonments. It was allowed to collapse. Rose had lost her interest in politics. She was contemplating setting up a Family Planning Clinic in London, as her friend Margaret Sanger had done in New York. She would have liked Guy to drop his political activity and join her in the project. But although Guy was sympathetic, he had no inclination in that direction. He thought the revolution should come first, and all else would follow.

A new member of the A-P.C.F. was John McGovern. He was an able speaker at a superficial level. He could hold and rouse an audience, and was probably the most active member during Guy's absence. He concerned himself with visiting Guy 'at least once a week, and attending to his many demands' (McGovern in *Without Fear or Favour*: Blandforth, 1960) — written at a time when Guy was no longer in favour. According to McGovern (he invariably needs to be checked for truth or exaggeration) a break was already developing between Guy and Rose, and this was evident in the 'many stormy scenes which took place between them in front of the warders.' This combination of resentment and impotence cannot have contributed much to Aldred's peace of mind.

Aldred had been sentenced to one year. That meant, with good conduct remission and the four months already spent in remand, that he was due out in five and a half months, about the end of November. The time came and passed, and there was no move to release him, which meant that, although he had caused no trouble in jail, he had forfeited all remission, probably to balance the political status treatment. That meant three more months in that coffin of a cell. Now he had to look forward to March 2nd, the date of his arrest. But that, too, came and passed, with still no sign of

release.   Then he was informed that the four months' remand did not
count.   This was most unusual.   Time on remand in custody was
always taken into account, even in criminal cases.   This was the first
time that it had not been part of the sentence.   Writing in *The Daily
Herald*, Patrick Dollan said:

> 'Guy Aldred, in prison for exercising the traditional right of
> free speech, was imprisoned four months before his trial, then
> sentenced for a year and not allowed to count the four months he
> had already served as part of this imprisonment.   The brutality
> of this sentence is a disgrace to the country, and nothing can
> remove that disgrace except the organised power of Labour.'

Two days later, George Lansbury, editor of *The Herald*, writing of
Communists in prison, said:

> 'Then there is Guy Aldred, editor of *The Spur*, whose case is
> well-known to all *Herald* readers.   He was born on November
> 5th thirty-five years ago.   His life has been a strenuous one all
> through, and during the past ten years he has spent more time
> inside prison than outside.   His one crime in the eyes of
> Scotland Yard and the Government is that he has desired to
> serve his fellow men and women.   Today he is serving a
> monstrous twelve months imprisonment, with four months
> added because of a failure to grant bail, and the charge which
> has landed him in prison is the old one of sedition.'

In his lonely cell, Guy Aldred continued to write, and to dream.
Aldred held the view of the Victorian radicals, that man was a self-
perfecting creature.   He was the biological expression of an upward
striving, reaching ever higher levels of consciousness from ancient to
modern times, passing through stages of savagery and barbarism to
civilisation, which he had almost within reach, dimly within sight.

To Aldred, the motivation was in the very nature of the animal.
That is how he was.   The expression of this biological will revealed
itself in the actions of nonconformists and heretics.   These were the
advance guard, the forward thrust, the dialectical imperative.   Driven
by the 'inward Must', tormented by 'divine discontent', they pioneered
the new age.   This meant opposition to the old, and it meant
rebellion.   In turn, that meant persecution, martyrdom — it meant
the dark dungeons and the grim gallows.   Not just for this generation
but for countless generations before.   He saw Jesus, the itinerant
preacher and prophet of ancient Judea, as one called by his nature to
be the voice of a new consciousness, to be the Word, to be the
rebel.   He saw his followers ready in his footsteps for martyrdom,
and this sacrifice becoming 'the seed of the Church', till the believers

of the first generation became the 'half-believers' and the 'semi-believers' of the second and third generations, till rebellion was institutionalised and the cross was crushed by the altar and the rebel became the priest. So it was also with Socrates, immortalised by the hemlock: slaughtered in the academy.

As Aldred thought on these things one Sunday afternoon when the sun was slanting across the fields outside his prison, and as he thought of all the good, respectable folk in Sunday best walking in the sun, he felt that his loneliness was a mirage, for his cell was filled by a host of those great and glorious dead. He wrote an essay, which he called *The Magnificat*, of which one part is relevant:

'....They have taken the Bible out of my cell, because I am an atheist. I may not have this book to read because I am the only person in the place who would understand it....Barlinnie's good chaplain wanders the fields this glorious afternoon in absolute freedom of body. He strolls abroad in the strange garb of masquerading piety and self-righteousness. And I, for my sins, as it were — the sins of enquiry and social struggle —am condemned to the monotony of this prison cell. Yet I am not entirely alone. Magnificent ghosts keep me company from the past. And this glorious choir from the shades is singing to me, as I sit here seemingly guilty and forsaken, in their mystic chorus, the Magnificat. I make the Chaplain a present of his inane complacency and stupid ramble. Poor, poor dullard that he is. What a magnificent company of the immortals have seen to it that, this very afternoon, when joy seemed so very far away, the silence to which I have been condemned should not make me eat my heart out with longing and sadness. The sun passes below the horizon, and the Chaplain's walk is over. Before him lies an evening of oppressive respectability, the penalty of being a man without a soul....But I have communed and am strengthened. My heart rejoices.'

It would seem that Aldred used his time in prison to sort out for himself, as much as for others, many of his thoughts on a wide variety of subjects. He concluded that the real Commons, that is, the Commons of wealth-producers, was above the House of Commons, and that the workers as active political thinkers, being the industrial creators of society, *were* the nation. What they willed was the true political constitution.

He also reflected on the Freethinkers. He had been an atheist since he was eighteen. He had found orthodox Christianity repugnant, and later had the same lack of respect of orthodox socialists, and his dislike of orthodox atheists was just as intense. He castigated what he called the 'professional' freethinkers — the journalists, editors, lecturers and others who propound freethought, and also the members of freethought societies, who, he says, meet every Sunday to tell God he doesn't exist as faithfully as the Christians meet to tell Him he does, and whose theology is to deny the Bible with as much conviction as the Christians assert it.

Perhaps the most interesting essay written in Barlinnie prison by Guy Aldred was *The Word to the World*. It is the most revealing of his inmost thoughts. It underlines what we have already indicated, that to Aldred the human species was on an upward development, and that his needs went beyond the satisfaction of basic requirements. This would have been sufficient if the human species had existed in a static condition, and not in a dynamic state of complex consciousness. Guy believed that wider awareness of far-off horizons — as well as material necessities — came from the vision and word of prophets, rebels and agitators often the denizens of dark dungeons or the lonely martyrs on the scaffold.

'....The old-time prophet was poor, and his authority was the inward wisdom generated of poverty. He died, as such men die, mourned by a multitude of half-believers....The "Word" oulives the prophet himself. He dies scorned and neglected. His word continues and increases till the struggle ends in triumph. The word is the verity, and is embodied in the scheme of things that serves men by using men.....

'The powerful cannot believe, and even the poor find it hard to sense, that the power of the word consists in the very poverty of its machinery. The Jews could not believe that Jesus was the Messiah because he came without armament, and was clothed in rags and had not where to lay his head....How could truth have where to lay its head when the palace was built on falsehood and the hovel rests on lies?

'....He who has vision is more than an angel! He is a man and an agitator, not a serf, not a stomach, not a brain, subordinate to digestion....He is a mortal, arrayed in the invincible armour of light. His manhood stamps his word with authority.'

4: BIRTH CONTROL PROSECUTION

Guy Aldred came out of prison in time to be nominated for Shettleston, Glasgow, in the 1922 General Election. The circumstances were not at all favourable. The Groups had weakened, as was usual in his absence, and there was neither *The Spur* nor *Red Commune* to keep them together. The A-P.C.F. did not endorse his candidature, considering it a breach of anti-parliamentary principle, but they helped him unofficially. John McGovern, who had supplied his needs while he was in prison (and who later became the Independent Labour Party Member of Parliament for Shettleston) assisted as his election agent.

Aldred worked with his usual great energy, but the campaign was badly conducted, which must have affected the poll. Only four hundred votes were cast for Aldred, and this created the public image of Aldred as a freak candidate. Nevertheless the poll was not taken as a measure of his worth or significance as an agitator. Edward Scrymgeor, who defeated Winston Churchill at Dundee, warned the Commons in his maiden speech against 'one whose name will be familiar to all in this House. I mean Mr. Guy Aldred. Mr. Aldred is a very able man, and he is desperately in earnest. He was cheered to the echo when he was committing himself to the most drastic line of action.'

The election echoes had hardly died away before Guy was in the news again. On December 22nd 1922 he was prosecuted for publishing Margaret Sanger's pamphlet *Family Limitation.* Aldred had taken the precaution of having a printed slip inserted into every pamphlet. This was to be signed by the purchaser. It was a declaration that he/she was over twenty-one, considered the artificial limitation of the family to be justified....and wished to know the various hygenic methods which could be adopted.... and 'undertakes to keep this booklet out of the hands of unmarried persons under the age of twenty-one.' This declaration having been read and signed, and sixpence paid, the problem of over-production was solved.

In the United States a few years earlier (1915) William Sanger had been tricked into giving a copy of his wife's pamphlet to a government official. He was immediately arrested, kept in jail for two days, sentenced to thirty days imprisonment and fined 150 dollars. The outraged judge told him: 'Your crime is not only a violation of the laws of man, but of God as well in your scheme to prevent motherhood....If some people would go around urging Christian women to bear children instead of wasting their time on women's suffrage this country would be better off.'

In Britain the Director of Public Prosecutions was uneasy in his mind. The printed slip did not satisfy him. He suspected that people not producing a lot of children might get a thrill out of reading the pamphlet. He summonsed Aldred and Witcop to court to show why 'this obscene publication' should not be destroyed.

Rose and Guy had known Margaret Sanger since 1914 when she had stayed with them in London. She was then a young nurse whose husband was serving a prison sentence in the United States for writing on birth control. She returned to Britain from the United States in 1920, and spoke with Guy at public meetings in London, and on Glasgow Green. She describes her Glasgow audience in her autobiography: 'About two thousand shipyard workers in caps and baggy corduroys (who) stood close together, listening in utter silence, without cough or whisper'. In the evening she spoke to a 'Ladies Only' meeting in Bakunin House.

Now, in 1922, she was back in Britain, speaking for the New Generation League, with Bertrand Russell and Guy Aldred among the speakers. The Government was worried. Unemployment was mounting: revolution was smouldering: and now there was this assault on the nation's morals, with notorious subversives selling a sixpenny pamphlet on Birth Control.

Four detectives were detailed to act as *agents provocateur* to collect evidence of indiscriminate sale. One of them called at the London Office of the Bakunin Press and had the good fortune to obtain a copy without having to sign a form himself. The young man who served him obligingly did the filling in, dismissing it as 'just a matter of form.'

To give more weight to the damning evidence, Inspector Miles had four letters written, purporting to come from four harrassed women who didn't know what to do, because they couldn't stop doing it, but didn't want to face the possible consequences. This booklet might help. They — figuratively, of course, for they didn't exist, except in the shape of Inspector Miles and his confederates — sent off sevenpence, to include the postage. The booklets arrived, each with a printed slip to be returned, signed by the recipients, stating age and giving assurance of pure moral intention. The wily officers did not return the slips, having immoral intentions of fraud and deceit. The quarry was in the bag. Scotland Yard swooped for the kill.

Guy Aldred conducted his own defence. Among the witnesses he called was Sir Arbuthnot Lane, consultant surgeon to Guy's Hospital. This eminent authority declared that the booklet should be in the hands of every young person about to be married. Despite this, and a very favourable Press, the Magistrate ordered the books to be destroyed 'in the interests of the morals of society.' This birth control activity increased the strains between Rose and Guy. Rose wanted them to develop a full-time committment to the establishment of a Birth Control Clinic in London. Aldred saw that the problem of unwanted children was one that must be tackled by the overthrow of the existing social system, which piecemeal reforms would only perpetuate.

Rose Witcop defied the Court by having the destroyed pamphlets replaced and sold surreptitiously. But the authorities were watching her, and were hatching a plot for her undoing. Guy returned alone to Glasgow, and made his home at Bakunin House, joined subsequently by his growing son, Annesley.

On May Sunday, 1923, Aldred's new paper *The Commune*, appeared. The name set the idea of 'commune' organisation above that of the 'party', because Aldred saw the centralised monolithic party as detrimental to the cause of socialism. *The Commune* made common cause with the Dutch and German anti-parliamentarians, and exposed the persecution of Russian socialists. On the domestic front its first task was to engage in the struggle for free speech on Glasgow Green.

5: THE BATTLE FOR THE GREEN

The Green lies in the heart of the city, on the north bank of the river Clyde. It is the oldest of the city parks, and owes its origin to the common lands of the burgh. An historian of the Green, writing in 1894, notes a civic function of that open space:

'One of the old customs of the Green still remains almost as vigorous as of old....From time immemorial it has been the custom for all classes of preachers and debaters to air their eloquence upon the masses who frequent the Green, and on Saturday and Sunday afternoons numerous knots of people are to be found listening to discussions upon all varieties of subjects.' (*Glasgow Public Parks.* Duncan MacLellan)

Another writer of the eighteen-nineties declares:

'....But there are other shows which have long characterised the space between the Court Houses and Nelson's Monument, and which still continues with unabated vigour. From time immemorial it has been classical ground to the East-End controversialists: the Orangemen and Romanists have fought bloodless battles by the thousand....There the stupid Tory and the lofty-souled socialist annihilates with ease all shades of orthodox political opinion. On the Green the atheist readily confutes the earnest Salvation Army, while the total abstainer has it all his own way in praising the mission of temperance. Let it not be thought that the whole matter is bvbble and froth: the phenomenon represents a vast aggregate of serious purpose, if not of deep thought, and it forms a most efficient safety valve for blowing off social, political and religious sentiments, which might otherwise attain explosive force.' (*Glasgow: Its Municipal Organisation and Adminstration:* Sir John Bell.)

Glasgow Green belonged to the Church till the Reformation, then it became civic property administered by the City Council. On the Green the townsfolk cut peat, bleached linen, pastured cattle, hanged felons and martyrs, and gathered to gossip, harangue and debate.

On April 13, 1916, the Glasgow Corporation passed a bye-law restricting the right of assembly on the Green, but it was not operated until 1922. Then it was challenged by John Maclean's group, the Scottish Workers' Republican Party, and Guy Aldred's Anti-parliamentary Communist Federation. On July 30, 1922, this bye-law was amended to make an exception of the space outside the gates of the Green — Jail Square — which was also a traditional meeting place. This was meant as a concession: meetings were being cleared from all the park gates, and Guy was contesting the use of the entrance to the Botanic Gardens. But he considered the right to speak inside the Green as a special case, because of its historic associations. On July 6 1924 he addressed an Open Letter to the 'Lord Provost, Magistrates and Council of the City of Glasgow' with respect to the right of free assembly on the Green.

'Sirs and Citizens: Today I shall be one of seventy participating in a quiet and orderly meeting, duly advertised, which will be held at the Monument....Our purpose is to maintain....the age-long right of public speaking on Glasgow Green....At present Edward Rennie (S.W.R.P.) is serving a sentence of fifty days as an ordinary criminal in Barlinnie Prison for speaking on Glasgow Green without a permit....'

(The S.W.R.P. was the Scottish Workers' Republican Party, founded by John Maclean to replace his Scottish Communist Party.)

This meeting was held in defiance of the ban, and was followed at weekly intervals by four others. On each occasion names were taken and Police Court summonses followed. Aldred contested every charge and gave note of Appeal by Stated Case. The Communist Party sneered at those 'anti-panties' and 'Claymore communists' — the latter reference being to the nationalist nature of John Maclean's Scottish Communist Party. Willie Gallacher described the free speech campaign, as 'a stunt, pure and simple.' The editor of The Worker, Aitken Ferguson, gave a derisive headline to an article by E. Clarke which described the Green as a bedlam of racing tipsters and medicine men. '....a Catholic layman proving that the only way to heaven was via the R.C. faith....I.L.P., B.S.P., S.L.P., and so many other P's hurling defiance at each other....'

The unequivocal note in this censure did not prevent the Communist party from performing a characteristic somersault a year later when their prospective parliamentary candidate was refused a permit to speak in the City Hall. The editor of The Worker then wanted to know 'When is the Glasgow Trades Council going to make an organised stand against the suppression of free speech on Glasgow Green? The Council would have taken action long ago if prominent Union and I.L.P. officials had been arrested instead of Guy Aldred of the A-P.C.F. and members of the S.W.R.P.'

At a meeting of the Glasgow Parks Sub-committee held on 29 November, 1926, a report was read from the Magistrates' Committee.

This referred to the abuse of Jail Square by 'racing tipsters and other undesirable persons' who had, since the ban had been lifted from Jail Square, crowded into the place, attracting 'a rowdy and troublesome element'. The Magistrates' Committee recommended that steps be taken to prevent the use of the Square by such persons. A motion was put to the Sub-committtee that the proviso exempting the Square from the restrictions on the Green be repealed. There was an amendment to take no action. The motion was carried by eleven votes to eight. So the police moved into Jail Square.

Aldred was in London at the time, conducting a campaign to gain the right to sell literature and take collections at meetings in Hyde Park. He was also involved in answering charges of blasphemy, having said unkind things about God. In this he successfully defended himself. When he heard that Glasgow Corporation had made application to the Sheriff-principle for the deletion of the clause which had protected Jail Square, he gave notice of objection. The hearing was held on March 29 1927 before Sheriff-Principle A.O.M. Mackenzie. The Corporation was represented by Mr. Campbell of the Town Clerk's Office.

Aldred quoted Acts and authorities to support his contention that the Bye-law was repugnant to the laws of Scotland. It was a gross abuse of language to place tipsters in the same category as public speakers. In London the authorities had extended certain laws which prevented tipsters from going into Hyde Park, but public meetings still went on. The Corporation's ban was contrary to the good government of the City, for this act of regulation was really an act of prohibition.

He was interrupted while he was drawing a distinction between tipsters and public speakers by the Sheriff-Principle, who remarked (amid laughter) 'You mean that free speeech is more important than free tips.'

He adjourned the hearing without stating a decision, but on April 1, 1927, he confirmed the reverted bye-law.

The *Glasgow Herald*, in a lengthy editorial, approved the Sheriff's decision, concluding:

> 'We hope the Corporation may be stirred up to make such use of the powers they have, or if they have not got them, to take steps to get such powers as may be necesary to enable them to regulate street corner oratory anywhere within the city.'

The Rev. Richard Lee, then Minister of Ross Street Unitarian Church, and sometime Labour Town Councillor, wrote to *The Glasgow Evening News* for March 31, 1927:

'It is lamentable that the citizens of Glasgow should treat so lightly the passing away of the freedom of Glasgow Green. How strange it is that the main defence of free speech should be left to a Sassenach, Mr. Guy Aldred, who made such an impressive case on Tuesday from the point of view of ancient usage, legal right and public interest....When Socrates laid down the foundations of rational research, he had no official caucus to back him up. When Jesus established the principles of spiritual religion, he had no support from official ecclesiasticism. Today there is little hope from any body of hide-bound ecclesiastics or politicians. This proposal of the authorities means the choking up of the fountains of rational liberty and social justice.'

The *Daily Herald* for the same date carried the headline:
SILENT GLASGOW GREEN
All meetings banned on Jail Square.

Meanwhile Scotland Yard had been watching Rose Witcop and her Family Planning activities. The police had received such a bad press when Aldred had been prosecuted that they tried another tactic. Rose Witcop, they discovered, was a Russian Jewess. She had been brought to Britain before she was five years of age, but she was still an alien. So she had a visit from the Yard, and was told that she must register as an alien, or face the probability of deportation. Rose did not speak Russian, and had no friends there. Her association with Aldred would have made her imprisonment certain, had she been deported to Russia. She came to Glasgow to ask Guy to help her in an application to the Scottish Court of Session for a Declarator of Marriage based on 'habit and repute'. Discovering that this would mean a delay, during which the Home Office might act, they decided to go through a civil marriage ceremony, after which they parted again.

That was in February, 1926, the year of the General Strike. The history of that event is too well documented to detain us here. We are concerned with Aldred's attitude. To him the strike was not general, and was not intended to be. The members of the T.U.C. General Council were more scared than the Government that it would get out of hand and show some degree of insurgency. The streets of Glasgow were plastered with the slogan 'ALL POWER TO THE T.U.C.' That was Communist Party policy. Aldred countered this with 'ALL POWER TO THE PEOPLE'. He issued a special *Anti-Parliamentary Communist Gazette*. In this he wrote: 'Base Wednesday has succeeded Black Friday. Once more Thomas has triumphed officially. May 12, 1926 will live in the history of the working class movement as the day on which the British Trades Union Congress Council made abject and unconditional surrender of the workers' cause...'

He quoted articles from *The Scottish Worker*, one entitled 'The Greatest Response in History' and the other 'Stand Fast'. Yet while those articles were being written, the T.U.C. was preparing an unconditional withdrawal of the strike notice. *The British Gazette*, edited by Winston Churchill, displayed a more truthful heading 'Total Surrender'.

Aldred wrote:

'This "total surrender" was being engineered and connived at by the leaders, and those responsible for *The Scottish Worker* (and *The British Worker*), while they were bidding the workers "stand fast", and boasting of "the greatest response in history". And the self-seeking knaves who write up *The Scottish Worker*, having assisted in betraying "the greatest response in history", continue to lie and deceive — in the official labour interest. We impeach them in this sheet that the workers may know their small worth. To treason they have added the further crime of hypocrisy, not merely before, but after the event.'

The rest of the *Gazette* was devoted to an attack on J.H. Thomas. It was recalled that he had said before Mr. Justice Darling *in 1921* that if a constitutional issue were involved he would *seem* to lead a General Strike in order to 'take steps to defeat it'. This was in a trial in which he won £2,000 in a slander action against the Communist Party. Yet the C.P. had placed the fate of the strike in his hands.

There were several branches of the A-P.C.F. in London, and several more in the North of England, but Glasgow was the centre of the Federation's activities. It comprised the Central, Eastern and Springburn branches. The Central had its headquarters in Bakunin House, 13 Burnbank Gardens, off Great Western Road, and a bookshop in Buchanan Street. The Eastern branch had its headquarters and bookshop combined in Shettleston Road. Someone had the bright idea of calling this *The Olde Redde Booke Shoppe*. It was also known as the *Red Spot in the East*. It was the centre of much vigorous propaganda. The Springburn branch had to book a hall for its public meetings and its domestic deliberations.

Though they preached the Utopia of universal harmony, there was nothing soft or yielding about the A-P.C.F., either in their treatment of their opponents or in their fraternal dealings with each other. At some tumultuous group meetings, capitalism stood on the side-lines while comrades (metaphorically) blooded noses.   Guy seldom exercised the natural authority of his personality on those occasions.   Although a raging torrent on the platform he was most often a placid stream among friends.

Practically all the A-P.C.F. members lived in poverty, and some of them in the greyest of the back streets.   Yet they were cheerful and vigorous.   The chief speakers were Guy Aldred, James Murray, Willie McDougall and Charles Doran, with a couple more from the Paisley branch.   Aldred and Murray toured the London and other branches as often as funds would permit.   Guy could always attract a crowd, and his debates could rally the customers in char-a-bancs, and fill St. Andrew's Halls.   One such debate was that held with Father Vincent Mcnab.   Its echoes stayed with the audience for a very long time, and it was still a warm topic when the present writer joined the group several years later.   Another notable debate was that involving Brigadier General R.B.D. Blakeney, a pre-Mosley fascist.   That took place in the Town Hall, Govan, on 17th December, 1925.

The A-P.C.F. was in favour of the Fourth (Anti-parliamentary) International.   There was quite a considerable anti-comintern movement in Europe at that time.   Aldred, as editor of *The Commune*, was in continuing correspondence with the Dutch and German groups, and also with the Mjasnikow Group, formed to defend an imprisoned Russian anti-parliamentarian of that name.

In nationalist circles in India it was recalled that Guy Aldred was the only Englishman to speak out on their behalf when they were abused by the Tory and Socialist Press alike following the assassination of Sir Curson Wyllie in 1909.   Aldred, they said, was the only Englishman to go to prison for India, and there had been a continuing flow of correspondence between Aldred and several Indian leaders over the years.   Most of his contacts were of Savarkar's persuasion, strongly nationalistic, touching socialist sympathies only incidently, and usually on the common ground of opposition to imperialism. Aldred sometimes printed articles on India in his paper, but it is doubtful if they held much interest for his Glasgow readers.

Guy Aldred had been, more than once, praised or blamed for expounding socialism with religious fervour.   The truth lies in the fact that to him socialism was not merely a change in the economic system.   In a compendium of definitions called *What is Socialism?* (ed. Dan Griffiths: Grant Richards Ltd., 1924) Aldred records: '....It is the term we use to define the next step in evolution....It is the next station to capitalism in man's forward march....It embodies all religion and includes all ethics'.   With this in mind it is easier to understand why Aldred had called his mission to make communist converts in 1919 the 'Red Evangel', and why, now that he was flaying careerists and traitors in 1928 there should occur to him the symbol of a *Red Scourge*. He would weave his words into a lash of knotted cords to whip those charlatans out of the forecourt of the Temple.

There was no shortage of offenders deserving chastisement. All who had climbed to place and office within the system had betrayed their trust: MacDonald, Tillet, Cook, Clynes, Wheatley, Kirkwood. Up they all went on *The Commune* pillory. J.H. Thomas with his 'ducal junketings' was blatantly exposed — since he blatantly exposed himself. Arthur Henderson rushed to meet trouble when he agreed to speak with Wheatley on the I.L.P. platform in Glasgow.

Two special issues of *The Commune* were published for the occasion: one for circulation in Clydebank and the other for Shettleston. They denounced Henderson for his membership of the Ministry of War, the wartime deportation of rebel workers from the Clyde, complicity in the execution of the socialist leader James Connelly following the Easter uprising in Ireland, and many other treacheries against the workers, who were urged to STOP THIS SCANDAL! — by which was meant Henderson's appearance on the socialist platform.

When the meeting was held on 8th January 1929 in Shettleston Public Hall, the uproar was greater than Aldred had anticipated. His point was that the workers should let the Divisional Labour Party know that Henderson was neither welcome on the platform nor tolerable in the Party, not that he should be howled down. As he *had* appeared on the platform, he should be questioned, challenged and discredited by exposure. That was Aldred's way, and he tried to put it into practice. An unfriendly critic describes him standing on a seat haranguing the platform 'like a latter-day Danton.'

Aldred could not be heard above the din. The choir tried the charms of music and sweetly emitted 'Scots Wha Hae', and the audience erupted into the 'Red Flag'. The police were called and seventeen arrests were made, most of them anti-parliamentarians. An exception was Willie Gallacher, who was included when he jumped on the back of the policeman arresting Guy Aldred.

Then followed the usual legal process of stated case and appeal, but eventually the fines had to be paid. The high-pressure free-issue campaign had exhausted the funds of *The Commune* and it ceased publication. Guy Aldred said its title was too tame: he would shortly publish a new journal called *The Red Scourge*. It did not appear, and it was two years before the next paper was published, but the propaganda continued.

Glasgow was still a city of street-corner diversions. The late afternoon stroller might be entertained, saved, damned, cured or emancipated, or he might buy a comb that would also cut his hair, just as he pleased. *The Lily of Laguna* was the music of many mendicant tap-dancers. The short-statured evangelist Wee Willie Murray, with his messianic message, was the good-natured butt of laughing boys in big caps, grimy mufflers and worn-out shoes. They cheered Wee Willie's evengelical exhortations, in mocking enthusiasm, and they sang with him in treble or cracked voices. And when he had had enough, they seated him on his platform-chair and carried him off shoulder high in joyous procession. He smiled through it all, not approving of the mockery, but happy at the youthful boisterousness of his tormentors.

The city stroller might come upon the Tramp Preachers, dressed in worn hodden grey suits, dusty, proud of their empty pockets and unfilled stomachs, calling the reprobate to share their blessed redemption. The 'Clincher' (William Petrie) might be afield, a contrast to the preachers, in tall silk hat and frock coat, selling his little journal of wit and wisdom, and declaring that he was the only sane man in Glasgow, and had a certificate to prove it. This was true. Arising out of some quirk of a court case, he had been required to show by medical certificate that he was in his right mind.

And there was Sam Bryden, kerbside atheist. A tall, gaunt, elderly man, he had no platform. He stood, or strode agitatedly back and forth, in the centre of his audience, whom he held entranced by his husky oratory. He spoke, his head thrown back, his eyes closed, pouring from his wet lips a cascade of abuse at the Old Testament patriarchs, the New Testament Apostles, and priests of every time. He believed that God could not exist with such unsavoury associates. He sometimes gave a change of programme. Then his bubbling lips erupted in a fulsome eulogy of Robert Burns, which remained delightfully fresh in hyperbole despite a hundred tellings.

More seriously, there were the political groups, in wide variety, mostly known by their initials. There were the I.L.P., the C.P., the A-P.C.F., the S.W.R.P., the S.P.G.B., the W.O.F, and, for a time, the B.S.I.D.L.P. (the British Section of the International Socialist Labour Party), and several more. The Labour Party was in power in the Town Council, and stood in the wings at Westminster.

In their progressive zeal, the Council members were determined to make Glasgow a modern city with traffic lights to facilitate the flow of the multiplying motor cars. This meant the closure of street corners which were traditionally platform sites, places where their own party had planted its roots not so long ago. Where there were traffic lights there could be no meetings, and even where there were as yet no lights, the invading motor car imposed its own veto. So the evangelists, the entertainers and the politicians had to go.

They did not go quietly. Free speech fights erupted at many of the cherished places. Foremost in the battles were the A-P.C.F. and the S.W.R.P. In 1929, the Glasgow University Students' magazine *Ygorra* printed a photograph of Barlinnie Prison, describing it as the 'Headquarters of the Communist Party Anti-Parliamentary Confederation, where non-workers of the world unite.' Aldred denounced this as a disgraceful picture, sneering at the free speech struggle of the common people. Certainly the reference to 'non-workers' was obtuse and unfeeling in a city of poverty-stricken unemployment. At that time the students were mostly Tory. They had tried to break the General Strike, and had taken over the running of the Glasgow trams. They would have been better employed at their studies, and could have left the breaking of the strike to its 'leaders', the General Council of the Trades Union Congress.

In 1931 Glasgow Green once more became a freespeech battleground. As we have already noted, a bye-law prohibiting meetings there without a permit had been passed in 1922: Guy Aldred and others had defied the ban and had appealed against the convictions of himself and others. The appeal was heard on November 21st before the Lord Justice Clerk, Lord Hunter, and Lord Henderson. The Lord Justice Clerk had agreed that as the law stood a small boy could be prosecuted for playing a Jew's Harp on the Green. The Appellent had argued his case well, but while His Lordship was not enamoured of the terms of the bye-law, the Appellant had failed to convince him that it was repugnant to the laws of Scotland to regulate the admitted right of public speaking. As a result of those remarks, the Glasgow Corporation Parks Committee withdrew the ban on that part of the Green lying outside the gates, and known as Jail Square. But two years later, in 1926, on the recommendation of the Magistrates's Committee, the prohibition was reimposed. There was a lull in the contest, and the few infringements were ignored, but in 1931 the Green became again the centre of attention, this time with less excuse by the authorities that it was a bedlam of tipsters and medicine men. The Tramp Preachers were the first to be charged with illegal speaking on the Green.

The Tramp Preachers belonged to the 'Brotherhood of the Way'. They tramped through the United Kingdom, as they conceived Jesus to have tramped through Judea, penniless, and with nowhere to lay their heads. When they were fined for speaking without a permit they had no money to pay the fines, nor would they appeal unto Ceasar. So they were sent to prison, in a court emblazoned with the civic motto: 'Let Glasgow Flourish by the Preaching of The Word.'

John McGovern had just gone to the House of Commons as the I.L.P. member for Shettleston, and was making a name for himself by his disruptive conduct. He decided that the case of the Tramp Preachers was just cause for more disruption. On 2nd July 1931 he asked the Secretary of State, Mr. Adams (Labour), if he could order the release of those men. Mr. Adams said he would make enquiries. McGovern pressed the point, despite the Speaker's intervention, and subsequently 'disgraceful scenes' ensued. The *Daily Express* had headlines the following morning:

LAST NIGHT'S BIG FIGHT — IN THE HOUSE
Glasgow member Dragged Out.

McGovern had refused the Speaker's order to leave the House, and refused to go quietly with the doorkeeepers — four stout fellows, but of advancing years, in morning coats, linen fronts and gold chains — so:

'One attendant took Mr. McGovern's hands. Mr. Becket pulled the hands off. The others arrived and seized Mr. McGovern by the legs and shoulders. Messrs Becket and Kinley threw themselves on the attendants. Mr. Maxton, sitting immediately behind leaned forward, his long locks dangling over his face and joined in....Slowly the struggling heap moved towards the door. As each successive pillar supporting the gallery, was reached, Mr. Maxton was dislodged, but renewed his hold on the other side of the pillar. Mr. Becket, seeing that his side was losing, took a leap on an attendent's back. Down they went in a heap on top of the others. Miss Jenny Lee, nearly a couple of yards away from the ring, shrank back a little. Messrs Brockway and Campbell Stephen (ILP) played an unhappy part. They were neutral. They neither moved out of the way of the attendants nor attempted to obstruct them....and they were thoroughly ruffled by the wave which swept over them.'

So the struggling mass reached the door, and John McGovern was ejected, under suspension until the new Session, before which there would be a General Election. A 'Free Speech Committee' had been formed in Glasgow, and Guy Aldred, the Rev. Tom Pickering (Tramp Preacher), Edward Rennie (S.W.R.P.) and Harry McShane, who at

217

that stage was acting without C.P. endorsement, had already appeared in Court for speaking at The Green without a permit. Now McGovern, in doubtful standing with the I.L.P., which had mixed feelings about his unparliamentary behaviour, joined them. On July 5th a crowd of about six thousand gathered on the Green and was addressed by a number of speakers. The police did not try to stop the meeting, but 'took names', which led to the appearance in court of Aldred, McGovern, McShane, Pickering, Rennie, John Heenan (I.L.P.), Willie McDougall (A-P.C.F.), Andrew Reilly (Irish Workers' Party), Daniel Lanaghan (Irish Labour League), and Joseph McGlinchy (Distributist). Aldred defended all the accused and asked for a Stated Case for Appeal.

The Communist Party was not anxious to get involved in a struggle for free speech, which was not surprising, considering the suppressions taking place in the Soviet Union. Harry McShane had to 'drag them in.' (*No Mean Fighter*. Pluto Press, 1978). Yet such huge demonstrations could not be ignored, especially as there was a roving representative of the Communist International in the city at that particular time.

The problem was solved by using Harry McShane. He was organiser and leader of the unemployed. By using him, the demonstrations could be reported to Moscow as unemployment protests — which, in fact, he made them to a great extent — but to those who preferred to think of them as demands for free speech, they could be considered as such. With McGovern, they began as one thing and merged into the other.

Aldred was not greatly interested in demands for the 'Right To Work'. He did not think wage slaves should demand burdens for their backs, but should work to abolish wage slavery. The more youthful members of the Group, and of the S.W.R.P., used to answer the slogan-shouters': 'We want Work' with the counter-slogan: 'We want Nourishment'. To reformist demands for more Parish relief, they would add sardonically 'And a bag of coal and woolly drawers.'

However, to meet this new dimension of the demonstrations, the Free Speech Committee was turned into a permanent Council of Action at a meeting of two hundred delegates from a number of organisations held in Central Halls, Glasgow, on September 19th 1931. It was agreed that the Council evolve the machinery of organisation necessary to set up other Councils of Action to deal with the 'Chronic economic condition which is the normal condition of capitalist society.' Aldred started a new monthly Journal *The Council*, as an unofficial organ of the Council of Action.

John McGovern says in his autobiography (*Neither Fear Nor Favour*: Blandforth Press, 1960) that the Communist Party wanted to take over the unemployed movement.   This is probably true, as it was the policy of the party to seem always to be the spearhead of the workers' struggle.   McGovern says he wanted to prevent this.   Maybe, but his methods were strange.   On the day of the big riot he and Harry McShane addressed a meeting at North Hanover Street, next to the City Chambers.   They both urged their audience to rally to the Green that evening.   McShane had addressed a meeting the day before in similar terms.   He then led a procession of unemployed from Warwick Street in the direction of Glasgow Green, but had stopped at Albert Bridge, short of the forbidden territory.   There he had mounted the parapet and had urged the crowd to gather in Glasgow Green the following evening, and to 'bring your sticks'.   The excited crowd took up the cry.

It seems that after the meeting in North Hanover Street and an unemployed deputation to the City Chambers, the police Superintendent of the Central Division sent a message to C.P. headquarters to the effect that no meetings would be allowed in the Green, and no processions would be allowed to assemble there on the night in question.   If any crowds assembled there, it would be quite in order to lead them off in small processions, but not to address them.   This information was not passed on to John McGovern, nor to the Council of Action.

So on October 1st McGovern led the East End contingent of unemployed to Glasgow Green, where, he says, one hundred thousand persons had already gathered (the police estimate was forty thousand), but there were no communist leaders.   McShane, who had urged his audiences to rally in their thousands and to 'bring their sticks', did not arrive till it was 'pitch dark and we could not see a thing.' (N.M.F.)   He did not bring a stick because the Party had instructed him not to.   He did not lead a crowd because the police had instructed the party not to.   He arrived with one comrade, Bob McLellan.   He and McLellan were getting a section of the crowd into marching order, presumably to march them away, as he had obeyed the Party orders up to that point, but he maintains it was to withstand the onslaught of the two hundred police who had gathered there.   In the event that is not what he did.   The appearance of McGovern and his followers was, to the police chief, a defiance of his warning.   He ordered his men to charge.

McGovern was assaulted and arrested at once.   McShane found himself behind the charging police, and, happily not recognised, got into the darkened Green.   There he met a crowd, evidently with their

219

sticks, for they wanted to 'have a go at the police.' McShane, having urged them to bring their sticks, now urged them not to use them, for they would be slaughtered. (N.M.F.) He led them, not to the affray, but away from it, over the suspension bridge to safety.

The Communist International Representative was not pleased. He sent for McShane and told him that, as McGovern had been arrested, he (McShane) must go and get himself arrested also. In abject obedience, characteristic of the party leaders of the time, Harry was putting on his shoes to get arrested when news came that two policemen had been thrown into the Clyde and killed. The Representative then instructed McShane not to get arrested, but to be ready to leave for Moscow. Fortunately, the rumour was false, and Harry was allowed to stay at home.

The rioting lasted over the weekend. McGovern, having his injuries dressed in a police cell, was told by the doctor: 'The city is in a grip of terror. The boys are smashing windows and stealing in every street. They are playing mighty hell.'

On the Monday Guy Aldred held a meeting in the Green. Two I.L.P. members of the Council of Action also spoke. Aldred trounced McGovern and McShane. They had stirred up the people, he said, for no other reason than to lead them. McGovern had now made sure that he would be nominated as I.L.P. candidate, a champion of the unemployed. McShane was using the free speech issue to establish himself as a leader of the unemployed, in pursuit of palliative reforms. There was no attempt to place power in the hands of the people.

McShane mounted the platform. In his autobiography he says he *demanded* a hearing. As Aldred made a point of giving a hearing to his antagonists, little demand would have been neccesary. McShane said: 'We have had the demonstration. A number of people have been arrested, a number of people are in hospital. The casualties are all on our side. We have got to organise for next time and make sure the casualties are on *their* side.' (N.M.F.) This was the kind of rabble-rousing Aldred had just condemned, for, having induced a hundred thousand persons to assemble on the Green when it was 'almost pitch dark', neither McGovern nor McShane knew what to do with them, or with themselves. One got arrested right away, and the other hastily departed.

McShane was arrested a few days later, at his home in the early hours, and charged with mobbing and rioting. It was not till January 18th. of the following year that he, McGovern and ten others appeared before the Sheriff. McShane was the only one not charged

with assault.   Superindent Sweeny of the Central Division confirmed
that he had sent word to the C.P. headquarters that processions to the
Green would not be allowed, but small separate processions could be
led away from the Green.   McShane had conformed to this instruction
and was acquitted.   McGovern was acquitted because he was in
custody before the violence erupted.   The ten others, rank and filers,
who had 'brought their sticks', were each sentenced to three months
imprisonment.   There is no firm statement on the number of
demonstrators injured, but four policemen were injured, and seventy-
seven shops had plate glass windows smashed.   (Full account in
Glasgow evening papers, January 18th, 1931.)

The appeal against the convictions of Aldred and others for
speaking on the Green on July 5th 1931 came before the High Court
of Justiciary on October 17th, 1931.   The appeal was unsuccesful,
and the fines imposed by the lower court confirmed, but observations
made by the Lord Justice General in disposing of it were brought to
the notice of the Parks Committee, and on March 3rd, 1932, the
offending bye-law was repealed, and replaced by a bye-law which
gave the right of public speaking on such places as would be set aside
by Notice for that purpose.

The part of the Green set aside for public meetings was known as
'The Old Bandstand'.   The Council of Action accepted this arrangement — with the exception of the C.P. and the S.W.R.P.   The C.P.
Delegate, Aitken Ferguson, said that they would be satisfied only
with the Green 'from Jail Square to Nelson's Monument' — ignoring
his former contention that freedom to speak in the Green was just a
licence for racing tipsters and cranks.   One meeting was subsequently
held at the designated spot.   This was addressed by Aldred, Maxton,
McGovern and Jean Mann.   Then the agitation was dropped.
McGovern went to parliament, McShane, obediently and reluctantly,
went to Moscow.   Aldred maintained that this was only the first step
in a campaign which should press for the bye-law to be generally
implemented in every one of the City Parks and Open Spaces.

In July 1932 Rose Witcop died in London.   She was forty-
two.   Guy Aldred and Jenny Patrick, friends for several years, now
set up a free union.   Jenny ran the domestic side of Bakunin House,
and as a time-served compositor (although, as a female, not union
recognised), supervised the printing in the basement.   Bakunin
House kept open house, and the table was always laid for all present.

Those were years of intense poverty.   Money was scraped together
for each meal.   For two years Bakunin House was without gas or
electricity, for the bills could not be met.   Paraffin supplied light and

cooking, and an old, evil-smelling motor cycle engine gave power to the press.

There were often tensions of personality within the Group.   These expressed themselves in opposition to policies.   Aldred felt that they could not continue propaganda on a negative note.   Labour parliamentarianism had been discredited.   'Now let us preach *socialism*. To propound anti-parliamentarianism above socialism was to destroy socialism.'   He would remain an anti-parliamentarian, but the stress should now be on the formation of the United Socialist Movement. The ballot box could be used for anti-parliamentary propaganda.

But the A-P.C.F. had uncompromising anarchist traditions, held with an almost religious conviction.   They did not believe in the ballot box, even as a tactic, and firmly adhered to a negative line of propaganda.   In the February issue of *The Council*, Aldred announced that he had left the A-P.C.F.   The next issue of the *The Council* was the last.

Guy Aldred was declared bankrupt. This was a personal bankruptcy, caused by a chronic inability to meet the usual bills of living — rent, rates, and so on.   It was soon discharged, as it had to be, since, had he been bankrupt, he could not have stood as any kind of candidate.

6: THE UNITED SOCIALIST MOVEMENT

Now Guy Aldred and Jenny Patrick moved to a tenement in Baliol Street, and there they lived for the rest of their lives. The A-P.C.F. found new headquarters in a shop in Commerce Street. Those who left the group with Guy Aldred — and these included a new young comrade, Ethel Macdonald — formed The Workers' Open Forum, with a rented hall at 3, Balmano Street.

Unity of the workers was the aim. Career-hungry politicoes were marching the unemployed all the way to London for a look at Westminster, pretending that this was doing something of value for the workless people. The workers should stay at home, form their own local Councils, and invest them with the power of the producers. The I.L.P. had recently left the Labour Party, and was being wooed on two sides: by the Communist Party for a United Front, and by Trotsky to form a Fourth International. Aldred later attacked the Trotskyists, but at this early stage he wrote: 'I appeal to my comrades of the A-P.C.F., to the Communist League of Opposition, and to the I.L.P. to rally together to form a Fourth International. Trotsky is right: we must have a united proletariat.'

The upshot of this line of persuasion was that the Townhead Branch of the I.L.P was expelled from the Federation and joined with the Workers' Open Forum to become the United Socialist Movement. Under the banner of this group Guy Aldred carried on his propaganda for the next thirty years.

The United Socialist Movement resolved that the group would make use of the ballot box at the coming Municipal Elections to bring the issue of open spaces for public speaking before the electorate. Aldred decided to hold a referendum by being nominated for every ward in the city. There were thirty-seven wards. He managed to get nominated as candidate for fourteen of them.

In his election address, Aldred 'outlined the history of Bye-law 20. He explained: 'I am not seekingTown Council honours, and I shall pursue none of the usual methods of obtaining votes. If you realise the vital nature of these questions, you will vote for me as a protest against the studied neglect of your citizens rights by the Lord Provost, the Magistrates, and the Councillors of the City of Glasgow, without distinction as to their political complexion....When the Town Council enacts bye-laws in the terms of certain statutes, those bye-laws are binding not only upon the citizens of Glasgow, but also upon the members of the Council....'

Aldred held outdoor meetings every night and a final rally in the City Hall. His political opponents said that the old 'anti-' was changing his coat. Guy replied that he had always believed in appealing to the people, and that this was what he was doing. To dissipate his energy over fourteen wards was not the way to gain a seat on the Council. When the votes were counted it was revealed that over a thousand citizens understood and cared enough to cast their votes for Aldred. As the 'referendum' covered only half the city, and for each vote cast there would have been perhaps three sympathisers not prepared to give their vote away, it may be reckoned that six thousand Glasgow folk agreed with Aldred on the matter of open spaces for Public Speaking in the city parks.

Aldred's line of action was to agitate for public speaking places in every park. Here the citizens could gather in democratic assembly and discuss their grievances and suggest remedies. From this would arise Communes which would challenge the bourgeous Government. He advocated this in opposition to party leaders who were promoting Hunger Marches. Aldred denounced these marches as stunts at the expense of the poor, contrived by the leaders to establish themselves and advance their careers. They would lead the unemployed workers, ill shod, ill clothed, all the way to London, to stand cap in hand before the House of Commons, supplicating their rulers for the right to be wage slaves, at the same time recognising the supremacy of England and Parliament. But indignation at the imposition of the means test required an outlet in noisy demonstrations. Aldred's attitude cost him much support, and his influence began to decline.

The Means Test was imposed on the demand of American bankers who insisted that Britain cut public spending and repay some of the War Loan owing to them. The pay of the Armed Forces was slashed, causing a mutiny at Invergordon, but worst hit were the unemployed. The current rate of unemployment pay was seventeen shillings per week (One shilling=five new pence) for a man, and fifteen shillings for a woman. If there was one or more adult wages coming into the household, no benefit would be paid at all, even if the wage was being paid to a son, or daughter or brother. The second unemployed person in the household got ten shillings, and the third only five.   Eight shillings would be paid for a wife, and two shillings for each child.

Aldred had always lived on the verge of poverty.   He took no fees for speaking, only the income from the sale of his paper and pamphlets, to the extent of his immediate needs.   When this source declined, he opened a second-hand bookshop in Buchanan Street. He was a hopeless bookseller, and was easily persuaded to 'lend' a book rather than sell it.   The shop failed, but not until many of Guy's own books, and almost all of Caldwell's little stock, had been sold, or 'borrowed'.

Then Guy opened an office in Queen Street and advertised it as an 'Advice Bureau.   Legal Advice.   Letters Written.   Typing done.' It was a miserable little office with a table, one chair, no lighting, no heating, no toilet (the one next door, belonging to the renting office, had to be used.)   A paraffin lamp supplied the light.

The customers were few.   Most were concerned with inablility to pay debts.   Would Guy write a letter?   Guy did not charge for his services, but left it to the client to make a donation.   He often received nothing from folk who thought he must be making something out of it somehow.   Mostly he was rewarded with a shilling, which was as much as could be expected from his poverty-stricken customers.   Fortunately there were no customers for typing, because his assistant, Ethel Macdonald could not yet type, although she was teaching herself, and quickly succeeded in reaching a high degree of proficiency.   Ethel, at that time in her mid-twenties, had joined the A-P.C.F. from the I.L.P., and was one of those who left the A-P.C.F. with Guy Aldfred.   She had worked at various jobs, in a news agents, as a waitress and so on, but now she worked full-time with Guy, sharing his poverty.

The Guy Aldred 'Advice Bureau' was a flop, at least financially, although without doubt it fulfilled a desperate need in the city of those days, a need that still exists, of course, and is today met, partially at least, by free legal advice and the Citizens Advice Bureau.   Once again, Aldred was far ahead of his time.   However, it hardly paid the rent, but it did at least serve one good purpose.   A member of the Group got a job selling Gestetner Duplicators.   He was able to allow prospective customers a month's free trial of the machine.   He gave Aldred's name as a prospective customer, and left the machine in the Advice Bureau for three months.   Ethel mastered it, and energetically turning the handle, she and Guy produced a spate of broadsheets dealing with a variety of subjects of social concern.   They even produced an issue of a new paper called *The Attack*.

The U.S.M. had taken over the I.L.P. hall in Stirling Road.   Indoor
meetings were held there on Wednesdays and Sundays during the
winter months and a fund raising social was held on a Friday.   A new
recruit to the movement at that time was John Taylor Caldwell, the
present writer.   He was a sailor, but still a dreamy, introspective
young man, dwelling much in his mind on the Why and the Wherefore
of existence.   He looked for answers in books and in human
intercourse.   He listened to all the street corner meetings — the
religious ones at first, because they were in touch with the eternal.
When he discovered them to be a moronic bunch he turned to the
politicos.

Here was something more down to earth, more recognisable, more
amenable to cognitive digestion, but there was still something
missing.   There was an element absent from the soul-saving godly
sycophants, but missing also from the stomach-based morality which
called for proletarian justice.

The first Sunday in May 1934 Caldwell was strolling along
Glasgow's Trongate, deep in the depression of disillusioned youth,
with sad heart despite the golden sunshine of early Spring, when he
heard the distant music of fife and drum, calling voices and marching
feet.   It was a procession, and when it swung round from Glassford
Street, to the Square and on to Glasgow Green, he saw that it was a
May-Day Labour Procession, of several thousand men and women,
tramping along over square setts and tramlines, waving flags and
chanting slogans.   The women were not the slender girls of outlandish
dress and strident voice of later times, but buxom women in grey
shawls, the fading fashion of proletarian women, waving arms as big
as hams, and calling 'A pound a week to feed a polissman's horse: two
bob a week to feed a worker's wean!'   In the procession Caldwell saw
a lad he knew, and was told that they were all going to Glasgow Green
to hear Guy Aldred.   Caldwell fell into step.   A marching band
gives a sense of security, an 'at-one-ness' of common identity.

The procession wended its colourful way along the Trongate and
the Saltmarket and into the Green, and beyond to Fleshers' Haugh,
so-called because it was there that in the past the city butchers were
required to slaughter their beasts, instead of outside their shop doors
on the common highway, as they had done in medieval times.

Here the procession poured like water into a dust bowl, breaking
into droplets and being reconstituted as dark islands of white upturned
faces as each speaker drew his audience.   Each stood on a coal lorry,
with upturned shafts, while the great horses, freed from their labour,
too, for the day, raced and snorted in the sun.

Even Aldred's enemies, and he had many, could hardly deny that he was the greatest orator there. That, though, was not of first importance. Of more importance was the fact that even when he spoke of mundane things there was in his delivery, and implied in the content of his utterance, something indefinable, which spoke clearly, even without words that 'Thou shalt not live by bread alone.' He gave socialism a soul.

Caldwell did not join the Movement for another two years, having in the meantime attended many meetings. When he did join, his claim to notice was earned by his constancy and durability. With the other three, Guy Aldred, Jane Patrick and Ethel Macdonald, he first opened the door of the Strickland Press in 1939, and he locked it for the last time in 1958 — alone.

The black sea of economic depression swept over Bakunin Hall, and it foundered. Only the little office was left. Among the campaigns mounted from that tiny headquarters was a denunciation of the Empire Exhibition of 1938 staged in Bellahouston Park.

Guy Aldred was incensed at the effrontery of the Government in staging this display of Imperial wealth and power in a city of high unemployment, where the ragged and half-fed overcrowded the crumbling tenements, where only two shillings a week was allowed to feed a worker's child (and £1 was required to feed a policeman's horse).

Did the workers not see that this Exhibition was a deliberate taunt, an insult? It had been located in Glasgow, centre of the notorious (or glorious) Red Clyde, home of the wild parliamentarians who had set off for Westminster with revolutionary manifestoes in their pockets. That the Exhibition should have been held at all in a depressed Britain angered him, that Glasgow should have been chosen as its site infuriated him, that the Labour members of the Council, and in parliament, did not protest, but actually welcomed this parade of colonial exploitation as an economic boon to the city left him speechless — almost.

Another matter which received his attention was the appointment of a Commission to enquire into the marriage law in Scotland. In a letter to *The Evening Times* dated December 24th, 1935, he said: 'I do not think the Secretary of State for Scotland is to be congratulated on the Commission he has appointed to enquire into the marriage law of Scotland....I have studied the Scots law of marriage....and have collected a host of information on the subject, and I hold that this is an institution upon which the clerics, with their empty pews and their stupid English allies, have no right to speak. It is a sound, ancient institution based on common law and justifed by results.....'

The report of the Morison Commission was published fifteen months later. Aldred, who had gone to Edinburgh to put his point of view before the Commission, returned to the attack in the columns of the *Evening Times*: 'It is to be hoped that the people of Scotland will not be satisfied with the dull and mediocre report on the Scots law of irregular marriage....The doctrine of marriage by interchange of consent is the most rational and moral doctrine of marriage in the world....Because marriage is a spiritual union and not a union of bodies, the Scots irregular marriage must remain....irregular marriage requires consent, actual, living, ever-present consent and consecration....It requires no ceremony....Real marriage is not a rite but a fact....'

The meetings had not stopped.. With the outbreak of the Spanish Civil War they were held every night, and drew bigger crowds than at any time since the General Strike. Guy had been in correspondence with the anarchists of France for several years, and Andrew Proudhommeau, of Nimes, suggested that a Scottish anarchist would be welcome in Barcelona. Ethel Macdonald, secretary of the United Socialist Movement, was asked to go. Jenny Patrick was not a member of the U.S.M,. and her name was not considered, but she pointed out to Guy that she was more representative of the anarchists than Ethel. Ethel had come from the I.L.P. Guild of Youth, and had never even been an anti-parliamentarian, whereas she, Jenny, had been the secretary of the Glasgow anarchists as far back as 1916. So Guy co-opted Jenny as the A-P.C.F. representative, and she and Ethel set off for Spain. Jenny worked in the Ministry of Information in Madrid, and Ethel became the English-speaking radio propagandist in the Barcelona Radio station. Her Scottish voice was a special attraction, and her broadcasts aroused comment as far afield as the U.S.A.

When Ethel Macdonald joined Guy Aldred as a fulltime worker she lived in Cathcart Road, some distance from the centre of Glasgow. This was inconvenient. Guy and Jane Patrick lived in one room of a decaying tenement in Baliol Street, near Charing Cross. It was obviously better if they lived nearer each other. This was made possible by a sympathetic house factor. He rented Ethel a top flat in Gibson Street, half a mile away. The rent and rates were £8 per quarter. The idea was to have a girl lodger to share the expense.

It was just a coincidence that J.T. Caldwell, the present writer, decided at that time to leave seafaring, which had been his occupation for the past eleven years, and work fulltime for the Cause. It was suggested that, as he had no permanent residence, having lived between voyages in the Sailors' Home, he might care to share the house in Gibson Street. He agreed, and he stayed there for the next thirty-two years.

It was also a coincidence that he had been there only a week when Ethel and Jenny departed for Spain, and he and Guy had to cope on their own. Caldwell had enough wages coming from his last voyage to pay the firt quarter's rent of the house, but apart from that there was no dependable income for him and Aldred to live on. Aldred ceased going to his office at the Advice Bureau. Caldwell went there for several hours each day, and sat waiting for the possible call of somebody helpful, or to be helped. Nobody called. Guy sat at home writing material he had no means of getting published. It may be that he wrote the speeches Ethel delivered on the radio in Barcelona. They seemed beyond Ethel's experience or capacity at that time, and bore some of Aldred's characteristics. Neither party ever confirmed or denied this.

There is no room here to go into the intricacies of the Spanish Civil War. We may say simply that it was a conflict between the Left Wing Republican Government, properly elected, and the land-owning and property-owning classes. The Government were introducing reforms in land and factory conditions. Farm workers would receive a working wage, instead of a serf-like pittance. Unions would be recognised and wages in the factories increased. The Government was under fire from two directions. The monied people did not like the reforms, and the poor folk did not like their inadaquacy and tardiness. The explosion came when the land-owning Army officers, backed by the land-owning Church, revolted, and, under General Franco, attacked Government positions, in July 1936. The war lasted for three years, and was won by Franco with the help of Germans, Italians and Moors, and with the connivance of the Western Governments.

On the Government side there were many factions. Their differences were reflected in the many street meetings held in Glasgow and other cities, where much acrimony filled the air. The Stalinists, weakest to begin with, had resources to enable them to challenge the others and have some measure of success in taking over.

Eventually, of course, the elected Spanish Government, weakened by internal dissension and isolated by the policy of (very selective) non-intervention followed by the Western Governments, fell to the forces of reaction and international fascism, and a dark night of

Ethel Macdonald, reading the English language news over the Republican Radio, Spain, 1937.

Francoism and fascism fell over the Land and the people of Spain for many years.

Eventually, Ethel MacDonald was jailed by the communists in Spain during the struggle between them and the anarchists. She helped some comrades to escape, and became known as 'The Spanish Pimpernel'. When she returned to Glasgow she spoke in McLellan Galleries on 'Spain — a Lost Horizon'. She told the story of the communists' attack on the anarcho-syndicalists. It was a very stormy meeting, and there were several ejections. The uninitiated were confused. They did not know that, if the ghost of Marx haunted central Europe, Bakunin and Proudhon had their own domain in the south of the continent, and the old authoritarian spirit was still afraid of them.

In March 1938 a Socialist Anti-Terror Group was formed in Glasgow. It comprised some Trotskyists, a few I.L.P. members, and the U.S.M. Guy Aldred published a pamphlet *Against Terror in the Workers' Struggle*. In the preface he said: 'When Bakunin wrote of two communisms, of an authoritarian communism that would persecute like an autocratic State, and of a free communism, his remarks were viewed with scepticism. In those days no socialist dreamt that one socialist would take power in order to murder another.'

And still at the street corners of Glasgow, and in dingy halls, another wordy battle wss being waged. It was hoary in origin and fierce in execution.. It was the Aldred/Goldman contest. Emma Goldman had been an international anarchist when Guy still a youth. She had praised him in *Mother Earth*. During the war they quarrelled. Now Emma was no longer active, but, Guy said, she sailed into selected situations as the grand lady, and was surrounded by admirers and supporters, and was credited with work she had not done, and then would sail away again when the excitement was over. She had gone to Spain and had been accorded the attention to which she felt entitled. Now in Britain she was sponsored by the London Freedom Group, and befriended by Ethel Mannin and several intellectuals to whom the Spanish Civil War was a Cause. Aldred felt she was cashing in on a reputation too easily earned too long ago. *He* was the active libertarian-communist, the biographer and champion of Bakunin, the one who had suffered imprisonment. Sympathisers of Spain should have given their support to *him*.

He was made more angry when the rump of the A-P.C.F. roused itself from a state of desuetude and remembered that it was the Glasgow Anarchist Group before Guy Aldred had made it the

Glasgow Communist Group, and later the A-P.C.F. Now it changed its name to the Anarchist Federation and established a connection with the London Group. Guy had made Albion Street-Trongate corner his central outdoor meeting place, (not Brunswick Street, as some article writers have supposed), and here the Anarchist Federation pitched their meetings to answer the 'abuse of Guy Aldred'. An impartial arbitrator was sent from London to investigate and reconcile. He was Captain White, D.S.O., a Protestant Ulsterman who, disagreeing with Anglo-Irish policy, had resigned his Army commission in 1913. In October of that year he helped James Connolly to form a defensive corps to protect the striking workers against the onslaughts of the police. From this grew the Irish Citizen Army which played such a heroic part in the Easter uprising of 1916. The execution of their leader, James Connolly, changed the course of Irish — and indeed world — history.

Captain White managed to get both sides together. His first task was to get the mountain (Frank Leech, leader of the anarchists, was a big man) to come to Mohammed (Guy Aldred was turbaned with a bandage because he had recently been knocked down by a car). Eventually he had them all together in Bakunin Hall. The debate went on till 2 a.am., and an arrangement was made. A new name was thought up for a new group, but as the Captain disappeared in his battered old car and the comrades set out for their respective homes, everyone but the Captain, knew that nothing had changed. The Anarchist Federation brought Emma Goldman to speak in Shettleston Hall. There was nothing glamorous about Emma now. She was middle-aged, dumpy-figured, darkly dressed, and spoke quietly, rather like a returned missionary, about the organisation of the communes in syndicalist Spain.

On the early death of Frank Leech about two years later, the Anarchist Federation declined. It fell into the hands of two speakers of great wit and popular appeal, Edward Shaw and James Raeside. They drew big crowds and caused much laughter with their scathing denunciations of capitalism, communism and careerists. But they had little understanding of anarchism, believing it to be summed up in the sentiment 'Every man for himself, and the devil take the hindmost.' When they emigrated, to Canada and Australia respectively, the Group declined. But it revived, and operates today, as this book is written, with a broader range of enquiry and an appeal to the young, rather than to the hide-bound traditions of outlook.

William McDougall left the anarchists at the end of the Spanish Civil War and formed a Workers' Open Forum. This eventually had its headquarters at 50 Renfrew Street. The Open Forum lasted into the late 1950s, and when it closed it marked the end of the period of proletarian meetings in austere halls of wooden benches and bare floors. But the U.S.M. remained.

Guy Aldred had not heard from Sir Walter Strickland for several years when, late in 1937, a letter arrived. Alarmed by the approach of war, Sir Walter, who was 87 and intended to live to be 100, asked to have his letter published as an appeal to men of science to stop 'this march of homicide.' He said that he intended to come to Britain, where he had not been for fifty years, and to visit Glasgow, which was the best centre from which to operate. With Aldred's help he would launch a peace campaign, using his wealth (which 'was considerable' — reckoned to be about £100,000) to bring influential world figures together. Guy had the letter, which was three thousand words long, published in *The Malton Messenger*, the local paper covering the region of the Strickland estates in Yorkshire, and in the Cambridge University paper *Varsity*. However, Sir Walter died in August 1938.

The Yorkshire estate was entailed. His money was left for the furtherance of peace, and Guy Aldred was the executor. Unfortunately, Strickland had been so opposed to Imperial Britain that he invested all his money abroad, and in countries which were at war with Britain before the will was probated. Only a fraction of it was recovered (about £3,000) enough to buy some second-hand machinery and re-establish the Bakunin Press, but it was called the Strickland Press in memory of Sir Walter.

The Strickland Press was established at 104-106 George Street, facing Albion Street, Glasgow. Number 104 had an interesting history. The departing tenant was Mr. Brown, 88 years of age. He had started work in that shop as an assistant to his father, tin smith and gasfitter, at the age of eleven, and for seventy-seven years had worked nowhere else. When he was twenty-two, his father had been knocked down and killed by a horse carriage in busy, congested George Street. 'Everybody told me I was too young to carry on the business,' the old man told Caldwell and Ethel Macdonald, who were checking the premises for suitability, 'but I did.' He attributed this success, somehow, to the patronage of Dr. Lister, the well-known pioneer of antiseptic surgery, who was consultant at the nearby Royal Infirmary. Dr. Lister had called into the shop and asked the young man to make instruments which were required for his surgical innovations. 'He often came into this shop,' the old man proudly recalled. He showed off the heavy-barred fireplace where he had forged the metal and shaped the glass to the eminent surgeon's directions.

The Strickland Press was run by Guy Aldred, Jenny Patrick, Ethel Macdonald and John Caldwell. They worked as a family unit: no wages were paid. The basic hours of work were from 9 am. to 9 p.m., with an hour and a half off for dinner and about three quarters of an hour at tea time. The women took Saturdays off for housekeeping. Everybody worked from a sense of personal responsibility. Ethel laid it down as a firm dictum that, unlike Bakunin House, there would be no open house, and no welcome to gossips and idlers. Once a month a happy company of young fellows cycled through the blackout from Paisley after their days' work, seven miles each way, to help in the despatch of *The Word* to postal subscribers.

Many of Guy Aldred's pamphlets were republished at this time, including a third edition of ten thousand of *John MacLean*, also *Bakunin, Richard Carlile, Studies in Communism, Pioneers of Anti-Parliamentarianism* and *The Story of the Communist Party.* These and other re-issued pamphlets were bound in two volumes under the title *Essays in Revolt.*

During the war the Strickland Press published the anti-war and monetary reform pamphlets of the (then) Duke of Bedford, cousin of Bertrand Russell. The Duke was not a socialist. His association with Guy Aldred was because of his pacifism, and his inability to have his unpopular writings published during the war. Aldred and the Duke spoke from the same platform on several occasions and became good friends. A few years after the war ended there was a parting of the ways, but the friendship did not altogether fade. For twelve years the Duke wrote regularly for *The Word.*

The Word was Guy Aldred's last journal. It appeared every month for twenty-five years. *The Word* was a strange title for a socialist-atheist paper. Friends puzzled over it and detractors sneered at it. It was chosen after much deliberation. The concept was not new in Guy's thought. It was present in his Boy Preacher sermons and appeared again in agnostic garb in his Barlinnie Prison essays. To him it was the inexpressible element in man's unconsciousness that gave rise to a change (hopefully an improvement) in the species. It worked in conjunction with material conditions. *The Word* was also a challenge to the Establishment in Glasgow, whose City motto was 'Let Glasgow flourish by the Preaching of the Word'. It was a taunt at the Church, which had forgotten 'The Word' in blessing 'The Sword'. It was a challenge to the parliamentary socialists whose representative, in the person of Sir Patrick

Dollan ('He'll be Sir Patrick before he's Saint Patrick', John Mclean had predicted) now appeared in military uniform to review the troops in George Square, in his double capacity of Lord Provost and Lord Lieutenant of the County.

The United Socialist Movement which had been formed to offer a wide front for varying socialists, was often little more than the working squad for Aldred meetings. It met for Group meetings, and for years maintained a Discussion Group. A public meeting was held in Central Halls every month, but despite the abilities of Ethel Macdonald the Group was really held together by Guy. For a time he was chairman of the No Conscription League, but resigned when a resolution was passed making the League funds available for objectors who accepted conditional exemption. Aldred held that the Fund should be expended only on the requirements of the absolutists. He helped conscientious objectors in every way — to formulate their Statement to the Tribunal, by appearing before the Tribunal as spokesman and as witness, and he helped to carry many cases to the Appeal Tribunal in Edinburgh.

After the war, during the years 1946 to 1948, Guy Aldred promoted the idea of world government, and his office at 106 George Street, Glasgow, became the headquarters of the World Federalists. He explained his thinking at a meeting held in Central Halls on April 7th, 1946:

'Consider the world today, and see how stupid, how thoughtless, is all our activity. In this city tonight a meeting is being addressed by a leading freethinker, Joseph McCabe, a man of about eighty years of age. He had travelled nearly five hundred miles in wintry weather to address a meeting in a cinema. And what is his subject? "Can Christiantity Survive?" It shows how far we have fallen when the leader of a once radical movement can travel so far to speak on such an inane subject. What does the survival of Christianity matter when we are faced with the possible destruction of millions of human beings? A more important subject would be "Can Man Survive?" What we need to consider is, what to do to prevent world chaos.....

'Surely it is evident that our past propaganda is getting out of touch with the world of fact. We must change our method of approach. In a world where distance is annihilated we must alter the focus of our vision. In a world growing smaller we must develop an all-embracing world outlook. We must propagate the idea of a world republic, with a world citizenship.

Nationalism must be ended. And so must inter-nationalism, for internationalism implies nationalism, and the representation of national governments. What we require is the direct representation of the people of the world as world citizens in a non-national assembly. By the policy, practice, and feeling of cosmopolitanism we must do away with national states, and the treaties and intrigues that lead to war.'

Aldred said that he did not forswear any of his socialist or anarchist beliefs, but there was no use letting disaster overtake us. We could not walk into a socialist society if we were corpses. Many of his anarchist friends objected to the word 'Government'. Let them call it 'Administration' if they liked. He stood for the complete world citizenship, the direct enfranchisement by right of every person in the world, irrespective of sex or creed. He did not want anyone to think that the propagation of world government, or some system of world organisation to end war need interfere with their activities as socialists, anarchists, freethinkers, or even Christians. He wanted more, and not less, dynamism of opinion.

Aldred was now entering his sixties, but, with the ending of the war there was an increase, rather than a lessening of his activities. He wrote innumerable articles and letters; he addressed meetings from London to Aberdeen, he helped opponents of peacetime conscription, and he tried to build the new organisation of World Federalists.

7: THE BALLOT BOX

In May 1945 Guy Aldred was asked by the Scottish Union of Ex-service Men and Women to stand as Peace Candidate at the forthcoming General Election. Aldred agreed, and was nominated for the Glasgow Central Division where the United Socialist Movement had its Headquarters. There was also a Communist candidate as well as the three usual parties. Aldred stood as an Independent Socialist.

He knew that the stage had a different setting from 1922. So much had changed in the scenery, although it was the same drama that was being enacted. The Labour Party had settled in as part of the Establishment. It had been a stairway for the ambitious from work-bench to Treasury Bench. Some of the young men who had shared the platform with Guy in his youth were now peers of the realm, adding but little lustre to the Upper House. The Labour Party had become respectable and was a career structure for some young men and women, just as happened in the Trade Unions, where the ladder led from Shop Steward to Union leader.

Aldred made a pledge, which he repeated on each of the other five occasions on which he stood for parliament, that, as ten citizens of the constituency had been required by regulation to nominate him, the same number should be able to bring about his recall if he were elected. Those ten signatories should be able to demand the calling of a public meeting at which the candidate would be required to answer criticism, and if the meeting so willed he should be forced to present himself again to the electors for re-endorsement or rejection. The candidate should be paid by the constituency and should have a permanent office or 'Surgery' there.

In his election address he made no concessions to reform, except to say to the nurses in the Royal Infirmary (in his constituency) that hospitals should be 'socialised, not nationalised', and that, if elected, he would discuss with them radical readjustments of their conditions of service. To the soldiers awaiting demobilisation he said:

237

'All the parties are competing in promising you homes when you return. There can be no homes unless you take control of society and establish a Workers' Commonwealth. This smoke-screen of pretended immediate reform hides from you the irresponsible foreign policy the Government are pursuing, which means a Third World War.

'.....A last word. The Tories are opposed to fraternisation (with the ex-enemy or the people of the ex-enemy nation). The common soldier won the war, and, when war is over, he is a missionary of peace and healing. I do not say that any soldier should be told that he *must* fraternise, but I do say that, having won the war, he has the individual right to decide for himself.... After all, he and his dead comrades decided the issue.'

Aldred put in a staggering amount of work during the campaign, sometimes addressing three meetings in one day, yet on polling day, July 5 1945, he polled only 300 votes. He was still a freak candidate. Aldred did not expect to be top of the poll, but he can hardly have expected such a low vote. Yet he was not unduly dismayed. He had intensified his propaganda; he had secured a fair amount of press coverage; his election address had been delivered to almost every house in the Central Division. *Some* good must have been done.

In 1923 Guy Aldred had written a pamphlet entitled *Socialism and Parliament*, subtitled *The Burning Question of Today*. In 1928 he wrote a second part, which was subtitled *Government by Labour: A Record of the Facts'*. Those two pamphlets had several reprints, and by the time they appeared under the Strickland Press imprint in 1942, they had grown into booksize publications.

The first part is an exposure of those agitators who preached socialism and emancipation to the oppressed workers and thereby. elevated their own social position, and in most cases actually regarded this as a laudable achievement. Their names have slipped from public memory, and only the student need recall them and their deeds and misdeeds. Our reference to them here need only be brief. The general story is typified in the title of J.R. Clynes's autobiography *From Cotton Mill to Downing Street*. Clynes described what happened when King George V sent for MacDonald to form the first Labour Government.

'As we stood waiting for His Majesty, among the luxurious gold and crimson magnificence, I could not help marveling at the strange turn of fortune's wheel which had brought Mac-Donald, Thomas, Henderson, Clynes etc. to this pinnacle beside the man whose forebears had been kings for so long.'

His Majesty was very understanding, as a press report noted. '....Amusing jests were made regarding the transition from corduroy trousers to black silk knee breeches and gorgeously braided uniform trousers. Only those who were behind the scenes will ever thoroughly appreciate how much King George was responsible for putting the new ministers at ease. He was blind to minor breaches of etiquette, and appeared to be wholly oblivious to the fact if a ceremonial sword was on the wrong side of its flustered Ministerial wearer.'

Aldred had been attacking this careerist 'socialism' since the inception of the Labour Party in 1906. In those pamphlets he piles up the evidence for his case in an intricate denunciation.

Most of the issues are no longer of interest in themselves, but in the first part Aldred goes deeper into the subject and explains his approach to anti-parliamentarianism. Briefly, Guy Aldred believed that working-class history took a wrong turn when it entered into the parliamentary lists. The direction had been that of craft organisation and an emancipated working class organised on a basis of production guilds. But then they were caught up in the middle class agitation for the vote just at the time when their cottage industries were breaking up and they were being herded into factories. The working class were transformed into proletarians, and their agitations became more intensely political, expressing their aims in the Charter movement (1836—1848). When Chartism collapsed, the working class turned to industrial organisation once more. This might have given rise to Sovietism or Syndicalism had it not been felt that labour should be represented in Parliament. Hence an *independent* Labour Party, then the Labour Representation Committee, which became the Labour Party, wherein socialism was not an undisputed or wholly accepted doctrine. Bargaining *within* the system warred with the object of *changing* the system. The rise of the Labour party gave birth to a new professional class of politicians, whose personal interest was in the maintenance of the system and the improvement of the status of the members of Parliament.

Aldred wrote:

'The history of organised labour begins in the 18th century public house. No visions of Labour Premiers inspired the workers who gathered in the Masons' Arms, the Bricklayers' Arms, the Blacksmiths' Arms, the Jolly Painters', etc. In their humble way they pioneered two vested interests — the breweries and parliamentarianism. They pioneered a third thing — association and the workers' desire to struggle. Those festive societies gloried in beer drinking and the practice of initiating apprentices by grotesque ceremonies and weird incantations. Not much promise of an International Working Mens' Association is foreshadowed by such proceedings....But slow changes are recorded in the early Minute books of the associations, and we witness the rise of real unions. The bar atmosphere merges into that of the Committee Room. Records of penny fines for swearing or drunkenness give place to accounts of money being voted to the "Turn-Outs", that is, the strikers....

'From 1825 to 1832, when the Reform Bill was passed, the proletariat, now in actual existence, still followed the middle class leaders. Their political consciousness had not yet evolved the idea of Labour representation at Westminster....

'From 1832 to 1835 the working class protest against disfranchisement was industrial. The British workers entertained ideas of a Soviet Republic, and knew exactly what they wanted. The Builders' Union was formed in that very year that witnessed the passage into law of the Reform Bill. The Builders' avowed object was the Social Revolution, and a year later it became prominent by its activities. It subscribed to the message urged by Robert Owen, who maintained that capitalist competition had ruined the workers, and that the only way out was to take over industry and run it on a co-operative basis. The Unions were to set up guilds of producers who would strike in each industry for an eight hour day and control of the job. This would force out the capitalists and absorb their businesses into the guilds.

'In January 1834 this programme was adopted by the Grand National Consolidated Trades Union. The Grand National proposed to replace the House of Commons by a Workers' Industrial Administration, which was actually a Soviet system of society. For their association with this activity the famous Dorchester labourers were arrested and deported. The Union was broken by persecution and the employers throughout the country compelled the workers to sign the infamous "renunciation" of Unionism. By January 1835 Unionism had collapsed, and the Grand National Consolidated was a memory. The idea of emancipation remained, and the workers turned from direct action to political or parliamentary action. Sovietism was replaced by Chartism.

'In London one of the many Radical Clubs, called the London Working Mens' Association, headed by Lovett, propounded the six points of the famous Charter. To the surprise of the London Radicals the working men of the Black Country throughout England and Scotland rallied to the cry, and Chartism, with its tremendous socialist propaganda, preached by men like Ernest Jones, took the country by storm. The flame of Chartism survived till the year 1850 when its Great Petition fiasco ended the movement in scorn. Just as the workers turned from industrial to political action in 1835, so, on a larger scale, they reverted to industrial action. Trades Unionism now determined that the workers should move along the quiet paths of industrial negotiation and peace, with the strike threat as menace, rather than the strike itself. The cry of "No politics in the Union" replaced the Chartist agitation which had urged avowed insurrection in the event of political reform being denied. The peaceful slogan of "A Fair Day's Wage for a Fair Day's Work" was developed. Economic circumstances favoured this development down to 1867 when once again a crisis compelled the workers to demand a Commission of Inquiry and turn to legal and political action. In 1867 the Master and Servant Act placed masters and workers on an equal footing in the case of a breach of contract. Five years later the Unions were given legal status and their funds protected. Another four years saw picketing legalised. The year before this occurred, 1874, the Trades Council and the Trades Union Congress sanctioned the first two Labour members, who, in 1874, with great diffidence, carried the Labour standard into the House of Commons. This brings us to the threshold of the eighties, when the modern Social Democratic Movement was developed fully in Britain'.

Aldred's pamphlet went on to note that almost at once there were protests at the way the Socialist movement was headed. He quoted lengthily and with appproval from a pamphlet written by William Leibknecht in 1874:

'On the grounds of the class struggle we are invincible. If we leave it we are lost, because we are no longer Socialists. The strength and power of Socialism rests in the fact that we are leading a class struggle; that the labouring class is exploited and oppressed by the capitalist class, and that within capitalism effectual reforms, which will put an end to class government and class exploitation are impossible.

'Every attempt at action in Parliament, every effort to help in the work of legislation, necessitates some abandonment of our principles, deposits us on the slope of compromise and of political give-and-take, till at last we find ourselves in the treacherous bog of Parliamentarianism, which, by its foulness, kills everything that is healthy.   Socialism is no longer a matter of theory but a burning question which must be settled, not in Parliament, but in the streets and on the battlefield, like every other burning question.'

Aldred certainly believed in the power of the streets — the local Commune as against the National Party — but in the 1934 issuue of *Socialism and Parliament*, at a time of demonstrations and marches, he wrote:

'The power of the streets has been travestied and mocked by the absurd mass demonstrations of the Communist Party.   They had made the word "demonstration" the synonym of "meeting", and by making their demonstrations a daily occurrence have reduced them to a habit.   Although people may be war-like, even in war-time battles require preparation and cannot take place daily.   In addition the mass struggles of a revolutionary epoch rise spontaneously and are not organised like parades or gala days....The Communist Party organisers cannot distinguish between a revolutionary struggle and a political masquerade. Their manouvres are essentially reformist and parliamentary, notwithstanding the seeming wildness of their slogans.'

The second part of *Socialism and Parliament* is an examination of the records of the Labour Governments of 1924 and 1929.   It goes into details which need not be repeated here, as they are intended as supports to the central argument.   Aldred's criticism of parliamentary socialism, and his exposures of careerism had been main features of *The Commune* and they received full treatment in *The Word*.

When the Labour Party won the General Election of 1945 so decisively, the leaders of the I.L.P. felt that that was the organisation they should be in.   The question of re-affiliation arose.   According to John McGovern in his autobiography *Neither Fear nor Favour*, James Maxton, leading figure in the I.L.P. was willing to merge the two parties but hesitated to make a move.   When he died on 26th June 1946, there was a scramble out of the I.L.P. into the Labour Party.   McGovern stayed in long enough to speak for James Carmichael at the bye-election in Bridgeton caused by Maxton's death.

The writ for the bye-election was issued on August 16th, 1946, and polling took place on August 29th.   Five candidates were nominated.

They were:

James Carmichael   (I.L.P.)
John Wheatley (Labour)
Victor Warren (Conservative)
Wendy Wood (Independent Scottish Nationalist)
Guy Aldred (Independent Scocialist)

The Conservative's only hope, and that a slim one, was that the two Labourites would split the vote, for Maxton had held Bridgeton as an I.L.P. stronghold since 1922.   At the General Election only a year earlier, his majority had been over six thousand.   Wendy Wood was a personality candidate, working on her own.   She tried to look specially Scottish by wearing her everyday dress of Balmoral and a tartan skirt.   Aldred considered James Carmichael and John Wheatley as two *Labour* candidates, for, he said, Carmichael would join the Labour Party as soon as he had made use of the I.L.P, tradition to get himself elected.   He (Aldred) had been accused by some of splitting the left-wing vote.   It was not he who was splitting the vote but Wheatley, who, apointed by the Labour Party National Executive, was standing against the local man, Carmichael.

Aldred opposed them both on several specific points, apart from fundamental differences concerning the definition of socialism.   If elected he would be the representative of the constituents, not the delegate of a party.   He gave the same pledge that he had given at the General Election, to the effect that he would resign if called upon to do so by the electors.   He opposed the other two on the question of the proposed increase in M.P.s salaries from £600 to £1,000, and their target of thirty shillings for Old Age Pensioners.   On this, he said that the current average wage of £5 per week should be enough for members of parliament, since they were dedicated men and women anxious to serve the community without thought of personal gain.   If pressed on the point he would agree to an allowance for travel and London residence.   But this must be accounted for in every case.   As £5 was the amount required by the cost of living index, that should be the sum given to pensioners.   His suggestion that M.P.s should be content with the current industrial wage was regarded as derisory and flippant by his opponents who were, after all, in the running for a wage of £20 per week, with many benefits and an elevated social status, and it was so regarded by many of his audiences who were somewhat appalled by the prospect of electing an M.P. who would be no better off than themselves.   His demand that Old Age Pensioners should receive £5 and not thirty shillings was dismissed by one very poorly-dressed woman as disastrous.   'Does the speaker think,' she asked, 'that my husband is going to work if his old fellow gets £5 for doing nothing?'

It was a lively and interesting campaign. In the Labour-I.L.P. camp there was a fascinating babble of forked tongues. Every one of the I.L.P. notables (with the possible exception of Annie Maxton, sister of Jimmy) knew that not only were they about to join the Labour Party, but that Carmichael would join them with as little indecent hesitation as possible once he was elected. McGovern said from the platform that it had been Maxton's dying wish that his friend Jimmy Carmichael should take his place in Bridgeton. In his autobiography he tells a different story. He makes the dying Maxton say: 'I think the I.L.P will go down, and it is steadily losing its finest stock, and has a small unstable element that has no united policy. I feel I must go down with it. My wife and sister are very hostile to the Labour party, and I do not want to start a controversy in our family circle.'

Aldred issued a leaflet in which he said, among other things: 'SINCE THE I.L.P. CANDIDATE STANDS FOR REAFFILIATION TO THE LABOUR PARTY AND GENERALLY SUPPORTS THE LABOUR GOVERNMENT, I ACCUSE THE OFFICIAL LABOUR PARTY CANDIDATE, AND THE OFFICIAL LABOUR PARTY HEADQUARTERS, OF SPLITTING THE WORKERS' VOTE.
AND FOR WHAT REASON? BECAUSE BOTH PARTY AND CANDIDATE STAND FOR POWER AND CAREER, PLACE AND OFFICE UNDER CAPITALISM: THE DICTATORSHIP OVER DEMOCRACY OF ONE ESTABLISHED GROUP.
SINCE THE I.L.P. CANDIDATE STANDS FOR REAFFILIATION, I ACCUSE HIM OF SPLITTING THE WORKING CLASS VOTE ALSO, NOT BECAUSE HE HAS A DISTINCT POLICY BUT BECAUSE HE WANTS A PARLIAMENTARY CAREER.
QUESTIONS FOR MR. CARMICHAEL:
Why, if he supports Labours, does he oppose Labour's candidate?
Why does he not resign now from the I.L.P.?
Will he jilt the I.L.P. if elected and join the Labour Party?
What have the members of the I.L.P. to say about Carmichael's attitude?

Reporting the campaign in its news columns, *The Scotsman*, Edinburgh, said:

'It is a matter of supreme indifference to Mr. Aldred whether he becomes member for Bridgeton or ends bottom of the poll. As publicist and propagandist for his conception of Independent Socialism he takes the view, quite logically, that it is as well to spend his time and money on electioneering as on pamphlets and other media.'

An article in *The Bulletin*, Glasgow, describes a meeting which took place in the early afternoon in a back court, surrounded by grey, crumbling tenements:

'A van equipped with loud speaker and electioneering paraphernalia makes a noisy arrival at the piece of waste ground near London Road. A young man with a red tie does the "Oyez! Oyez!" act through a microphone and a young woman in a red mackintosh distributes "Vote For Aldred" leaflets.

'The microphone has a magically magnetic effect. The audience has already swelled to 100, in addition to the occupants of a dozen "Box seats" — housewives who lean curiously over window-sills and remain to be amused and amazed by this most independent and unorthodox of all candidates.

'A stout figure, carelessly dressed in a knickbocker suit prepares for his oration by sucking a throat pastille, then he mounts the platform. The practised street orator scorns the microphone as "artificial", but even his voice cannot compete with a three-cornered canine contest, and he waits laughingly till the dogs have barked themselves out before he starts his tirade of scorn and accusation.

'Almost at once he is calling for old-age pensions of £5 per week, justifying his claim by "collaring" all the money spent on armaments. And what is good enough for old-age pensioners is good enough for Guy Aldred, if, and when, he is M.P.....

'He makes it very clear that it would be no personal favour for him to go to Westminster. "I'm not going to scramble to get into parliament," he says. "Parliament isn't a very desirable place. There's better company in Barlinnie Prison. And I should know: I have been to jail for eight years because of my beliefs, and I've an unconquerable readiness to go to prison again if necessary."

'He pauses and reaches for the lemonade bottle which serves as a carafe, and, refreshed by water, he tells his audience of "common people" that he believes in them, then flays them. "Goodness knows you need a lot of believing in sometimes, but if there's no hope for you, then there's no hope for anybody."

'There's no pleading for votes with Aldred. He tells the people that if he isn't at the top of the poll the loss will be theirs.

' "You look on me as a roughneck, don't you?" he asks, and adds that in some respects they're right, but he is a roughneck with a love of truth and culture who believes in the common people....'

In its 'Pertinent and Otherwise' column, *The Bulletin* brought out, under cover of amusement, two essential items of criticism in Aldred's campaign.

LOOSE TALK

'That was a pretty shocking proposal that Guy Aldred made in Bridgeton the other night. He said, if you remember, that if ten electors could propose a man for parliament, it was only fair that ten electors should be able to call him to account after he was in. Golly, it's as well Parliament isn't sitting, or there would be some question about that. What a way to carry on. Where does he think he is? In a democracy?

'But apparently Guy wasn't fooling, because he said that if he was returned and people started taking a dim view of him, he'd call a public meeting, and if the general vote was agin him, he'd resign.'

The same column, three days later, read:

'Seriously, though, this chap Aldred who is standing simply isn't playing the game. Remember the other day he promised that if the electors didn't like what he was doing he would resign? That was bad enough, but now the man is saying that he only wants £250 of the £1000 salary if he is elected, and that the rest can go into a trust fund for the benefit of the Constituency.'

The London *Times*, which away back in 1819, had, in its editorial columns called Thomas Paine and Richard Carlile monsters for their writing and publishing the *The Age of Reason*, now, in 1946, acclaimed Aldred as a man similar in character to Richard Carlile.

The result of the poll was:

James Carmichael (I.L.P.) 6,351
John Wheatley (Labour) 5,180
Victor Warren (Conservative) 3,987
Wendy Wood (Ind. Scot. Nat.) 2,575
Guy Aldred (Ind. Socialist) 405

After the election the exodus from the I.L.P. continued. Mc-Govern and Campbell Stephen were among the first to shake the Maxton tradition from off their feet. Brockway had already done so. Carmichael waited a year, then the hard core of I.L.P. voters in Bridgeton who were not prepared to give their allegiance to a Labour candidate found that they had voted for one in the person of James Carmichael.

One of the I.L.P. members of Parliament who went over to the Labour Party was Campbell Stephen, representing Camlachie, where he had been returned with a vote of 15,000. Not long afterwards,

Stephen died, and a bye-election was held in Camlachie in the cold inclement January of 1947. Six candidates were nominated: Charles MacFarlane (Conservative), John M. Inglis (Labour), Annie Maxton (I.L.P.), R.B. Wilkie (Independent Scottish Nationalist), Guy Aldred (World Government and Independeent Socialist), R. Goodfellow (Liberal).

There had been four I.L.P. members in the Commons: Buchanan (Gorbals), McGovern (Shettleston), Maxton, (Bridgeton) and Stephen (Camlachie). These were the four Marx brothers. George Buchanan had not waited for the death of Maxton before he deserted to the Labour party. This desertion (writes McGovern in *Without Fear or Favour*), was one of the greatest blows dealt to Jimmy Maxton. So McGovern waited will Maxton was dead, then he 'felt free' to leave the barren I.L.P. for the more fruitful field. Next to leave was Campbell Stephen, but he died before any benefit could accrue. James Carmichael had to *use* the I.L.P to get into Parliament before he could betray it. He had told the electors of Bridgeton:

> 'It will do no harm to have a Labour Government kicked from the Left, because at the moment they are being kicked from one direction only....We have been told by a Socialist Brass-hat that it is their intention to crush the I.L.P.....That is a new way of expressing their desire for democracy and freedom.'

Now, a year later, having kicked himself in a hopeful direction, he was helping the Labour brass-hats to crush the I.L.P in Camlachie. Maxton's dying wish, so tenderly recalled by John McGovern, that Carmichael inherit Bridgeton, was quite forgotten.

Aldred wrote in *The Word* (Feb. 1948):

> 'The "Maxton Tradition", an absolute legend, was exploited by the I.L.P. to secure the return of Carmichael for Bridgeton. Now that he has joined the Labour Party, the local I.L.P. has issued a manifesto demanding his resignation, and stating that the I.L.P. had done more for Carmichael than he had for the I.L.P. This may be true enough, but why was this not said at the time of the election? And what right had Maxton to nominate his successor?'

If Maxton had such a right, he evidently did not have much sound judgement to go with it. But MacGovern was not one to let truth disturb a good story: it is likely that Maxton made no such claim. Now, at Camlachie, to McGovern, Carmichael and all other erstwhile I.L.P.ers, Maxton and his tradition had become an embarrassment. The seat had become vacant because Campbell Stephen had died only a few weeks after handing it and himself over to the Labour Party. The I.L.P. considered the seat to be theirs because their candidate had been voted into it. The Labour party considered it theirs because their man, who had had been voted into it, had made them a present of it, intending to become their man. Annie Maxton, who had considered Aldred an interventionist at Bridgeton, was now so regarded herself at Camlachie. When she, who stood for the I.L.P., and Inglis, who stood for the Labour Party, between them lost the seat to the Tory, she was abused as the one responsible. In *The Word* Aldred quoted from *Reynold's News* for February 1st, 1948:

> 'One lesson of Camlachie is that *splinter parties* — I.L.P., Liberals, or Nationalists —have no serious place in Scottish urban politics, except to aid reactionaries.'

The election result was: Charles McFarlane (Con.) 11,085; John Inglis (Labour) 10,690; Annie Maxton (I.L.P.) 1,622; R.B. Wilkie (Ind. Scot. Nat.) 1,320; Guy Aldred (Ind. Soc.) 345; R, Goodfellow (Lib.) 321.

For once, but not for the last time, Guy was not at the foot of the poll. The Duke of Bedford, who did not usually comment on Aldred's election activity, on this occasion wrote in his commentary column in *The Word*:

> 'A capacity to display intelligence at election time is never a strong point in the British public, who show singularly little concern with regard to that all-important factor, the personal character of one who offers himself as their parliamentary representative, and not much ability even to estimate the merits of the policy which he advocates. Provided a candidate be not an atrociously bad speaker and does not happen to represent a Party of whose misrule the people are getting sick, he is likely to be successful if only he has behind him more Party funds, and a larger volume of propaganda than his rivals. At Camlachie, as far as I can judge, the electors' first choice was the second worse candidate offered them, their second was the worst, their third, who gained far less support than the other two, was the fourth best, their fourth the third best, their fifth the best, and their sixth the second best.'

Guy Aldred had booked a hall in the heart of Bridgeton — the Town Hall — to denounce the I.L.P. parliamentarians in particular, and parliamentarianism in general. He was in the heartland of Maxton territory, where Jimmy Maxton had flourished so long, and had been stifled so hastily. His subject was 'The Meaning of Camlachie'. Here he denounced all concerned in 'this disgraceful episode of careerist betrayal.'

Aldred had described himself as a World Government candidate, and so devoted much of his campaign to the propagation of that idea, but just as much time was spent on anti-parliamentary propaganda. This probably accounted for his consistently low vote. People did not understand why he should stand for Parliament if he did not want the privileges that went with the job. Nor did they understand any better when he quoted Proudhon's dictum that 'Universal suffrage leads to reaction.' (Expounded in *General Idea of the Revolution in the 19th Century.*) He meant much the same as he did when he wrote in *Socialism and Parliament* that 'Parliamentarianism leads to fascism.' To state the case in absurd brevity (Proudhon takes a whole book), it is that the history of government travels in a circle, giving us Absolute Power, which gives place to Constitutional Power, which gives place to People's Power, which gives place to Dictatorship. So we are back to Absolute Power. Hence, for the radicals of the 1830s to call for manhood suffrage in a governmental framework was simply to give another push to the roundabout. What was required was a new concept of social organisation — the administration of things, in place of the perpetuation of power and authority.

The pretence that Parliament was a democratic law-making body was false. It had originally been a bargaining chamber between the powerful land-owners and the Crown; then the merchants moved in, to debate on charters and concessions, then the industrial capitalists had used Parliament to protect their interests, and finally finance capital had taken over. Members of parliament were always motivated by an *interest*, — a class interest, a Party interest, a personal interest — and only if it furthered those interests were they concerned with the voters' interests. The ruling class had personal interests before they became M.P.s. That was often *why* they became M.P.s. Labour members rarely had personal interests outwith Parliament, but with 'M.P.' after their name, they hastened to acquire them. This was part of the deception of Socialist Parliamentarianism.

The delusory nature of this assembly could be noted by the conditions the members accorded themselves: conditions of club-like comfort, as of men (and women) there on an amateur occupation, engaged in something ancillary to their prevailing interests. Could we tolerate a situation in which miners or factory workers stayed away from the job for which they were paid in order to make money in other interests? Should there be a lounge, a restaurant, a licensed smokeroom at the pithead, from which miners could proceed to the coalface only when they felt like it, and often somewhat the worse of alcoholic lubrication? Was it not time our alleged representatives ceased to be over-paid part-time workers; ceased, in fact, to be delegates of a Party, and became the spokesmen of their constituents? He proposed in this election, as he had on other occasions, that M.P.s be controlled by their constituents, subject to recall to answer criticism, and paid the national average wage for industrial workers, plus expenses. This would make parliamentary work a 'calling'. Only sincere, dedicated men and women would want to go there. Few familiar faces would remain.

Aldred's arguments for World Government tended to evaporate in the heat of the Korean War, and to perish in the chill of the Cold War. He said there were forty-four M.P.s associated with World Federalism, but none of them dared support him. It was not that the Labour members did not know of *The Word*. A free copy of every issue was sent to every one of them for over twenty years. In spite of his poor opinion of parliamentary socialists he had several friends among them, but only if many of their ideas were in accord with his own. Rhys Davis (West Houghton) visited him several times, spoke with him on the pacifist platform, and wrote for *The Word*. Fred Longden (Deritend) also wrote for *The Word*, and had his book *The Proletarian Heritage* published by the Strickland Press. Creech Jones, Secretary of State for the Colonies in the Attlee Government received full support in the columns of *The Word* for his ideas in reference to the African colonies. Aldred called him the 'Member for the Colonies'. But many of the advocates of World Government were begining to stress a distinction between 'peace-loving nations' and 'bully nations'. In these circumstances the idea became a mockery, and in any case, quite impractical.

Guy Aldred used the ballot box on three more occasions. He stood for Glasgow Central, where the Strickland Press was situated, at the General Election in February 1950; and again the following year at the General Election, October 1951. He stood as 'Peace Candidate' on both occasions, describing himself as an Independent Socialist. Although he spoke on some local issues, his main theme was as before — the deception of parliament as a means of attaining Socialism. The last time he made use of the ballot box was in 1962, when he stood for Woodside. We will tell that story when we come to it.

8: ETHEL MACDONALD

The public meetings continued without pause over the years. 'The vote-catching politicians come and go,' Aldred said, 'but I am always here.' He never in his life took a holiday, and except when he was in prison he never ceased to write or speak, or give help to the wronged. He was a champion of lost causes. Eventually he did allow himself one little weekly relaxation. Every Friday evening he went, with the three others of the Press, to 'the pictures', and there he slept noisily through the performance. With a care which amused his colleagues he would gravely study the advertisments to find a good picture —to sleep through. Strangely, he would afterwards recommend or dissuade with more confidence than the wakeful ones.

The Strickland Pres had some hard times financially, for Aldred always worked to the limit of his capacity. He had little sense of 'market potential' and over-printed enormously. He never estimated a cost to find a price, and consistently under-charged. He was lavish in the distribution of free copies, and conducted a postal mission which took *The Word* to most parts of the world where a glimmer of political awareness was manifest. But the price Aldred had to pay was a constant struggle to keep abreast of his creditors. He had constantly to appeal for funds. This position worsened when, the war over and the soldiers back at work, the Typographical Society refused to allow suppliers to serve The Strickland Press because it 'employed women'. Those responsible for imposing the ban knew well that Ethel Macdonald and Jenny Patrick were not 'employed' by the Press, and that whatever reason (if there could have been any) for not allowing women to work at the trade, the Strickland Press was a special case. Guy, Jenny and Ethel were veteran socialists, and they had all been in prison for upholding the cause of the workers. The phrase 'male chauvinist pig' had not been coined in those days, but it is still not too late to have it engraved on the tombstones of the Typographical Society officials of that time.

Ethel Macdonald, with Guy Aldred on his platform, Hyde Park, 1936.

The Press was still struggling from the result of this ban when something more serious happened, and the last shadows began to gather over the four comrades. Near the end of February 1958, Ethel Macdonald had what seemed a slight accident. She fell from a box on which she was standing to make an adjustment to one of the machines. She was more distressed than the accident seemed to justify, as if she knew that this was the onset of dreadful illness. She continued with her work at the Press, though within a few weeks she needed the aid of a stick. One of her legs seemed to be gradually losing its power.

Another cloud had been hanging over George Street. Now it began to settle down on the Strickland Press. It had been known for some time that the Town Planners had their eyes on that entire block of buildings on the north side. It was too near the City Chambers to be overlooked. Its doom was certain, but its future was not. There was some speculation among the tenants, and the most favoured notion was that the Maternity Hospital in Rottenrow was going to be extended over the hill into George Street, making a grand centre for pre-natal and maternity care. This idea was either mistaken or shelved. The safe arrival of healthy babies was important, but this technological age had another consideration. Just as compulsory primary education had to be be enforced in 1871 to produce a literate proletariat, so now a scheme had to be devised to train adolescents for the age of science and technology. So the old Technical College had to be extended and expanded into Glasgow's second University — the University of Strathclyde.

Gradually the tenants were rehoused in various schemes, and left their habitat of dim closes and dank stairs, not always with unalloyed joy. Nostalgia wears a rosy hue. Insanitary smells and back-court squabbles resolved themselves into a remembered miasma of 'warm humanity'. One young man was more specific in his objection to his new abode in an area of gardened semi-detached. 'There's nae closes fur staunin' in wi' yer lassie,' he said. To him that was a monstrous oversight on the part of the planners. And he was probably right about that.

In the late 1950s Guy was still able to call on support from the Glasgow districts, and from the Lanarkshire towns, and *The Word* maintained a fair circulation by postal subscription. But the ranks were thinning around him. The old anarchists and 'antis' were fading from the scene. Jenny Patrick was still active, setting up the headlines by hand as she had been doing since she was a teenage girl. Mrs. Haining, who had been Guy's hostess when he had come to Glasgow in 1912, had hardly missed a meeting since as seller of

Guy Aldred with the Banner of the United Socialist Movement in the 1930s. It claims Jesus as 'The First C.O.' (Conscientious Objector).

pamphlets and taker of collections. Her daughter, Josie, who worked as linotype setter for Willie McDougall, gave two twelve-hour days to the Strickland Press each month, and during Ethel Macdonald's illness set up the entire *Word* herself.

In the life of the pioneer there are many people not less worthy in themselves, perhaps, but less insistent in their call upon the attention of posterity. In the main they cannot be mentioned individually, but no life of Aldred should be written without a reference to the self-sacrificing, modest and scholarly Miss Helen Brown Scott Lennox. She was the daughter of a clergyman, a graduate of Glasgow University, with an honours degree in classics, a poet of fair talent, and street-chalker extraordinary. Before the Second World War (and the First, for that matter) it was the custom of Glasgow political groups to advertise meetings by chalking in the streets with pipeclay. It was generally understood (and observed) that the chalking had to be on the smooth tarmac of the side streets, and not on the pavements, and certainly not on walls. It was also an unwritten rule that no party deface another's chalking. The letters were usually made as broad as the cake of pipeclay, and many cakes had to be carried to complete an evening's work. Helen Lennox chalked far and chalked well, her sensitive soul warding off the taunts or abuse occasionally hurled by disagreeing passers-by.

Despite her education and her quick mind, Helen Lennox worked in junior positions as office typist, and she donated practically all her earned money to the Group, which she had joined in 1926. When the Americans set up air bases in the United Kingdom after the war she made a placard showing a map of Britain with the words
'AMERICA'S LARGEST AIRCRAFT CARRIER
S.S. GREAT BRITAIN.
SEVERAL MILLION CHILDREN ABOARD.
She died while Ethel lay ill, suddenly, without fuss, when the group was too harassed to mourne her and could ill-afford to lose her. Her death took place on April 27th 1960. She was cremated in Maryhill Crematorium, Willie McDougall saying a few last words of tribute.

By the end of 1958 Ethel's condition was so bad that she was unable to board a tram, and had to travel to and from the Press in a taxi. Guy Aldred never owned a car, and was inclined to think that proletarians who did so were halfway to betraying their class. Ethel lived in a flat three stairs up in Gibson Street, Hillhead. The disease, having paralysed completely one of her legs, now attacked the other. In November 1958 she went into hospital, though she and her friends were beginning to fear the illness was incurable. Six weeks later she was discharged. She had walked into the hospital with difficulty.   She was unable to walk out.   The consultant told her she must give up hope of ever walking again.   Her hopes, too, of pause or remission of the disease began to fade.   In fact, she was suffering from a particularly virulent form of multiple sclerosis.

It was decided that it would be better if Ethel were at Baliol Street where she could be looked after by Guy and Jenny.   A year from the time of her 'accident' she had lost the power of both arms and legs, but there was no lessening of her mental powers.   She once said to Guy, 'I'm inside watching this happening to me.'

Aldred wrote: 'Having rendered her legs useless, the disease spread to her arms.   First her left arm, then her right — as though the virus possessed a malicious consciousness that caused it to gloat over its dastardly work.   It was a painful business to serve her so anxiously and yet so purposelessly.'

For a year she was nursed at Baliol Street by her three comrades and by members of her family who visited her regularly.   By the end of 1959 she was completely paralysed and had to be propped up to prevent her powerless tongue from falling back and choking her.   Only her eyes were alive, and only by these could she express her dreadful mental agony.   She was still a woman of great power and vitality, imprisoned in a dead shell, and she knew that she must die.   There was no acceptance or resignation in her last agonised look at Guy Aldred and John Caldwell as they sat by her bed, waiting for her relatives, who arrived too late.   She died in Knightswood Hospital on December 1st, 1960.

The world had forgotten Ethel Macdonald after her brief appearance on the stage of international politics in 1936 to 1938.   During her illness many remembered, and she had a full mail-bag.   The *Glasgow Evening Citizen* headlined her obituary 'SCOTS SCARLET PIMPERNEL DIES.   **She became a legend in Spain.**'   The text read, in part, 'The small, dark-haired woman — once called Scotland's Scarlet Pimpernel — is dead.   And so ends the legend of Ethel Macdonald.'   The article then outlined Ethel's connection with Spain during the Civil War.   As a radio announcer her 'audience was world-wide.   Then she disappeared (arrested by the Commumists, following the "May Days").   An American editor received hundreds of letters from people who had listened to Ethel Macdonald, not because they agreed with what she had to say, but because they thought she had the most wonderful radio-speaking voice they had ever heard.'   The article then went on to recall Ethel's description of her arrest.   'Then she was taken to prison in a lorry that looked like a tumbril.   While in jail she organised escapes for fellow prisoners — and managed to free several.   Finally she was released after a British

Government official called to see her....At Queen Street station a crowd of 300 cheered her. But there was sadness in Ethel Macdonald's face as she said: "I went to Spain full of hopes and dreams. It promised to be a Utopia realised. I return full of sadness, dulled by the tragedy I have seen." '

The *Scottish Daily Mail* headed the report 'STORMY PETREL OF THE THIRTIES' and told its readers that Ethel Macdonald had left her body to medical science and had also willed her eyes to the Glasgow Eye Infirmary, but because of the nature of her illness the Infirmary could not accept the legacy. The story was also told in *Reynold's News*. Many tributes were sent to *The Word* and were published in that paper.

Ethel's death was a great sorrow for Guy Aldred, a sorrow from which he had not yet recovered when death took him as well three years later. Yet he did not let this interfere with his work, which continued unabated till the last few days of his life. He never allowed anything to turn him aside from what he conceived to be the 'Cause', neither poverty, illness nor mental distress.

Without Ethel's help *The Word* had to be reduced in size and in circulation. Debts piled up as income dropped. Now all the tenants had been moved from the houses above the Strickland Press; from broken windows and gaping roofs the rain found its way through the ceiling of the Press and dropped on to the paper stock and the machinery. The smell of damp and decay pervaded the place, and the sensitive may have felt in the basement an invisible brooding sorrow, as though Ethel Macdonald, old Mr. Brown, Dr. Lister and a host of others, erased from time, were lingering there awaiting the dissolution of their earthly haunting place.

9: WALLY CLOSES AND SINGLE ENDS

In November 1959, while Ethel MacDonald lay in the final stages of her illness, Aldred wrote once more to the secretary of the Scottish Typographical Association, explaining the difficulties which now faced him. *The Word* was a Socialist paper, non-competitive and non-profit-making. The Press was operated by four partners, not in a position to employ anyone. If it did, surely it was obvious that the conditions of employment would be in line with Union standards. Meantime, since Miss Macdonald was no longer able to work at the Press it would be necessary for the maintenance of the Socialist propaganda to have some of the setting done by a trade typesetter. In the circumstances he asked that the ban on supplying Strickland Press be lifted. The secretary replied:

Dear Mr. Aldred, Many thanks for your letter of 19th October relative to the difficulties you are at present encountering regarding the Strickland Press. You will appreciate that the Executive Council of the Scottish Typographical Association is an administrative body, not legislative, and the amendments to rules are submitted every three years for alteration. The present Rule Book appears to satisfy the membership so that I have no further comment. Harry Girwood (Gen. Sec.)

This was *thinking to Rule Book*, which, like *working to rule*, is more an exercise in aggressive tactics than an expression of principle. Aldred's knotted cords still stung in some sensitive quarters. He printed the letter in *The Word* with the comment: 'Does a Rule Book justify sex discrimination in these days of growing recognition of sex equality?'

The *Glasgow Evening Citizen* for May 13th 1961 carried a headline:

NOW THE WORD IS HOMELESS
After 22 years it has to move from George Street.

Glasgow's amiable knickerbockered anarchist, Guy Aldred, is having to find new printing headquarters for *The Word*, organ of the United Socialist Movement. He has been given notice to quit his George Street premises after 22 years tenancy, but cannot find anywhere to go....'

258

In *From All Quarters* in the *Glasgow Herald* on August 3rd, 1961, 'Pursuivant' wrote:

> *'Battle of Words.* To a younger generation of Glaswegians the name may mean little or nothing of Guy Aldred, the city's kenspeckled, plus-foured politician *extraordinaire*. He is still rebelliously printing and publishing from his Townhead offices *The Word* —editorial by Guy Aldred, printing by four dedicated unpaid associates — runs up to 10,000 copies a month. "We send out free copies, but we do have our subscribers from Madrid to Moscow." But now the indefatigable Mr. Aldred (who once fought fourteen wards simultaneously in the Glasgow municipal elections, and been in his time an Independent Communist, an Independent Socialist and an advocate of World Government) has had to shift ground — physically, not politically. Redevelopment plans for Townhead are forcing him to leave his old stamping ground, and, if present plans materialise, may even see him settle, comfortably if rather incongruously, in the West End.'

The plan to settle in the West End was one of several abortive efforts to settle *somewhere*. There was a shop in Montrose Street, a short distance from the Press, which Aldred considered suitable, though much smaller than the George Street shop. But the Rehousing Department seemed determined not to offer it to Aldred, and he was determined not to move his machinery till he was given somewhere suitable to move to. 'We will sit tight,' he repeated. The City Corporation sent printers' engineers to make an estimate of the cost of dismantling the machinery and presumably piling it in the street. Aldred continued sitting tight. The plaster fell from the ceiling onto the paper as it was being fed into the machine, rain plopped into buckets, and the air of desolation grew heavier and more pungent. The machinery was not dismantled. A bluff had been called. The bulldozers began eating away at the corner of the block and daily crept nearer; hoardings went up around the Press — but *The Word* continued to appear. Then, in February 1962, Aldred was given the keys to the Montrose Street shop.

With the removal of the Strickland Press the demolition continued. The *Glasgow Herald* for March 29th 1962 described the passing of George Street beneath the headline:

PAST RECOGNITION

'The grey block of buildings in George Street, now rapidly disappearing amidst clouds of dust and falling debris as the demolition men clear the way for Glasgow's latest development scheme, has a history curiously compounded of respectability and religious fervour.   Yesterday the workmen were hard at it with pickaxes at No. 136 — once the site of the Kale Kirk, which belonged to a small independent sect and was so-called because the members of the congregation were always given platefuls of kale, though whether as part of a secret ritual or simply for sustenance is uncertain.   Already the Congregational Church is rubble.   Soon the bulldozers will move on towards the site of the tenement (demolished about 1930) which was the birth-place of Sir George Burns, co-founder of the Cunard Line, then relentlessly on round the corner to the little blue organ factory in North Portland Street, which was once a Quaker meeting house.   Even the building recently vacated by the left-wing press in George Street (once considered a very superior residential quarter) seems already to have moved into the distant past.   Through the greased windows can be seen some tracts and pamphlets they left behind them, including one on *Discarded Dogmas*.'

This time was the hey-day of the town planners.   With devilish delight they set their iron-jawed monsters to work, devouring the city, levelling it to dust and rubble, and erecting on its ruins 'living units' for humanoid habitation.   It is only now, forty years later, that the obtuse frenzy for destruction and reconstruction has passed, and the result comes home to us in bleak dissatisfaction.

Now, in a surge of creative energy which has lain dormant in the lassitude of decay, comes an ambition to make Glasgow a City of Culture.   How far that will be for the benefit of the inhabitants, and how far chiefly a show piece of the tourist trade is not yet clear.   A step in the latter direction has already been made.   A piece of derelict dockland has been transformed for 1988 into a Garden Festival, capable of attracting a million visitors.

In opening this Exhibition the Prince of Wales, who seems to have a genuine interest in inner city rehabilitation, expressed the confidence that the Festival would mark the city's rebirth in significance and character.   He deplored the wanton destruction that had taken place of fine tenements, and was moved to quote a folk song which expressed those sentiments of regret.

The song told sadly of the vanished 'wally closes', of the 'wumman upstairs', of the friendly wee corner shop where the shopkeeper never failed to ask 'How's yer mammy?'

Lovely stuff, and commendable, coming from the lips of a Prince.   But it is coloured into inexactitude by nostalgic imagination.

Wally closes were closes faced with porcelain tiles. Few wally closes still exist, and the individual tiles have become collectors' items. The vast majority of Glasgow folk, the frontline workers in shipyard and factory, did not live in wally closes. Their closes were of the cheapest reddish-brown paint and flaking whitewash. The wally closes were in the outer districts, between the inner city and the suburbs, with their vistas of 'semi-detached'.

The wally closes were clean and bright, with shining unbroken stairhead windows, sometimes with coloured glass panels. There were usually only two dwellings on each landing. The occupants were upper-working class or lower middle class. They spoke proper English with a Scottish acent, and never had nasty loud arguments over the wash-house key. Their children wore school uniforms, were in the Scouts or Guides, and would probably go to University, to become respectable members of the professions, and be the backbone of middle management. It is unlikely that they would loiter in corner shops, and surely no-one would ask of them 'How's yer mammy?'

Yet from the heart of that respectability and civic responsibility would come many of the world's inventors and innovators. They would also supply many martyrs for rebel causes, and would dream of their wally closes as they lay enchained in dark dungeons.

Nostalgia plays many tricks. The corner shops of wistful memory and dramatic folk-song never existed, except in rare, uncharacteristic cases. The corner shop owner, usually a woman, was as hard as nails, and as relentless as the grubby sign which hung on the wall behind her: NO TICK HERE. She didn't give a toss for anybody's mammy. She was too busy watching that wet-nosed urchins did not steal a caramel — which they were not above doing. She kept the empty lemonade bottles well out of their reach, for they would pinch one and ask for a penny on its return.

Nor did the customers gather to gossip in a spirit of loving kindness. Nor would they, on the slight hint that old Mrs. McJimmy was unwell, be seen hurrying off in her direction with a bowl of hot soup. More likely, they speeded off to the factor to put a name in for her house. Softness was rare enough to be remembered.

George Street went into decline in the 1850s. But even before that there must have been a surprising mixture of affluence and poverty dwelling side by side — as there was, indeed, in all Scottish cities. The Strickland Press had once been a doctor's house. In the basement where the printing machine stood was the flag-stoned evidence of a large kitchen with space for a huge range, and a door leading from the kitchen to a scullery, low ceilinged and windowless.

261

A stair led to the tradesmen's entrance, with steps so worn that for a hundred years menial feet must have pressed them.

Yet the doctor's house must have been surrounded by slums, one of which, still standing, had the date 1820 on its wall, and another 1798. No wally closes here, and they were typical of many Glasgow houses still occupied then. The closes were narrow and dark, leading to steps worn concave by generations of use. At a turn on the stair was a sentry-box water closet, usually seatless and chainless, with broken window and puddled floor. This served six dwellings, whose doors were in dark passages leading off the landing. There were three such landings. The caller (such as was this writer on many occasions, handing out political leaflets) found his way along by the guidance of door handles and letter-boxes.

When the door opened he could see the official plaque on the door lintel stating the cubic capacity of the single room within and the ordained number of persons it should house. Some splurge of civic conscience in the forgotten past had ordered this tabulation. Nobody took any notice of it.

The door opened directly into the room, exposing to the visitor all the inhabitants and their activities. Some of the single ends were spotlessly clean with well-scrubbed table and polished brass — an oasis of pleasant smells in the miasma of cat stink and urine spillage on the common stair — some, and their occupants, matched their surroundings.

Of special fascination for the imaginative was the tenement bearing the date of its erection: 1798. Once, sturdy workmen had built it, manhandling heavy stone onto stone. On its completion the first tenants moved in, overjoyed at their good fortune. There may yet have been no running water piped in, nor water closet, and they would live after dark by lamp and candlelight. But they would be the envy of their friends, and their foes.

The district would not have been so bad. Balmono Mansion may still have stood at the top of the hill, and what later became a street would have been an orchard. It was a time, as the poet said, when to be alive and young was very heaven. The ideals of the French Revolution were still in the air: Liberty, Equality and Fraternity: and the *Rights of Man* by Tom Paine, suppressed as seditious, made exciting reading for the daring mind. The poems of Robert Burns, with their twin themes of social protest and glorious bucolic life (a life half-remembered by the city dwellers of the day) were still fresh in the minds of everyone. In the Trongate, *The Reformers Gazette* was published, demanding parliamentary representation for the common people.

Yet there was a dark side.   Stockaded in the area now covered by the fruit market in Candleriggs were French prisoners-of-war, crowded together and inhumanely treated.   They made toys and ornaments as a pass-time, and sold them to the not unsympathetic people.

All that had gone now.   The prisoners gone, their place of travail smelling of oranges, Balmano orchard covered by cobblestones, the once new houses now ruinous hovels from which the inhabitants were departing to fresh fields.

10: THE FINAL BATTLE

The misfortunes of the Press were not greatly evident in Guy Aldred's public activity. He still addressed a meeting in Central Halls in Bath Street on the first Sunday of each month; he still took his turn at the weekly discussion group, and he occasionally spoke for the Workers' Open Forum in Renfrew Street Halls. He also fought the important battles of local and personal injustice. For nearly a year he had been engaged on the case of the unrecognised widow of a tram driver who had been burned to death when his tram car caught fire in Shettleston Road. Two passengers had also died, but it was evident that the driver had sacrificed his life in an attempt to save his passengers. The driver had died on the eve of his wedding day. He had taken on an extra shift of duty to earn a little extra for the occasion. The intended bride was a tram conductress. The couple had been living together for two years and had two children. Now the union was to be legalised in accordance with English law. But as the marriage had not taken place at the time of the man's death, the authorities considered him a bachelor and the children illegitimate.

Guy took up the case and it had wide publicity, all of it favourable, in the press and on television. Younger members of the United Socialist Movement had a petition drawn up and collected several thousand signatures. Prominent public figures wrote letters of support. Every effort was unavailing. The mother of the dead man's children was not his wife, because he had thoughtlessly given up his life one day too soon. For the woman there would be neither compensation nor pension.

Aldred commented: 'Scots Nationalists who should have known better, have allowed stupid English moralists to mutilate the marriage laws of Scotland. The Scots law is fundamentally moral, and based on true morality entirely absent from the ceremonial nonsense in England. As no Edinburgh solicitor will fight this case, I wrote to the Court of Sesssion asking permission to appear myself in application for a Declarator of Marriage. The principal Clerk of Session replied that he regretted that he could be of no assistance in the matter.'

A wider issue of concern was the proposed British entry into Europe. Harold MacMillan was the Prime Minister and Edward Heath the Common Market negotiator. In seven long essays printed in *The Word*, Guy Aldred put forward his objections to Britain joining the European Community. The first of those articles appeared in July 1961 and the last in March 1962. He wrote: 'On Monday July 31st, 1961, Prime Minister MacMillan ignored the opposition of the most intelligent members of the Tory party by opening his campaign on behalf of the Common market.'

Aldred's view was the the Commmon Market had been thought up by international finance as a contrivance to save capitalism. National states had been created in the fifteenth century to serve the interests of rising mercantile capitalism. Serfs, peasants and proletarians had been taught to regard love of country as more dear than life itself, and had marched and died to defend these mundane expediences as though they were eternal verities. Now finance capitalism found it expedient to erase these national boundaries so that an oppositional bloc could be formed against the Soviet Union and so that the socialist forces inside each country, modelled on national structures, would be set in a state of disarray. The Treaty of Rome means the re-emergence of the Holy Roman Empire brought up to date as the Unholy Capitalist Empire. Here was an object lesson in the operation of the materialist concept of history. The ideal concepts arose from the material conditions. But the material conditions were not basic realities. They were survival devices of the ruling class. The *realities* of the material world worked in the factories and the back streets. From thence would rise the ideal superstructures of the new era.

The idea of the Common Market was being advanced in the face of objections from the ruling class itself, and in defiance of the traditions it had established. Aldred quoted Winston Churchill in his address to the United States Congress: 'The British Commonwealth of Nations is not prepared to become a state or group of states in any continental system — on either side of the Atlantic.' He quoted from the Conservative *General Election News* for 1950: 'The Conservative party promise to guard (the British people's) freedom, to rescue them from Socialism, which is the half-way house to Communism, to fight the rising cost of living....Either Britain is great or she is nothing. Without the Empire and Commonwealth Britain would be a poverty-stricken and overcrowded island, with an insignificant voice in the world's affairs.'

He quoted Harold MacMillan speaking as far back as October 23rd, 1929: 'If we go into a European combine we must depress the standard of living of our people to that of the European standard. I am sure English people will not hesitate about this. We ought seriously to consider whether we should not be wiser to revert to the tradition of the Conservative Party, that of the Imperial tradition, rather than become too much involved in rather vague internationalism.'

Coming more up-to-date, Aldred quoted the recent utterances of Clive Jenkins, the General Secretary of the Association of Supervisory Staffs, writing in the *Daily Express*, on June 8th, 1961. 'Make no mistake, the Common Market was designed as a weapon to attack Britain's leading position as a world trader. I hope the Labour movement will fight and utterly defeat the proposal that Britain should join....The Germans are export hungry. They need Britain's markets to absorb their industrial output (built up with massive American gifts at the end of the war). And don't forget that it was the Germans who really engineered the Treaty of Rome four years ago....'

The October 1962 issue of *The Word* carried a headline:

DANGER: U.S. RISKING WORLD WAR OVER CUBA

Then followed an article from Havana detailing the build-up of United States forces against Cuba, by threatened armed invasion and economic blockade. These aggressive measures against an island which had chosen a form of government disliked by the Americans were a danger to the world.

By the time the November issue of *The Word* appeared the 'Cuban Crisis' had occurred. By a sleight-of-hand exercise in public relations, the Western World was led to believe that President Kennedy had performed a great act of statesmanship and had saved the world from nuclear war. Aldred took a different view, and expressed it in his article.

'As this paper goes to press news has come that Kruschev has agreed to remove "Offensive" weapons from Cuba. The American people are jubilant. This is hailed as a great victory for President Kennedy. It will be some time before the Americans realise the (for them) chilling truth that Kruschev has run diplomatic rings round Kennedy. Without moving a single Russian soldier, or even raising his voice in anger, he has defeated the intention of the entire military might of the United States, and he has honoured his pledge to go to the aid of Cuba if she were threatened. It should be remembered that the main issue was the *invasion of Cuba*. The U.S. was building up a force for that purpose *before* the discovery of the rocket bases. Now they are defeated in that intention. Time will show the Russian leader to have been the better man because (a) he (unlike Kennedy) was not prepared to destroy the world to have rocket bases removed from his doorstep. (b) By building up a secondary point (rocket bases) and then seeming to give way on that, he has scored a victory for the main issue. *Kruschev has not lost Cuba. Kennedy has.*

In July 1962 the Scottish Campaign for Nuclear Disarmament organised a march from Castle Douglas to Glasgow in protest against the American Nuclear base at Holy Loch. Aldred was not a member of the C.N.D.: his distrust of demonstrations as transient emotional displays persisted from the days of the hunger marches. He saw in them a breeding ground for careerists. But the object of the demonstration had his sympathy. He gave it a full-page announcement in *The Word*, and in his meetings supported the C.N.D. call for the removal of the nuclear bases. At one of his meetings a member of the audience asked Aldred why he did not stand for Woodside at the forthcoming bye-election. The point being approved by the meeting in general, Aldred agreed to stand. He was submerged in debt, and in the matter of full time assistance he was reduced to one man — Caldwell. But he agreed to stand, and set about raising funds and calling for volunteer help.

When Aldred launched his Woodside campaign he had less than a year to live. He was 76, a powerful man with a great voice and a sharp mind. He had joined the Anti-Nicotine League when he was twelve and signed the pledge not to indulge in strong drink when he was fourteen. Both pledges he had kept. He seemed indestructible. Yet weariness crept over him now, and sadness. The death of Ethel, the destruction of the old Press, and constant battles to raise funds, were beginning to have their effects. He walked more slowly and overcame his prejudice against motor cars enough to take a taxi to and from work.

He could no longer look forward to a new society in which he would participate, nor the rise of any movement which enveloped his ideas and ideals. He saw that his concept of socialism as a principle of living, unselfish, unmercenary, with banners inscribed 'The End of the Wages System', was something young men used to dream about, but no more. The guts were being torn out of the earth and the ultimate height of human thought expressed by politicians and Trade Unionists concerned how much each could grab for his own faction — and himself.

Yet optimism, by its nature, dies hard. Aldred, an atheist always ready with an apt Biblical metaphor, declared that he was the Rejected Stone. The one which the builders had rejected, but which

Helen Brown Scott Lennox of the Glasgow United Socialist Movement, who, before C.N.D., paraded the streets of Glasgow in a one-woman protest.

was the cornerstone of the Temple. Without the corner stone the edifice would not stand.

There was no suggestion of sadness or despondency hanging over Guy when he opened his election campaign in November 1962. He wrote: ' "The Red Clyde" was a parliamentary pink myth. It was a mockery of the workers' struggle. It was the wilful deception of the workers of the Clydeside. The parliamentarians went to Westminster and secured careers for themselves ....I enter the Woodside contest to challenge this, and to end this disgraceful humbug....It is imagined that the anti-parliamentarian has no practical programme. That is wrong....At this election I shall define a clear programme of action....'

The winter of 1962 had started as it meant to continue. November was bitterly cold and heavy with fog. There could not have been worse conditions for the conducting of an election campaign. Aldred went through cold streets to speak in stuffy school halls. It was weather for the fireside and television, but Guy always had an audience. The *Glasgow Herald* reported: 'The first shots in the Woodside parliamentary bye-election in Glasgow were fired last night —fireworks aimed in every possible direction by the Independent Socialist candidate Mr. Guy Aldred. Speaking in the Central Halls on the eve of his seventy-sixth birthday — and the sixtieth anniversary of his first public speech — Mr. Aldred called the Labour Party a party of crooks, and the Tories a party of tricksters. He wanted to sweep them and the "dedicated bureaucrats" who actually ran affairs, out of existence. He said he had spent his life trying to sweep away the rubbish caused by capitalism.'

There were five other candidates: the favourite to win was the Labour Party choice, Neil Carmichael, son of James Carmichael. Carmichael said the over-riding issue was the need for jobs: a quarter of a million people had left Scotland over the past ten years to find security. Other Scottish Labour M.P.s gave him their support, though, as the *Glasgow Herald* put it: 'Most of those do not endorse Mr. Carmichael's overstepping the party line on unilateral disarmament.'

Asked if he would support the Labour Party's policy on defence if elected, Carmichael said: 'The Party's policy on defence is clearly printed in my election address. At Westminster I shall accept the Labour Party Standing Orders.' The Tory candidate, Norman Glen, accused Carmichael of having accepted advice from his party to change his views, in case his unilateralist position might damage the Labour vote. Carmichael replied that his views were well known, and that within the Labour Party he would reserve the right to persuade his colleagues that his point of view was the right one.

It was, however, on this point of difference with the Labour Party that Carmichael got most of his campaign support. The Woodside Young Socialists, naturally vigorous, noisy and enthusiastic, were unilateralists in the extreme, and very much in favour of getting the Americans out of the Holy Loch. To merit their support Carmichael had to speak their language: to appease the Party he had to 'accept the Labour Party's Standing Orders': to confound Mr. Glen's accusation of performing a *volte face* he had to add a rider to his acceptance of the Standing Orders to the effect that he would endeavour to subvert them. It was not a happy position to be in.

Some of the Young Socialists explained to Aldred that Carmichael was 'a good lad', 'one of themselves'. He could do more to get the Yanks out of Holy Loch by getting inside and 'acting behind the scenes' than they could by demonstrations. This was a variation on a theme Guy had heard played many times.

On November 16th the six candidates were invited to address the lecturers in Glasgow University, as it was in the Woodside Constituency. Five accepted the invitation. Charles Graham reported the meeting in the *Daily Express* under the heading:
DUNCE CAPS FOR X-MEN.

'Lecturers at Glasgow University deplored the shortage of dunces' caps yesterday, when five of the six Woodside bye-election candidates came up to answer questions on education.... So fumbling and ill-informed were the candidates' answers to the first few questions on finance and the University Grants Committee that one lecturer felt obliged to ask:What *is* the University Grants Committee? To the chairman, Professor Esmond Wright, the question seemed reasonable, but he thought it just a little too insulting to be put formally....'

After describing the attempts of the other candidates to deal with the questions, Charles Graham continued: 'Hero of the meeting, to the surprise even of the lecturers, was Independent Socialist Guy Aldred. "I believe in a university education for every citizen who can benefit from it," he proclaimed. "And the new University should be built where it is most needed — in the middle of the slums. As well as Universities we need something else — places where people, especially young people, can meet and talk social, economic and educational heresy." His non-conformist audience cheered him warmly. For heresy of this kind is in the finest traditions of British Universities.'

A pen-picture of Guy Aldred during the election campaign was

given by Edward Ashton of the *Scottish Daily Mail* under the heading:
KNICKERBOCKER POLITICIAN.

'He has been called the "knickerbocker politician" because of his unshakeable loyalty to that Victorian fashion (probably the only conservative element in his make-up). He has been hated, feared, reviled and imprisoned for his political beliefs. But today, by the odd switch of feeling that only the British public can manage, Guy A. Aldred, Independent Socialist candidate in the Woodside bye-election, is regarded with a good-natured tolerant affection. None of the other candidates can even begin to match the experience and record of Aldred....It is impossible to believe that this vigorously articulate man is 76 years old. There is not much grey in the dark hair brushed straight back. The black, fuzzy eyebrows twitch as he emphasises a point. But the real gold is in the flow of words. The voice has the slightly brassy, carrying note of one who has learned his public speaking in the tough, street-corner, pre-microphone days, when a man with message had to make himself heard through his own fervour and lung power....The reason for Aldred's private strength and public ineffectiveness, lies, I think, in the fact that he is always the non-conformist who cannot compromise....'

The accompanying full-length photograph of Guy Aldred standing in a busy Glasgow street was captioned:
WHAT A GUY!

'Six times a good loser, the knickerbocker politician fights yet again.'

Polling took place on Thursday 22nd November, one of the worst days of a dreadful month. The cold fog swirled like a river of filthy mist in the streets. Towards evening Aldred and Caldwell took a taxi round the polling stations. It was a pointless journey. The Young Socialists created a little liveliness at the entrance with leaflets, placards and slogans, but inside the station apathy hung in silence. At former elections in which he had taken part, Aldred would have had a representative in each station, and a few Group members at the gates. Now the active members of the U.S.M. numbered no more than half a dozen. The visit to the polling stations was a mere formality.

At nine o'clock Guy Aldred and his agent, J.T. Caldwell, were at the Sheriff Buildings for the vote counting. It had been a hectic three weeks campaign for Guy. He had spoken every night in the week,

United Socialist Movement Banner, on Glasgow Green, 1939.

Jane Hamilton Patrick

without any supporting speaker, or even a long-winded Chairman to take some of the strain. He had been interviewed, questioned, telephoned, called upon, and at the same time had prepared the next issue of *The Word* for the press. He had taken bundles of his election manifesto home in the evenings, and he and Jenny Patrick (now nearly 80 years of age and house-bound) had sat up half the night addressing them by hand. He had caught a cold in the changing temperatures of stuffy halls and cold streets, and the fog choked him. At the top of the stairs leading to the vote counting room he was breathless and swayed unsteadily. An attendant quickly placed a chair, and asked if he would like a little brandy. Guy shook his head: for the first time words deserted him.

When the count started he had to move inside, for the doors had to be shut. He sat smiling and seemingly relaxed, but Caldwell knew that he was feeling ill and apprehensive with a foreboding of darkness. He seemed only half interested in the proceedings till the counted votes began to pile up under the different candidates' names, then he recovered a little.

Although in press and television interviews he had declared that he expected to 'win this time', he took this no more seriously than did anyone else. He expected the usual 400 votes, and perhaps, as this must be his final appearance before the electorate, a little more by way of appreciation. Just a mere flicker of disappointment passed across his face when the final count was announced. *Aldred, 134.* He rose from his seat and waited at the microphone where the victor, Carmichael, and the defeated were to make the formal speeches of thanks to all concerned. Aldred had recovered his voice. He was not dismayed by the result, he said cheerfully: he would be back, at the next election.

Then he and Caldwell went down the stairs to the street, jostled by the excited supporters congratulating the successful candidate. The policeman who had opened the doors for Aldred did not notice him going out. Outside, the cold fog was thicker than ever; through it came the exultant cries of the Young Socialists telling the world that the Labour man was A Jolly Good Fellow. Shadowy shapes showed them carrying him shoulder high to his car and depositing him inside, and off he went to Westminster, to execute the fulfilment of all his promises. And there he still is (Baron Carmichael of Kelvingrove in 1983) — and the Americans are still at Holy Loch. Guy and Caldwell went home to Baliol Street where Jenny made some tea, then Caldwell set off on the walk to Gibson Street, where he still lived — to keep Ethel's memory warm.

The excitement over, the lid-bashing, lorry-climbing, slogan-shouting all done, Woodside was a dull place for the Young Socialists. They stayed around long enough to be expelled by the Labour Party whose candidate they had just helped to return, then the interest had gone and life called them on their various ways. Guy Aldred had seen it all before.

11:VISION AND REALITY

The severe winter passed from fogbound November to freezing December and into wild January. The Press was draughty, and a chill rose from the dank cellar. Guy caught a cold but did not even consider staying away from work. He was desperately worried. Debts amounted to several hundred pounds, and despite the generosity of several loyal comrades there was little hope of raising the money. Yet he never thought of a future in which there would be no Press, and he would not be an active propagandist. He daily expected a miracle, and every day the old machinery shed more screws — and another line appeared on Caldwell's weary face.

Ethel Macdonald was still missed, as a worker, and as a friend. Guy had some consolation in seeing that she was not forgotten. It was two years since she had died, yet letters of appreciation and condolence still arrived at the office, and occasional articles on her appeared in the papers.

During the long nights, Aldred sat on his bed-chair, alone with his thoughts and his wakeful dreams. The door of his room had always to be open a little and a light left on, for darkness pressed on him like a suffocating black cloud. Those silent hours were now a time of melancholy thoughts and foreboding. He was in his mid-seventies: one by one his friends and enemies had departed, and he was becoming more and more alone in a world which was becoming more strange. He knew the time was not so far off when he would (as he put it) join yesterday's seven thousand years. (He had always loved his *Omar Khayyam*). It was a prospect fearful to him, for he was too rich in life to contemplate extinction with equanimity. Yet, regardlessly, he continued to expend the energy of a forty-year-old.

One night in January 1963 Caldwell had a phone call from Jenny Patrick. Would he come at once? Guy seemed to be in a fit. He had called for her, but was unable to speak properly. When Caldwell reached Baliol Street he found Guy semi-conscious and using all his will to say that he did not want to go into hospital. By morning he had recovered his senses, but was too weak to get dressed. A week passed before he would allow a doctor to be called.   Then he was told that he suffered from a heart condition and that it would be better if he would go into hospital for a time.   Guy agreed, but after one night in the Western Infirmary he signed himself out.   He spent another week at home, then he returned to work.   He had to travel by taxi now, because he could not walk to the bus stop.   But once back at his desk he was as vigorous as ever.

He denounced Franco, the dictator of Spain, for the execution of Julian Grimau, the communist leader who had been kept in prison for twenty-five years, since the time of the Spanish Civil War, for alleged crimes committed at that time.   He wrote on Kruschev's exposure of Stalin, reproducing the famous speech.   He wrote an essay on 'The Evolution of Stalin's Communism'.   He reproduced, from the columns of the *New York Times*, an 'Open Letter to President John F. Kennedy', calling for an end to the Vietnam war — an early protest, with the signatures of over sixty prominent Americans.   He continued his interest in the position of Cuba, and he devoted an issue of the paper to an exposure of police methods against the Negroes of Alabama, who were asserting their right to equality with their fellow citizens.

Guy had been warned against speaking in public: he had every intention of defying the warning,   In the event, he found he could not remain standing long enough to address an audience at the two-hour meetings, so substitute speakers were found for February, March and April.   But May Sunday was a special day, dedicated to the cause of Labour.   For sixty years — except when he was in prison — Guy had spoken on that day.   He could not let this May be an exception: it might be his last.   Fortunately a solution was found.   A sympathiser produced a tape recorder.   Neither Aldred nor Caldwell had known such things had been invented: they were grateful for the discovery. The microphone was set before Guy, seated on his bed-chair in Baliol Street on the Friday before the meeting.   Aldred and Caldwell discussed likely themes and titles, and when that was settled, Guy started to talk into the microphone, without notes or other preparation, for almost an hour.

Those tapes have been kept, and a few excerpts from them will give an idea of what was in Aldred's mind during those last months of his life.   The first lecture, for May Sunday, 1963, was entitled 'The Two Nations'.   After some observations on the traditions of May Day and its pagan significance, Aldred got down to his theme.   This contended that within every nation there is an economic divide which cleaves it into two nations: the nation of the rich and the nation of the poor.   What concerned him was the further divisions which beset the nation of the workers, and his plea was that those divisions should give place to reconciliation and unity. 'We must elevate the Nation of the Poor to the position of power. We must make the Nation of the Workers the supreme Nation, and define sedition and treason as offfences against the poor. In international socialism today we have loyalty to sects, loyalty to Parties, but not loyalty to Class, *not loyalty to a working class Nation....*'

The lecture for June 2nd was called 'Down to Earth'. The title referred to attempts by America and Russia to launch men into orbit round the earth. Aldred belonged to a generation which had implicit faith in the beneficial nature of scientific advance, for though knowledge may not give wisdom, it supplied the information which brought enlightenment. Scientific warfare had shaken that belief, and science was suspect.

'The title of my address is easy to understand. It arises from a consideration of the state of mankind on Earth coupled with Man's ambition to conquer the heavens. Whether this desire to explore the heavens is right or wrong, whether it is useless or useful, I cannot say. It has a touch of romance, and a touch of bravery, but it seems to me somewhat futile....In every generation Man strives to secure one thing — the conquest of the needs of his mortal existence, to extend his life as fully as possible, and also to procure some degree of happiness. He wants to overcome a sense of insecurity that clings to him and oppresses him. Whether he is doing so in these space operations or not I cannot say.

'It is said by those who are behind this very materialist concept of the conquest of the heavens, that Marxism is an expression of materialism. But the strange thing is that Marxists — and every kind of socialist for that matter — are moved by an idealism despite their economic interpretation of the basis of life. And the people who claim to be idealists are the very people who tend to continue a social struggle which destroys idealism and makes brutal and evil materialism the criterion of existence....We live in times of capitalism, that is, in times of self-interest.'

Guy Aldred went on to show how self interest, fear and compromise have fostered divisions in the ranks of the workers and have introduced a note of unreality into the struggle. But so has alleged scholarship and adoration.

'What none of these groups has realised is this. It is not important to perpetuate the name of Marx, or the ideas of Marx. It is not important to perpetuate the name or writings of

Bakunin. It *is* important to bring about the emancipation of the working-class. Jesus was am unemployed person who had nowhere to lay his head. He conquered, but he conquered as a shadow, and the worship of his ghost became the means of enslaving the people, instead of emancipating them....Deification is always the road to slavery. The deification of Marx has destroyed, to a large extent, the socialist movement. The deification of Bakunin has to a large extent destroyed the anarchist movement. The deification of the rulers of the Kremlin has helped to destroy the powers of communism as the final expression of the working-class in their struggle against capitalism....'

And so the plea to 'Come Down to Earth'. The last speech recorded was 'Vision and Reality.' This was relayed to an audience in Central Halls on July 7th 1963. Like the other lectures it was almost five thousand words in length, but it is even more difficult to summarise. Whatever its merit in content or in expression it surely rescues Aldred from the category of mere tub-thumper. The previous month he had asked his audience to 'come down to earth'. Now he wanted to show that on earth and from earth dwells and arises all the spirituality that man can experience, because it comes from himself. There is always implicit in Aldred's social analysis the belief in an improving society.

He tried to convey to his socialist, materialist and mostly atheist audience that man's highest dreams were not impaired by a materialist conception, but were thereby given a reality. In 'Vision and Reality' he began with a definition which makes the Greek meaning of *Vision* of greater significance than the Latin. The latter simply means 'to see'; the former means the same, but with an added implication, arising from philosophical usage, to 'see with the mind'.

'....Vision means sailing on uncharted seas which represent the mind, setting out from the base of reality, finding its own way, venturing forth, and as a result discovering new realities. We tend to despise the use of the word "Vision". It is regarded with disapproval and contempt. Nevertheless it is to men of vision that reality owes its development, and owes its worth to the people, whether they possess vision or not. All the realities around us, all the differences in our lives from that of our forefathers, the development of man from the brute animal, is due to the faculty of vision — as opposed to the mere observation of Reality.

'In the beginning Man was a product of brute reality. He possessed no *soul* — and that does not mean some supernatural manifestation of something which has *descended* into Man. It is an expression of Man reaching upward. It means that the animal has developed a new understanding and has therefore changed into a new being. But it is a growth from roots; it is a plant standing upright, stretching upwards; it is a challenge to dull reality. Each generation is to some extent led by that Vision. Always Man is seeking the promised land. Always the Vision arises on the horizon. Always, therefore, he is sailing the uncharted waters in search of Utopia. And the Utopians are the real founders of scientific society, the *real* founders of a *real* world; a world that will one day be an abode of fairness and beauty for all mankind.

'It was Vision that inspired Isaiah to prophesy the triumph of righteousness. He was scorned and rejected. It was Vision that led Jesus to the Cross. He also was despised, till at last he was deified, and in that deification his Vision became the stock-in-trade of priests. Today, those of us who think, are scornful of that Vision, debased into priesthood. Yet, behind that imposture is the history of righteousness in poverty and misery, opposing the false realities of purple and fine linen, and the alleged riches of life....It is the story of the struggle of science as well as of art for a world wherein science and art will work together for a fuller life of leisure and beauty for all mankind....

'Do not think I speak without experience. I speak with much experience. I speak with great bitterness....I have challenged the cravens of fact, and those who have debased themselves before fact, before the chimera of Reality, and I have stood for truth. Of course I am bitter. I am bitter at the lack of support. I am bitter because I am growing old, and the voice I have used for so long has not had the effect it should have had. In this I am wrong. There should be no bitterness, for I know that finally the Cause shall triumph.

'And so I have finished, Comrades. A very poor, limp ending to my address, but if you will take these seeds and plant them in your minds, and in the minds of your neighbours, they will probably yield a greater harvest than that yielded by this lecture delivered by me. I am probably not the best Sower, but someone other than myself will cultivate the seed that I have scattered, and gather in the harvest that I will never see, and in the reaping there will be well-being for all mankind. That is all.'

The following month Guy decided that if he could sit in Baliol Street and talk for an hour into a microphone, he could just as easily sit on the platform and speak to the audience, so no more speeches were recorded. The lectures of August, September and October were spoken extemporaneously from the platform in Central Hall, Bath Street.

The last meeting took place on Sunday 6th October, 1963. Guy spoke for an hour, his voice as powerful as ever, but at the end he was physically exhausted. He concluded: 'Next month I will be seventy-seven years of age. I will speak to you all again on that date, then I will say goodbye. Someone else will take my place. I hope you will give him your loyalty and support.' He was helped into a waiting taxi.

He struggled to the office on the Monday and the Tuesday, but the next day he allowed himself to be persuaded to stay at home. He sat in his bed-chair struggling for breath, at times sinking into semi-consciousness. On Saturday he rallied enough to tell the friendly taxi driver who called for him that he would need the cab on Monday, but by Monday Dr. Miller had ordered an oxygen cylinder. Two days later Guy agreed to go into hospital.

When the ambulance men arrived they refused to move him: they did not think he would survive the journey. Guy, seeing them arrive, and then go away again, probably wondered in his fading mind what was happening. After waiting patiently for two hours he said, in a loud, clear voice: 'I'm willing to go now,' evidently thinking that the delay was caused by his former refusal to go into hospital.

It was four hours before Dr.Miller was able to call, and order the ambulance to return. Although he was only half-conscious as he was being carried down the stairs, Guy must have known that he was leaving Baliol Street for the last time; that he was being taken from the city streets which he loved so well, and that slipping from him was the life that had filled him so abundantly.

Jenny Patrick and John Caldwell waited at Baliol Street all night for a dreaded phone call. It came at six in the morning, and contained a glimmer of hope, seized upon and magnified. Guy had survived the night. In fact, 'he had rallied a little.' But it would be well for them to come and see him.

His bed was near the door of the ward, curtained off. A physiotherapist was massaging his chest to ease his breathing. He called aloud for 'Jenny' and 'Caldy', his voice good for the whole ward as an audience. He was sitting propped up in bed. When his two friends came through the curtain he half turned and bestowed on Jenny the most radiant smile that can ever have come from any man or woman. His entire soul was in that smile. Jenny leaned towards him and said softly 'How are you, Guy?' He said — and it seemed as though he had made up the cheery remark in advance — 'Oh, I thought you said I was going home on Monday.' Caldwell told him that he had phoned his son, Annesley, and that the next issue of *The Word* would come out on time. Guy nodded.

After about fifteen minutes he tried to put his arm round Jenny, but Jenny was old and ill herself: she did not understand, and did not respond. Then he extended the rejected hand towards Caldwell, but he, thinking Guy was about to fall asleep, and that the disengagement of the handclasp would disturb him if they were asked to leave, hesitated. Then, suddenly, unexpectedly, Guys' head fell back, his eyes flickered, and with his hand still extended towards his friends, he died. The nurse was called, the doctor hurried, and the ward quietened. Guy Aldred was dead.

He had bequeathed his body to the Anatomy Department of the Glasgow University, so there was no funeral. There would be no gathering of friends to be sad, to remember, to eulogise, no reunion of forgotten comrades. Guy had gone as un-noted into the dreaded dissolution of death as he had into the prison cell, and as courageously. Jenny and Caldwell stood by the bed for a little while, trying to believe the unbelievable. Then they left him.

In the evening Caldwell made his way to The Strickland Press. He had to decide its future. But what choice did he have? Guy had died with ten pence in his pocket, and Jenny had given that to a small boy who ran an errand. The Strickland bank account stood at three pounds, and its debts in the region of three hundred. At the corner of Parliamentary Road —what significance in the name of the road! — Caldwell saw a placard of the *Glasgow Evening Times*. In bold letters it said GUY ALDRED DEAD. At the entrance to Queen Street Station he heard one news vendor call to another, 'Did ye see ma auld china's deid?' When the other asked 'What?', he replied, 'Guy Aldred. He's deid.' Caldwell bought a paper. The news was on the front page: still unbelievable.

The Strickland Press was dark, cold, and silent, in that silence which seems to speak its presence in disembodied sadness. Caldwell felt that there was something not to be disturbed. He switched on one light only and went no further than the shop counter. Guy's office door was open. On his desk lay the galley proofs of his last essay. It was a birthday musing written for the 5th November, and it was entitled: 'Please to Remember.'

It would be printed. He had promised Guy that much. The next issue — with its obituaries — would appear. But after that?

On the counter lay a copy of *The Word* for January 1961. Its leading article was on Ethel Macdonald, who had just died. Caldwell, looking through it, came to the words: 'I see no kindness, no friendship, no regard for mankind, no purpose in the universe. It is a miracle that cannot be explained. It seems to be a wonderful evolution from cause to effect, although there seems to be no cause and the effect is without intelligence or aim. So, for for my part, I do not believe in God. That was also the belief of Ethel....Yet for some strange reason a contradiction arises within us. We *do* change the world. One generation merges into another. The hopes of yesterday's heroes and martyrs become the inspiring slogans of today, passed on to the heroes of tomorrow....In this frame of sorrow I turn from the lifeless body of my comrade to associate with those in whom still dwells the consciousness of being....'

That is what Guy Aldred wrote when Ethel died: that is what he believed, and with that belief Guy Aldred died. Caldwell switched on the office light, and, seated at Aldred's desk, wrote his first headline:

THE WORD CARRIES ON!

Four sketches by Peter Miller. Guy Aldred is shown in a despondent mood, following the death of Ethel Macdonald, when the Press and his Group were in decline, and he was heavily in debt. A new political epoch had swept him aside. In such moods he declared himself a failure, but optimism constantly returned. His failure was not the defeat of his ideas. A sense of futility must never overwhelm us. 'The abiding sin is futility,' he often said. To the end of his life he refused to accept a state of futility.

Jenny Patrick is shown confined to a chair in her last long illness. The look of sadness and despair on her face touches me deeply even after twenty-five years. She was so bright, intelligent, and disdainful of weakness. Now she cannot even feed herself. Her mind is still clear enough for her to know and suffer from her endless helplessness.

Ethel was only fifty. A forceful personality with no time for weakness or indecision, and a habit of thrusting aside the incompetent, and with little maudlin sympathy. Now she is in the last stages of multiple sclerosis: completely paralysed, she can move only her eyelids. She has to sit upright to prevent her tongue from slipping back and choking her.

I nursed all three. I remember when they walked tall, confident that

Guy Aldred (1961)

they were the heralds of a bright new age. Now, at the end, see the terrible agony of despair. Surely the fable of the Cross is symbolic, and the cry is never stilled: 'My God, my God, why hast thou forsaken me?'

I am the last of the quartet. My despair has little depth, for despair can arise only from faith and hope.

John Caldwell.

Guy Aldred (1963)

Jenny Patrick

Ethel Macdonald (1959)

APPENDIX ONE

THE WRITINGS OF GUY ALFRED ALDRED

Born 5th November 1886, 24, Corporation Buildings, Clerkenwell, London. Died 17th October 1963, Western Infirmary, Glasgow.
Periodicals: Founder-Editor of various journals:
Herald of Revolt, 1910-1914. *The Spur*, 1914-1921. *The Red Commune* (one issue, suppressed) Feb. 1921. *The Commune*, 1923-1929. *The Council*, 1931-1933. *Attack* (One issue), 1934. *The United Socialist* (one issue) 1933. *Regeneracion*, 24 issues, duplicated typescript, then four fortnightly issues letterpress, 1936. *News From Spain* (one issue) 1937. *The Word* May 1938, then May 1939 - October 1963, continued under different editor till May 1965. *The Word Quarterly* (1) The Gandhi Murder Trial. (1950): (2) What War Means (1951).

Writings (Apart from fugitive writing in the above and other journals) The Last Days — War or Peace? (1902). The Safety of Unbelief (1904). The Possibility and Philosophy of Anarchist Communism (1906). Logics and Economics of the Class Struggle (1907). Open Letter to a Constitutional Imbecile (1907). The Basis and Exodus of Bourgeois Sectarianism (1907). Sex Oppression (1907). Anarchism, Socialism and Social Revolution (1908). From Anglican Boy Preacher to Socialist Impossibilist (1908). Representation and the State (1910). Trade Unionism and the Class War (1911). The Life of Richard Carlile (1912). (Editor) Jail Journal of Richard Carlile (1915). (Editor) Selected Writings of Bakunin (1913). The Life of Bakunin (1920). Communism and Religion (1920). Richard Carlile (Revised: 1923). Socialism or Parliament (1923. Revised as Socialism and Parliament, Pt. 1, 1942). Government by Labour (1928, Revised as Socialism and Parliament, Pt. 2, 1942). At Grips with War (1929). John Maclean (1932). Life of Bakunin (Revised Edition 1933). Towards Social Revolution (1934). Socialism and the Pope (1934). Socialist May Day Special (Broadsheet, 1934). For Communism (1935). Glasgow Empire Exhibition Leaflets (six issues, 1937-1938). Against Terrorism in the Workers' Struggle (1938). The Rebel and his Disciple (1940). Historical and Traditional Christianity (1940). Studies in Communism (1940). Dogmas Discarded (1940). Pioneers of Anti-parliamentarianism (1940). Why Jesus Wept (1940). The Conscientious Objector, The Tribunal, and After (1940). Armageddon Incorporated (on Jehovah's Witnesses, 1940). When did it Happen: A study of the Calendar (1941). Edited, Revised Edition, Carlile's Jail Journal (1942). Edited W.W. Strickland's This March of Homicide (1942). Convict 9653 - Eugene Debs (1942). Devil's Chaplain - Robert Taylor (1942) Communism, the Story of the Communist Party (1943). It Might Have Happened to You: An Exposure of Regulation 18b. (1943). A Call to Manhood: 26 Essays (1944). Sown in Dishonour (1945). Peace Now and Forever (1945). Rex. v. Aldred — Report of Trials for Sedition, 1909 and 1922 (1949). No Traitors' Gait! — The Life and Times of Guy A. Aldred (Issued in 19 parts. First part, December 1955, last part June 1963, Unfinished.)

The writings of Guy Alfred Aldred have been issued by World Microfilm Publications, 62 Queen's Grove, London, NW8 6ER. They can be consulted at major libraries.

APPENDIX TWO

CONSCIENTIOUS OBJECTORS: (1916 — 1919)

These statistics include the final figures obtainable from all sources in 1919. These figures do not include the men who refused to bear arms, but served in the Non-Combatant Corps, the Friends' Ambulance Unit, the Friends' War Victims' Relief Committee, or accepted alternative service in the form of 'Work of National Importance' as prescribed by the Tribunals or the Pelham Committee. Some 'conchies' who refused to respond to their calling-up papers were never arrested. Some successfully evaded arrest.

The grounds on which the conchies of 1916 — 1919 objected overlapped in many instances. Some were Socialists, and some were Quakers, and some claimed to be both. There were, of course, many varieties of belief of conviction expressed by the six thousand three hundred objectors who registered, and the unnumbered who did not.

In the following list, 'NL' means: Not Liberated till after the war had ended. 'NCC' means Non-Combatant Corps: 'ILP' — Independent Labour Party: 'BSP' — British Socialist Party: 'SPGB' — British Socialist Party: 'IWW' — Industrial Workers of the World: and, of course, the proud designation 'Conchie' means Conscientious Objector.

Conchies Registered	6312
Court Martialled Once	5970
Court Martialled Twice	655
Court Martialled Thrice	521
Court Martialled Four Times	181
Court Martialled Five Times	50
Court Martialled Six Times	3
Sent to France	37
Sentenced to Death	30
Served over two years in prison	816
Died after arrest	69
Died in prison	10
Became mentaly deranged	39
Discharged on medical grounds	362
NL 1919	1039
Accepted Labour Camp Scheme	3862
Accepted Military Duties	349
Disappeared after arrest or sentence	220
Socialist Objectors	1191
Unattached Socialist Objectors	245
ILP Objectors	805
SLP Objectors	21
BSP Objectors	78
Anarchist Objectors	27
SPGB Objectors	9
IWW Objectors	6
ILP Members (NL 1919)	211
Other Socialists NL 1919	122

```
ILP Members
released on medical grounds          71
Other Socialists
released on medical grounds          88
ILP: Work Camp Scheme               454
Other Socialists: Work Camp Scheme   159
ILP Objectors not traced             69
Other Objectors not traced           57
Quaker Objectors                    184
Quaker Absolutists: NL 1919          77
Quakers: Work Camp Scheme            57
Quakers released on medical grounds  28
Quaker Objectors not traced          22
Quaker Associates (Absolutists) NL   25
Quaker Associates
released on Medical grounds          12
Quaker Associates, Labour Camps      45
Quaker Associates not traced         13
Associations Unknown               3928
Of these: Absolutists               604
Released on Medical grounds         171
Labour Camps                       3155
```

CONSCIENTIOUS OBJECTORS
WHO DIED

The following sixty-nine after arrest, the first ten in prison

W. Bone, Birkenhead
O.S. Bridle, Brighton
E. Burns,, Failsworth
P. Campbell. Skye
P.I. Gillan, London
A. Horton, Manchester
F. Wilkinson, Dulwich
A. Wilson, Blackburn
J.G. Winter, Cornsay

P. Allen, Nelson
T. Allen, Nelson
W. Allen, Southgate
A. Barlow, Mansfield
A. Battenham, Downham Market
H. Beynon, Swansea
F. Bowden, Oldham
A.G. Brentnall, London
H. Brightman, Camden Town
T. Cainet, Manchester
N.A. Campbell, Glasgow
C.J. Cobb, Croydon
C.H. Dardis, Risca
L. Deller, West Brompton
P. Dunbery, Blackburn
A. Eungblut, London

J. Jackson, Theadore
A.L. James, Kingston
H. James, Worcester
S. Linscott, Newton Abbot
W.W. Malcolm, Glasgow
A. Martlew, York
T.D. Matchett, Bath
W. May, Edinburgh
J, Moss, Morley
J. Mountfoeld, Manchester
W.H. Parkin, Sheffield
F.L. Parton, Chiswick
A. Peddieston, Glasgow
H. Phipps, Harringay
R.A. Richmond, Brighton
J.A. Rigg, Barrow-in-Furness

R.G. Evans, Reading
W.H. Firth, Norwich
H. Goldsborough, Blackburn
P. Hall, Old Dalby
H. Haston, Chesterfield
A. Henderson, Dundee
A. Hurst, Southwark
H. Hoad, Chart Sutton
R. Hooper, Bradford
W. Hurley, Camberwell
H. Hurst, Manchester

W.L. Roberts, Stockport
A. Ruddall, Newport
A.J. Slater, Glasgow
N. Stafford, Hyde
W. Swettenham, Liverpool
J. Taylor. Silvertown
G. Thompson. Norwich
G. Todd,Willesden
G. Whinnerah, Barrow-in-Furness
E. Woodward, Birmingham
C. Zachnies, Glasgow

C.O.s Sentenced to Death

C. Barritt, Pinner
H.S. Beavis, Edmonton
B.M. Bonner, Luton
H.S. Brewster, London
J.H. Brockesby, Rotherham
C. Cartwright, Leeds
E.C. Cryer, Cleveland
A.W. Evans, Ilford
A. Foister, Cambridge
N. Gaudie, East Boldon
C. Hall, Leeds
C.E. Hicks, Burgess Hill
C.R. Jackson, Leeds
S. Hall, Leeds
B.P. Jordon, Little Milton
H.G. Law, Darlington
W.E. Law, Darlington
R.A. Lown, Stansford
H.C. Martin, Pinner
A. Marklowe, York
F. Murfin, London
A. Myers, Cleveland
A. Priestley, Stafford
L. Renton, Leeds
O.G. Ricketts, Petworth
J.R. Ring, London
H.W. Scullard. Sutton
H.E. Stanton, Luton
A.W. Taylor, London
A. F. Walling, London